Enlightened Sexuality

Enlightened Sexuality

Essays on Body-Positive Spirituality

Edited by Georg Feuerstein

The Crossing Press
Freedom, California 95019

Library of Congress Cataloging-in-Publication Data

Enlightened sexuality : essays on body-positive spirituality / edited
  by Georg Feuerstein.
      p.   cm.
    Includes bibliographical references.
    ISBN 0-89594-375-1 (cloth)   ISBN 0-89594-374-3 (paper)
    1. Sex—Religious aspects. 2. Body, Human—Religious aspects.
  3. Spiritual life.   I. Feuerstein, Georg.
  BL65.S4E5   1989
  291.2'2—dc20   89-36327
                                                  CIP

CONTENTS

PART THREE: ALTERNATIVES WITHIN EROTIC SPIRITUALITY

PREFACE

In 1983, ex-journalist George Leonard boldly declared that "sex . . . is an idea whose time has passed." He was right and he was wrong. Leonard was wrong because sex still seems to be on everybody's mind, notwithstanding the AIDS scare. However, Leonard was right, too, because a new orientation to sex is emerging today in our Western society.

This new orientation makes our conventional approach to sex obsolete. It is broadly sensual, erotic, and even ecstatic. It represents a great alternative to the modern obsession with self-centered genital sexuality and its pursuit of the thrill of orgasm. Truly erotic sexuality is not narrowly focused on a small area of the body—the genitals. Nor is it powered by withdrawal into private fantasies. Instead it requires that in our sexual play we are present as the whole body.

This entails, among other things, that we are in emotional relationship to our sexual partner and not least to our own body. "Making" love thus becomes a priority of intimacy and of self-giving. We stop depersonalizing our partner and ourselves. An integral part of this is that the near-universal concern for orgasm, which causes a great deal of unhappiness in sexual relationships, is relaxed. Orgasm is the ordinary person's substitute for self-transcending ecstasy. Once this is fully understood, we can begin to take charge of our capacity for sexual-erotic pleasure and happiness.

As we assume a more responsible attitude toward our own sexuality, we learn that our whole body-mind, not only our genitals, is a source of immense delight—ananda or bliss. In that delight we find that we are not really distinct from those whom our energies of love hold in eternal embrace, and we also begin to experience others in a new light. Thus sexual pleasure becomes spiritual bliss that grasps and moves us at a level where we are one.

Sex is *not* incompatible with spiritual life. For centuries we have been haunted by the opposite idea, namely that sexuality and spirituality are mutually exclusive. This unenlightened stereotype has traumatized millions of people, and continues to do so. The truth is that if we want to grow spiritually, we cannot merely deny the existence of our genitals, just as we cannot merely succumb to all our self-indulgent whims. Rather we must integrate our sexual urges into our spiritual aspirations.

Sex can be so much more than a valve for our neurotic need to feel good or loved. It can be joyous and illuminating. It can be a truly transformative force in our lives. Not only can it reveal to us a depth of pleasure that outdistances the nerve spasms of conventional orgasm, it can also yield a radical intimacy that penetrates the skin of our bodies as it penetrates the boundaries of our ego-personalities, until we recognize each other in the Mystery of existence itself. Sensuality and enlightenment do not lie poles apart, as our inherited Victorian morality would have us believe. Sex can be a means to, and an expression of, spiritual enlightenment.

How this is possible is discussed in this volume. The present anthology explores how sexuality and spirituality dovetail in a lifestyle that is dedicated to higher values yet is free from repression, or the unnatural suffocation of ordinary bodily desire. What is proposed here is *erotic spirituality* as a valid approach to inner growth: We do not have to deny our bodies in order to discover the spirit. Instead it is argued that in order to truly realize our spiritual potential, we must embrace our body-minds and bless them with our love.

As I was readying this volume for the press, it struck me increasingly just how badly our culture lacks a *Kama-Sutra*, a "pillow book" for those who seek to integrate their sexuality into a spiritually based life. I will pursue some of the ramifications of the thoughts expressed here in my next book, provisionally entitled *Sacred Sexuality*. I trust, however, that in the meantime the essays and interviews offered in the present volume will provide plenty of stimulus for deliberation, questioning, and personal experimentation.

I would like to leave the reader with the following twin questions: Can we discover the Divine, or Reality, without also discovering the mystery of our own body? Conversely, can we find fulfillment in sex without finding the Divine, or Reality?

Georg Feuerstein
Lake County, California

INTRODUCTION: SPIRITUAL SEXUALITY AFTER THE SEXUAL REVOLUTION

By Georg Feuerstein, M.Litt.

THE SEXUAL REVOLUTION

Not too long ago, sex belonged to the shadow side of human existence. Men had to hide their sexuality, and women were supposed to have no sexual feelings at all; at least not decent, self-respecting women. Because of this lethal ideology, sex had to go underground. Men cultivated double standards and went to the brothels, and women had to sweat it out in largely unfulfilling marriages that lasted "until death do us part."

Today, however, it is not uncommon for young teenagers to have sex, and promiscuity is rampant. According to one survey conducted in Britain, a staggering 65 percent of women aged sixteen to twenty-four years admitted to having had sex by the age of sixteen. Figures for the United States are similar. The institution of marriage itself has become an endangered species. In 1986, there were 2.4 million marriages in the United States and 1.1 million divorces, the average marriage lasting about seven years.

It was the countercultural quake rumbling in the mid-1950s and shaking vigorously in the 1960s that so profoundly affected the core values of our Western postindustrial society. It added new ways of thinking and feeling about the family, sex roles, and sexual relationships. These new standards are summed up in the catch phrase "Sexual Revolution."

The Sexual Revolution is first and foremost a revolution of ideas and attitudes, concerned with alternative perceptions about reality. Secondarily, it is about behavioral changes. We must first conceive of the possibility, say, of making love before breakfast, with the lights on and enjoying our lover's nude body, before we can do so. The Sexual Revolution represents a radical shift in what we consider to be possible, and it is this switch in our ideas and understanding that extends the boundaries of our morality and sexual practice. The Sexual Revolution has empowered the individual to find out just what it is that seems appropriate. The cultural watershed of the Sexual Revolution has both relieved anxieties and created new ones. On the one hand, it has alleviated repression; on the other hand, it has led to a host of new problems In an early study, psychiatrist Benjamin Morse wrote:

> Sexual freedom or sexual conformity, sexual license or sexual maturity, sexual disorganization or sexual stagnation, sexual promiscuity or sexual monotony—there seem to be an infinite number of approaches to the sexual revolution, an infinite number of speculations in regard to its causes and possible outcome . . . Yet the most important thing we may do in a study of [our] changing mores in the realm of sex is to realize once and for all that the sexual revolution is not all black or all white, all good or all bad, all progress or all regression.[1]

Journalist Vance Packard aptly titled one of his books *The Sexual Wilderness.* This was meant to describe the state of affairs in the 1960s, and it applies even more today, twenty years later.[2] The sexual wilderness refers to the moral wilderness of our modern postindustrial society, with its amazing complexity, its dearth of real intimacy, and its lack of a comprehensive philosophy, or faith, that can serve the individual as a guide through this perplexing terrain.

In preceding ages, people had a limited repertoire of life choices, which was both a blessing and a curse. It was a blessing because they knew their "place" in life; in particular, they knew what to expect of marriage and relationships. It was a curse because they could entertain little hope of changing their life circumstance if they grew weary of it.

Today, people are free to improve themselves and their lot: They marry young or old, or not at all; they divorce and they remarry or remain widowers, without being stoned for it; they marry within or outside their social status, age group, race, or religious creed; they have affairs and swap partners or are monogamous and faithful; they are heterosexual, bisexual, or homosexual (even though a same-sex relationship is still widely held immoral); they have children or not; they use contraceptives or not; they use the missionary position or playfully experiment with any number of other sexual positions; they have sex for procreation or for recreation; they ignore their sexual problems or consult a sex therapist and marriage counselor; they make love a lot or, as we shall see in this volume, practice voluntary celibacy together.

In the nineteenth century, women were still condemned to renounce their own sexual gratification in favor of their husbands' appetites. Nor were they given leave to explore their sexuality on their own. In fact, our nineteenth-century forebears held that women were by nature unorgasmic. Now, surveys show that around 80 percent of women are capable of having orgasms. This is part of the phenomenon of sexual equality, which has almost become a new tyranny. Orgasm has in fact become an important measure of self-worth. The new myth, sponsored by the studies of sexologists William Masters and Virginia Johnson, is that women have a nearly inexhaustible orgasmic capacity; potentially at least, they are the ultimate sexual consumers.[3]

This stereotype of women as insatiable nymphomaniacs, who have the "right" to experience orgasm, has placed a heavy burden on the men who now feel they are expected to "perform" as sexual athletes, maintaining erections to the point where they become priapic, and demonstrating their affection or love by turning their penises into piston engines. Not surprisingly, many men develop an inferiority complex, constantly wondering whether their sexual performance is on a par with that of the next man, and worrying whether they are able to satisfy the ever-hungry vagina of their partners.

One of the new male concerns is that if the woman hasn't had multiple orgasms, either something was wrong with the man's performance, or the woman is on the frigid side. Other preoccupations that men and women share are whether the woman "needs" a clitoral or a vaginal orgasm (though it appears that all orgasms are clitoral); how to find the G-spot and whether it is necessary to stimulate it; whether extended orgasms (ESO) are preferrable to multiple orgasms, and whether they should orgasm together in synchronous climax. As psychiatrist Rollo May observed:

> I confess that when people talk about the "apocalyptic" orgasm," I find myself wondering, Why do they have to try so hard? What abyss of self-doubt, what inner void of loneliness, are they trying to cover up by this great concern with grandiose effects?[4]

May has called this new performance-oriented approach to sex, which dehumanizes both men and women, the "new puritanism." It has three characteristics: a state of alienation from the body, the separation of emotion from reason, and the use of the body as a machine. As May pointed out, whereas our Victorian ancestors aspired to find love without succumbing to the sin of sex, today we crave sex without wanting to risk the virtue of love.

Some men, like some women, find this pressure to perform sexually, that is, to "work" at sex, too overwhelming and oppressive. In response, they explore other alternatives, such as solitary masturbation or complete sexual abstention. Masturbation

has for long been taboo, and masturbators have been indoctri-
nated with the pseudo-medical dogma that their "affliction"
causes hair loss, blindness, asthma, and insanity, and is apt to
lead to suicide. Women masturbators faced especially harsh
judgment and, worse, the threat of medical intervention: from
drugging, to wearing a chastity belt, to the quite sadistic remedy
of cauterizing (burning and rendering insensitive) the offending
organ, the clitoris.

It was sexologist Alfred Kinsey who took off the lid on the
lingering puritanical ideology when he showed, in his famous
1948 and 1953 reports on male and female sexuality, that 94
percent of men and 65 percent of women in the United States
have masturbated at times.[5] Roughly twenty years later, Betty
Dodson published her book *Liberating Masturbation*, which
reflected the new mood.[6] Nowadays, masturbation is considered the norm and perfectly "healthy" by the medical profession.
This 180-degree swing is a telling commentary on the changing
fashions within medicine.

The Sexual Revolution, to be sure, is an ongoing process.
As Kate Millet rightly noted in her *Sexual Politics*, the Sexual
Revolution can be considered complete only when the patriarchal system of male dominance is fully overcome.[7] This has not
yet occurred, though the present-day cultural reconfiguration,
spoken of as the "New Age" by some, is introducing values and
ideals into the mainstream of our culture that are geared toward
ending the war between the sexes. By the same token, however,
the Sexual Revolution will not be complete unless the politics of
matriarchy, or female dominance, has likewise been transcended.
There is no "first" and no "second" sex. Both men and women
must conjointly care for the human species and its planetary
environment.

BEYOND SEX-NEGATIVE RELIGION

We are flesh-and-blood beings, *embodied* spirit rather than
disembodied ghosts. To say that we are embodied signals, above
all, that we are *sexual* and *passionate*, capable of desire, enjoyment, love—the embrace of bodily existence. In the past, most
religious and spiritual traditions have either ignored this fact or
only paid lip-service to it; worse, they were antagonistic toward
the "flesh." We have suffered this religious ideology far too long,
and are entitled to experience the full picture—a picture that
leaves behind the dreary black-and-white depictions of the past

and celebrates all the colors of the spectrum of human existence.

Spirituality in the ancient world was almost synonymous with an orientation toward life that is essentially hostile toward incarnation, bodily functions, and ordinary impulses, especially sexual desires. Archaic spirituality sought human salvation outside the realm of forms in an idealistic paradisaical condition (or "place"), where beings are discarnate, or at least sheathed in ethereal and quite sexless bodies, with only the purest intentions and thoughts, forever absorbed in prayerful praise of the God-architect, or "heavenly father."

The philosophies of Platonism, Gnosticism, and traditional Christianity, Judaism, and Islam are examples of this otherworldly and antisexual orientation. They all look upon human existence as an inevitable struggle between the lowly structures and functions of the body and the higher aspirations of a saintly life, between the flesh and the spirit.

According to this age-old model, spirituality is essentially the ascent of human consciousness into the domain of the genderless spirit. Thus, archaic mystical spirituality is typically portrayed as a vertical path, or stairway, to the "other world" of the Divine—the heavenly regions—or as a ladder of increasing perfection. But always the movement is away from the physical body and the material world, away from worldly concerns, problems, and obligations, away from the present and the future and into the past (where the origin is thought to lie).

At the apex of the ascent, the spiritual seeker—or traditional mystic—discovers a transcendental Reality (be it called God or the Self or the Absolute)—a reality that is held to have nothing to do with embodiment, or form. It is described as the end of all human desiring, even of all human characteristics. "I am not this, not that," declares the Hindu mystic. In this view, the way to that Reality is through the eye of the needle of a consciousness that has divested itself of all content, that has utterly renounced all objectivity and materiality, and that is submitted to the higher reality. Such a vacated consciousness acknowledges no binds, moral or otherwise, but follows its own spontaneous impulse "back" to the source of all life.

But the vertical path of archaic spirituality is typically not a path into any external or objective dimension of reality. It is a journey *within* the field of consciousness itself. More exactly, it is an odyssey within the structures of the human nervous system. In other words, archaic mystical spirituality is principally an adventure in the wonderland of human neuropsychology. This is borne out by the fact that even the traditionally most prized state of formless ecstasy, called *nirvikalpa-samadhi* in Hinduism, is dependent on manipulations of the nervous system.

Through intense mental concentration, fasting, breathing, sexual abstention, and other similar means, the yogin remodels his internal environment. He may indeed fuse with the transcendental Reality, just as some drugs can catapult a person into the unitive consciousness of the mystics. But his enjoyment of that Reality is only temporary. When he returns to the ordinary waking state, he also returns to his ordinary ego-personality. In this regard, mystical virtuosos are no different from mathematical or musical geniuses. They have a highly specialized talent, but for the most part are rather ordinary individuals who can even be quite helpless, boring, and uncongenial outside their field of competence. Indeed, the mystic runs a high risk of succumbing to ego-inflation.

The mystical state of formless consciousness, immersed in the infinity of Being, can be repeated only by recreating the initial preconditions again and again: usually acute asceticism. Frequently, the yogin or mystic can meet these conditions only by denying the rest of life, by rejecting bodily existence in favor of a nonphysical state of being. Peter Campbell and Edwin McMahon (who also contributed to the present volume), observed:

> Being drawn beyond ego is not something that is wrested from the universe like some prized mineral that is arduously dug from the earth. Rather, it is given to us as butterfly wings emerge from the caterpillar when the time is ripe.
> The question of ego-transcendence, then, is not some esoteric adventure, a striving to achieve an altered state of consciousness. Neither is it an asceticism of willpower and control.[8]

In conventional mysticism and Yoga, the body is viewed as a corpse, and in fact it becomes corpse-like in the formless ecstatic state. For this reason, not a few medical commentators have confused it with catalepsy or other similar conditions involving a loss of body awareness. But even when criticizing the typical mystical or yogic viewpoint for its onesidedness, I in no way mean to suggest that what the mystic or yogin experiences is only a brain phenomenon or that he is merely unconscious. The content of formless ecstasy is indeed the transcendental Reality, but this realization is achieved only by excluding the physical dimension of existence.

In Christianity, the dualistic attitude of ancient religiosity is best reflected in the myth of Adam and Eve's discovery of carnal knowledge, for which they were expelled from the Garden of Eden. As a result of that original calamity, their numerous descendants are all presumed to be born as sinners. This potent idea, which has informed, obsessed, and troubled hundreds of millions of people throughout the ages, has been one of the main sources of Christian misanthropy and sex-negative ideology.

Traditionally, Christians have regarded sexuality as a necessary evil, and ever since Paul of Tarsus marriage has been hailed as the only legitimate channel for satisfying one's sexual passions. The only admitted purpose of sexual intercourse is that of procreation, and celibacy, according to Paul, is far superior to married life with its sexual entanglements. Sex for tension release has always been tolerated but never encouraged or commended.

It was not until Martin Luther that the *ancien regime* of the sex-negative Church patriarchs began to be somewhat challenged, for Luther looked upon marriage as a divine dispensation, with motherhood being a desirable goal in itself. However, even Luther—like his contemporary Calvin—taught that sex was for procreation alone.

The antisexual teachings of traditional Christianity imply not only a rejection of *sexus* but, more tragically, of *eros*. Puritanism or asceticism is not only troubled by the existence and persistence of carnal desires but by pleasure in general. Notwithstanding the mystical doctrine of the beatific vision and the delight in the company of God in the hereafter, traditional Christianity is deeply anti-ecstatic.

Matthew Fox, who has recently been silenced by the Vatican, observed:

> If I were asked to name in one word the message I have received from my religion regarding sexuality over the forty-five years of my life I would answer: *regret*. I believe that the Western church, following in the spirit of St. Augustine, basically regrets the fact that we are sexual, sensual creatures. "If only sexuality would go away," the message goes, "we could get on with important issues of faith."[9]

Fox contrasts this attitude of regret with the tradition of *praise*, which celebrates sexuality as a "suprising and imaginative gift." Fox's Creation Spirituality is among those contemporary efforts within Christianity that avow an eros-positive orientation. "The Cosmic Christ," writes Fox, "rejoices and is intimately at work and play when lovers make love. Angels flap their wings in envy at those times."[10] He envisions a renaissance of sexual mysticism, and in his book *The Coming of the Cosmic Christ*, he offers one of the finest commentaries on Solomon's *Song of Songs*, with its wholehearted endorsement of an erotic spirituality.

The fact that Fox, a Dominican priest of international renown, has been silenced by the Church holds little importance, for this enforced silence will be heard far and wide. What is important, however, is that Fox is not alone in protesting an antiquated theology and moral teaching. There are a growing number of Christian notables who do not hide behind dogma but are considering, questioning, and voicing their opposition against current Church attitudes.

Sexuality is now generally viewed as an area where genuine love and mutual delight can be expressed. Moreover, issues such as homosexuality, masturbation, as well as premarital and extramarital sex have come under more compassionate review, although opinions about them are still divided. It will take time for the more enlightened viewpoints to prevail.

There is some help in the fact that the religio-spiritual teachings of the ancient world were not all of the antisexual, Apollonian type. A scant few, but powerful, non-Christian traditions—notably Indian Tantrism and Chinese Taoism—early on developed an incarnational spirituality. Instead of taking flight from the basic and irrevocable fact of our embodied condition, they acknowledged and included the body and eros in the spiritual enterprise. Rather than denigrating the mortal coil as a "corpse," as did the Gnostics when they equated the body (*soma*) with the grave (*sema*), they saw in it the temple of a higher, spiritual reality, that is, a manifestation of a superior spiritual order.

These body-positive traditions succeeded only to a degree, however. They were hampered by the strong body- and sex-negative attitudes prevalent in their respective cultures at large, and therefore they unfolded as esoteric initiatory systems, burdened with the baggage of archaic beliefs and ideas, including a certain elitism and male chauvinism. Thus, in some instances, women were excluded from initiation or full initiation, or were otherwise treated as *means* of self-transformation for the male spiritual aspirant. Such attitudes and biases are not viable in any age, but they are distinctly out of place in our era.

Those of us who are searching for a deeper existential meaning within the context of our own Judeo-Christian or, perhaps more rarely, Islamic heritage are, for the most part, saddled with largely outdated and irrelevant ideas and beliefs. This would explain, in part at least, the attraction of contemporary humanistic substitute programs for religion: the do-it-yourself methods of personal growth that preach the right to sexual expression and erotic pleasure. While numerous people flock to the apostles of the new therapeutic "psycho-technologies"—from primal therapy to hypnotic regression, to creative dreaming, to bodywork—these approaches generally lack a deeper sensitivity to the authentic spiritual dimension of existence, which transcends conventional religiosity as much as it transcends the conventional understanding about human nature and psychosexual realities. They can put us in touch with our body and with the hidden aspects of our psyche, yet they still tend to leave us somewhat empty-handed (or, rather, empty-hearted) spiritually.

TOWARD AN INCARNATIONAL SPIRITUALITY

What is needed is a new spirituality that does justice to both the scientific-humanistic tradition and the vast body of religio-spiritual lore around the world, without succumbing to their inherent limitations. *Bio-spirituality* is proposed as such an approach. In their book *Bio-Spirituality*, Edwin McMahon and Peter Campbell characterized this orientation in a nutshell as follows:

> Once our entire consciousness is encouraged to open and mature, then the root of our biological connectedness to some vast Process of Unification can gradually reveal itself within our daily existence. There is an awareness within our bodies that leads beyond ourselves.[11]

Erotic spirituality includes the "verticalism" (the ladder of spiritual ascent) of archaic mysticism, as well as the "horizontalism" (the expansion of human consciousness through humanistic programs), but it sees neither as a final destination point. Rather, bio-spirituality is a *radical* response to life in which the ego-consciousness, the structural underpinning of our common dualistic notion of subject (psyche/mind/ego) and object (body/world) is itself transcended. The ego is transcended, not because it is inherently evil, but because its clench represents an unnecessary distortion of reality.

The ego is a "trick," as Alan Watts put it. It is a learned response and one that keeps us shut off from Being. This fact is one of the best-kept secrets of our human civilization. In the words of Alan Watts:

> The most strongly enforced of all known taboos is the taboo against knowing who or what you really are behind the mask of your apparently separate, independent, and isolated ego . . . The sensation of "I" as a lonely and isolated center of being is so powerful and commonsensical, and so fundamental to our modes of speech and thought, to our laws and social institutions, that we cannot experience selfhood except as something superficial in the scheme of the universe.[12]

The universe of discrete phenomena is a product of our insular ego. Bio-spirituality proceeds on the foundation of an experiential recognition that (a) body and mind form a functional unity or complementarity, and (b) the body-mind is not inherently opposed to the spirit, or reality-at-large, but is a manifest aspect of it. In this way, bio-spirituality is in consonance with the findings of modern psychology (e.g., psychosomatic medicine) and avant-garde physics. The latter discipline admits that the observing subject/consciousness is inextricably implicated in the world-process and, even more remarkably, that the quantum wave functions are, as pioneering quantum physicist Fred Alan Wolf puts it, "under our control."

Bio-spirituality is the sustained disposition of radical participatory openness to the multidimensional process that is life itself. It is radical because it goes to the bodily root, or matrix, of experiencing. It is participatory because the openness to life is a bodily openness: We risk ourselves—our very body—in a discipline of self-transcendence that discloses the spiritual dimension.

The "spirit"—an ancient word worthy of being retained but greatly in need of clarification—is not an entity but the *essential process* of a being. Thus, spirituality is an *essential* response to life, that is, a response that conforms to, or brings forth, the *essential process* of one's being. It is therefore a deeply *creative* response, by which we create our higher evolutionary destiny. By contrast, sexuality in its most primitive aspect is a *procreative* response that merely fulfills the biological design. Because of our unique level of awareness, we humans are singularly equipped to subsume our sexuality under a life of spiritual creativity. In fact, we are challenged by the present-day evolutionary crisis to integrate our sexuality with the rest of our lives, especially our spiritual needs and impulses. Unfortunately, the mature response we are called upon to make has so far not been forthcoming to any appreciable degree, and people, in default and in despair of spiritual meaning, are apt to treat the body as a machine of pleasure, and sexuality as the quickest and most convenient means of pleasurable excitation.

The much-vaunted orgasm has become the ultimate goal of the bored and long-suffering pleasure-seeker. But like alcohol or drug addiction, a despiritualized sexuality is little more than an effort to create a substitute for the "perennial" experience of *unio mystica*, the spiritual exaltation of humanity's great sages and mystics who participated most directly in the all-embracing mystery of the world-process, or life-at-large. As C. G. Jung remarked about a former patient in a letter to the founder of Alcoholics Anonymous: "His craving for alcohol was the equivalent, on a low level, of the spiritual thirst of our being for wholeness, expressed in medieval language: the union with God." Here Jung anticipated the findings of transpersonal psychology, as outlined by Roger Walsh and Frances Vaughan.[13]

Jung's insight also applies to our addiction to sexual pleasure, which is a manifestation of our frustrated (because unconscious) search for perfect bliss—the kind of flawless delight that is the substance of self-transcending ecstasy. In orgasm, we seek to emulate the ecstatic bliss of spiritual wholeness. As a matter of fact, spiritual ecstasy is orgasmic, in the broadest sense of the term, because in order to be authentic it must include the body.

At the same time, we must note that orgasm occasionally opens a window into a more comprehensive, spiritual reality. As Julius Evola, in his book *The Metaphysics of Sex*, observed:

> If any reflection of a transcendence actually experienced unintentionally takes form in ordinary existence, it does so through sex and, in the case of the common man, through sex alone . . . This is the true foundation of the importance that love and sex have and will always have in human life, an importance unmatched by any other impulse.[14]

When we are deeply in love, our self-consciousness is eclipsed by an ecstatic feeling vibrating throughout our body, and we are dynamic and uninhibited enough for our love to reach out and embrace others. In orgasm, when the feeling of bodily pleasure is so intense that we are lost to the world around us, we catch a glimpse of the bliss of self-transcendence. But these experiences come to us gratuitously and fleetingly. Still, the fact that they do happen to unsuspecting people is noteworthy and clearly a gateway to transcendence.

In the midst of the rapid changes of our age, we can witness pockets of genuine spiritual regeneration (as opposed to merely conventional religious revival). This spiritual renaissance goes hand in hand with a profound revaluation of our sexuality—its evolutionary significance and its role in our personal lives as bio-spiritual beings. Widely read authors like Sam Keen, George Leonard, Erich Fromm, and Rollo May have identified some of the initial issues, complexities, and implications of such a revaluation. The works of these men, among others, contain the seed for a sexual spirituality that we are called upon to articulate today if we want to reintroduce a measure of quality, sanity, and, more importantly, transcendence into our intimate lives.

But in our dealing with these profound issues, we can also not afford to ignore the cumulative wisdom of Eastern traditions like Taoism and Tantrism. Long before contemporary psychologists scrutinized the malaise of our mechanical sexuality and lamented the loss of authentic *eros* and *agape*, the body-positive traditions of India and China grappled with integrating our "natural" instincts with higher spiritual aspirations. The present volume honors this fact.

It is addressed to both men and women, churched and unchurched, Christians and non-Christians, in all parts of the globe. As Madonna Kolbenschlag suggested in her book *Kiss Sleeping Beauty Good-Bye,* women have suffered a dwarfing of their spirituality.[15] This also holds true of men. Both genders are victims of the erosion of the sacred witnessed over the past two centuries. They have also suffered a corresponding "gianting" of their sexuality. When religious or spiritual bliss is denied by a culture, people will turn to other sources of pleasure—notably their genitals. It is clear that a healthy balance needs to be restored.

This volume is a contribution toward an orientation in which spirituality is given its rightful place in our lives—a spirituality that without fear embraces the body and bodily existence—brain, heart, and genitals.

NOTES

1. B. Morse, *The Sexual Revolution* (Derby, Conn.: Monarch Books, 1962), 9.

2. See V. Packard, *The Sexual Wilderness: The Contemporary Upheaval in Male-Female Relationships* (New York: David McKay, 1968).

3. See W. H. Masters and V. E. Johnson, *Human Sexual Response* (Boston: Little Brown, 1966).

4. R. May, *Love and Will* (London: Fontana Library, 1972), 44.

5. See A. C. Kinsey, *Sexual Behavior in the Human Male* (Philadelphia, Penn.: W. B. Saunders, 1948). Also A. C. Kinsey et al., *Sexual Behavior in the Human Female* (Philadelphia, Penn.: W. B. Saunders, 1953).

6. See B. Dodson, *Liberating Masturbation*, (New York: Dodson, 1976).

7. See K. Millet, *Sexual Politics* (Garden City, N.Y.: Doubleday, 1970), 62. This view is independently endorsed by Jean Gebser, who envisions an "integrate" beyond "patriarchy" and "matriarchy." See his *The Ever-Present Origin* (Athens, Ohio: Ohio University Press, 1985).

8. P. A. Campbell and E. M. McMahon, *Bio-Spirituality: Focusing As a Way to Grow* (Chicago, Ill.: Loyola University Press, 1985), 72-73.

9. M. Fox, *The Coming of the Cosmic Christ* (San Francisco: Harper & Row, 1988), 163.

10. Ibid., 164.

11. P. A. Campbell and E. M. McMahon, *op. cit.*, 2.

12. A. Watts, *The Book: On the Taboo Against Knowing Who You Are* (New York: Vintage Books, 1972), 11-12.

13. See R. Walsh and F. Vaughan, eds., *Beyond Ego: Transpersonal Dimensions in Psychology* (Los Angeles: J. P. Tarcher, 1980).

14. J. Evola, *The Metaphysics of Sex* (New York: Inner Traditions, 1983), 273.

15. M. Kolbenschlag, *Kiss Sleeping Beauty Good-Bye: Breaking the Spell of Feminine Myths and Models* (New York: Harper & Row, 1988).

PART ONE
Eros – The Passionate Life

Therapist Jean Lanier argues, in simple but powerful terms, that we tend to treat each other and our sexual encounters as property to be owned. As a result, she notes, even when we rub our skins together we do not really contact each other and thus remain oblivious to the delightful mystery in which we arise and through which we have our being. Therefore, we need to reinstate person-hood in our sexual life, and in the encounter between two persons, two real human beings, discover the ecstasy of the shared Ground of Being. Hence the title of her essay is "From Having to Being: Toward Sexual Enlightenment."

FROM HAVING TO BEING: TOWARD SEXUAL ENLIGHTENMENT

By Jean Lanier

A man sits up in bed next to a woman. "Was it good for you?" he asks apprehensively. "It was marvelous," she replies. Satisfied with her response, he rolls over and tries to sleep. She, too, tries to sleep.

Instead of sleeping, however, they each lie awake, wondering in silence. In spite of minutes (all we seem to have time for) of exciting exploration of each other's bodies, and moments of thrilling abandonment, something has not been fully satisfying. The woman may decide that perhaps "sex" has been overrated, and the man may decide that perhaps he has overrated the woman.

There are obvious exceptions to this scenario. Nevertheless, as a therapist and as a concerned observer of cultural trends, I am persuaded that this scenario is played out all too often in people's lives. People are feeling empty at the very time when they thought they would feel full. For many people, sex has become a substitute for the kind of fulfillment that work or religious conviction might be expected to offer. But, like most substitutes, it is not ultimately nourishing.

The key to the emptiness experienced by this couple lies, in my view, in their use of the word "it." "It" could be "marvelous," or "it" could be a "failure," but the living truth of the matter is that between persons there can be no "it" when "it" refers to sexual encounter. Sex has become a thing to "have," and like most things we have, it does not offer the gratification that is imagined. Things that we "have" may be temporarily, but not ultimately, satisfying. What has happened in this reference to "it," is that the part has been taken for the whole, the genitals for the human being.

The freedom to experience release through genital excitement—a dubious reward for our so-called "Sexual Revolution"—has not liberated the whole person. For that, something else is needed. For that, the "I" needs to be present in the "it." This "I" who we are is a presence that cannot be reified. The "I" *cannot* be an "it." The "I" is rooted in the vast mystery in which birth and death take place, the Ground of Being itself, which some traditions speak of as God. Whatever view we take of what the "I" is or is not, in the final analysis, the "I" remains a mystery. And it is this mystery that is ignored when persons behave as if their intimate meeting could be reduced to an "it." When two "I's" meet, they meet in the Ground of Being itself, or as the Hebrews put it, in the "I am that I am." The mystery of the "I" is a reflection of the mystery of the "I am" of God. It follows that when "I" meet you who are also an "I," we are both meeting God.

This awareness of the mystery of ourselves as persons, as "I's," involves a total commitment to our sexuality that is far more meaningful than our partial commitment to "having" sex. "Having sex" is one of the most tragic and symptomatic phrases in common usage today. We believe that we can "have sex" as we have a meal, good or bad, but whereas a good meal can be satisfying, no one would claim that it is liberating. And yet, liberation is precisely the burden that we place on "having sex," a burden that such an attitude toward sex cannot bear. We have the freedom to "have" sex when and where we want it, but we still feel imprisoned. What is missing?

In gestalt therapy, we notice that when an experience is unfulfilling, it is because we are, in some way, out of contact with the experience. The experience is not complete; thus we don't feel completed by it. Something is missing in the contact. Genuine contact, which means "with touch," helps us to grow and realize ourselves. Incomplete contact diminishes us because it leaves something untouched. All living organisms need contact. Plants need to contact sun, air, and water; animals need to contact food; human beings need what plants and animals need, and much more. Human beings are faced with a variety of presences, manifested in other people, ideas, histories, events, emotions, religions, philosophies, languages, hopes, dreams, and memories. Human beings are fed by much more than food and drink. But just like the plants and animals, they grow only by contact with that which is truly nourishing to their *total* being.

It may seem odd to suggest that *contact* is what is missing in certain sexual encounters. On the surface, it would seem that contact is *all* there is. In fact, the genital contact may be so powerful that it overwhelms the feeling of self and other (of "I" and "you"), and draws the participants into a momentary fusion, a blissful feeling of mutual partaking in each other's being that promises a deeper transformation of separateness into oneness. However, as in the case of the couple described above, this transformation does not always occur. In fact, just the opposite occurs. We can ask, therefore, has contact failed in its purpose?

The point here is not that contact is not made, but *who* makes it. If part of me is left out of the contact, then contact is not complete, and I am not a complete beneficiary of that contact, nor am I a complete benefactor. It is important to understand that a person is something more than any, or all, of the parts that make up that person. I cannot add up your head, arms, legs, and torso, and arrive at *you. You* are a mysterious presence who inhabits, and is, all those parts without being defined by any of them. You are not a simple sum total of parts, of "its," you are an "I" who is *someone*, not a *something*.

A key concept in gestalt psychology is that the whole is greater than the sum of its parts, and thus is different from them. This whole configuration is what is called a gestalt. To illustrate this concept of a gestalt, we can consider water, which, as we all learned in high school, is made up of two parts hydrogen and one part oxygen. Together these parts form the gestalt of water, which is different from anything in hydrogen or oxygen taken separately. You won't find a hint of water in hydrogen or oxygen by themselves, but once water is created, it determines the behavior of hydrogen and oxygen. This is the mystery of relationship, of parts to the whole. The whole determines the behavior of the parts, not vice versa.

This mystery of gestalt formation is the mystery of the person, just as it is the mystery of water. If hydrogen were to imagine that it could be water, by itself, it would be not only foolish, but useless. Yet this is exactly the kind of foolish fantasy we indulge in when we imagine we can "have" sex without our whole person being involved. A person is a totality of mind, body, and spirit. A person is a gestalt, a presence, just as water is a presence that radiates its being in beautiful and nourishing ways. To imagine that a person can function partially is an illusion, and this is the illusion we suffer when we engage in sexual encounters that leave out the totality of our being.

In many ancient cultures, and indeed in our own up to the present era, the strict regulations against casual sexual behavior, were rooted in this awareness that the whole person is involved in sexual intercourse, and thus the whole person would suffer by being divided up into parts. Sexual activity was recognized as whole-person activity, which included the spiritual as well as the physical. To treat sexual encounters lightly, or without reverence, was to harm not only the person involved, but the entire community, because persons live in community.

In ancient Hebrew there was no separate word for body as

opposed to spirit. A human being was a living *nephesh*, a living body/spirit. Thus, to touch a person physically was to touch him or her spiritually. There was no escape from this totality, this wholeness of persons. Sexual contact was between persons as wholes, as "I's," who could not divorce the body from the spirit, nor the person from the community of persons.

Today there is very little evidence of this reverence for the person when we speak of "having sex" with someone. Instead, the reverence is for the idol of sex itself, as if we had ordained sex on its own with no regard for its sacramental nature, which is its power to connect persons to the very Ground of their being and therefore to God. This connection of being to being is grounded in the mystery of Being itself, and it is this connection that transforms us. Enjoyment does not transform us, thrills do not transform us, orgasms do not transform us. Ecstasy transforms us.

Ecstasy occurs when the being of one person touches the being of another person. This ecstasy occurs when the "I" stands (*stasis*) outside (*ex*) itself, and meets the other in the Ground of Being itself. Ecstasy reveals this Ground of Being as Divine Presence, as God, through the presence of each "I" for the other. If *I*, as a person, do not enter into a sexual encounter as a total presence, then *I* do not receive *you* as a total presence, and *we* have not met. To imagine that I can remove my wholeness, my presence as a manifestation of being, from a sexual encounter is to imagine that you can shake my hand without touching me.

It is commonplace today to remark that these splits between mind and body, body and spirit, individual and community, account for many of the problems that human beings are encountering on this planet. Many of us look to our sexual experiences to overcome these splits, and in this search I feel we are on the right track. While there is nothing so disappointing as the emptiness we can feel after "having sex," there is nothing quite so fulfilling as the ecstasy we experience in truly meeting and joining with another person in the spirit of reverence for the total being of that person. It is in such encounters that we can know and love the God who is love. This love has nothing to do with possession or obsession. It has to do with freedom, with spirit. It has to do with giving, not owning, or "having." When we give ourselves to each other as those mysterious presences we are as persons, we find ourselves not only in each other's embrace, but in the embrace of Divinity itself.

It is my suggestion that we consider our sexual encounters

as spiritual encounters, that we take thought as we embark on them, and that we enter into them as we enter a temple, with awe and reverence. Perhaps then we can journey from the era of Sexual Revolution into an era of Sexual Enlightenment.

Sexual enlightenment, or enlightenment, or enlightened sexuality, is always a personal encounter with the Mystery of life. This insight also underlies the thinking of maverick philosopher Sam Keen. His ideas on love and sex are explored in "Our Journey Toward Erotic Love." In this interview, conducted by the editor, Sam Keen draws our attention to the fact that learning to love is a graduated process with clearly distinguishable stages, which can take a lifetime to fulfill itself. He rightly insists that we cannot love in a mature way without first having become authentic persons. This involves the capacity to say No to convention as well as to say Yes to life, expressed in the ability to surrender the self and the discovery that we, as lovers, are a part of everything.

OUR JOURNEY TOWARD EROTIC LOVE

An Interview with Sam Keen, Ph.D.

GF: In your book *The Passionate Life*, you proposed a new model of individual development, comprising five stages. According to this model we proceed from childhood to the rebel temperament, to the adult personality, to the outlaw and, finally, to the lover. Can we look at this progression from the point of view of eros and sexuality?

SK: Right. What I was trying to do here was to find an answer to the question, "How do we become lovers?" Our culture has been fascinated with the I.Q., or intelligence quotient, of people. But we have given very little thought to what I call the E.Q., or erotic quotient, which we can also call the C.Q., or compassion quotient. Our society simply assumed that somehow love and compassion would take care of themselves. We didn't exactly know who taught people to be loving, compassionate, and caring. We assumed that the family should handle that, or the church, but probably not the schools. And then we noticed that families didn't do it, or didn't do it very well at all, and the church also failed at it. This situation prompted me to ask the question, "How would one increase someone's E.Q.?"

In considering this, I pointedly used the word *eros* instead of *agape*. Certainly theologians had been accustomed to talk about love in the sense of *agape*, of God's love, a kind of supposedly selfless love, the kind of love that had no need. It was Paul Tillich who began to redeem the idea of *eros* theologically. Personally, I have always believed that erotic love was also spiritual, and that eros was a more embracing term than *agape*.

GF: *Agape seems flight from the body.*

SK: That's right. Often it was understood as something that we as humans were not really empowered for, but that it was God's love for us.

GF: A purely platonic act.

SK: Yes. As I looked around, it was very clear to me that my heroes were those people who were lovers, not just in a sexual way, but lovers of the world about them. They were people who were passionately involved in all of their lives. So, I started to ask myself the question, "How does one become a lover?" I soon realized that what we lacked in our culture was a developmental theory about love, anything that would give us a normative idea of how a person might develop through the course of a lifetime into becoming a more loving human being.

So, I developed this model of the five stages, and I should say that it was always meant to be taken in a very loose and playful way. I understand it as a map of the ideal erotic development of an individual. Very few people ever follow that map, because we all go through different stages at different points in our lives; we start from different places, and we have different life tasks, as well as different kinds of impediments to becoming loving human beings. For instance, a person who has been sexually abused or battered as a child is going to have a very different trajectory than somebody who has hadn't that traumatic experience. Or, somebody who has been smothered is going to have a very different trajectory than somebody who has been deprived of love.

The itinerary of love proceeds through five stages. First of all, there is the child whose "task" it is to bond well with its parents. Children who had loving parents who cherished them will, as Erik Erikson and others showed, develop basic trust. They are likely to go further in their journey toward becoming loving beings themselves. What this implies is that people get a very uneven start in this world.

GF: What is it that is happening in the stage of childhood? Is it simply that the child is learning in a passive way to receive love and thus to develop basic trust?

SK: No, I don't think so. The idea of active and passive doesn't really apply here. Children are very active, even in their loving. They are learning that the ground of their being in this case, which is the mother, the father, and the family, is trustworthy. Later in life we all have to rediscover that same sense of safety with regard to a much larger world. The child has to learn to live in the mood of basic trust. This comes as a gift to a child. In the beginning our life is a gift, or grace. Of course, there may also be disgrace, because some children are brought up in disgraceful situations, where love is withheld from them.

We can say that the gracefulness and the lovefulness of a person is something that is created over many generations. You can't talk about love and talk about only one generation. If you really want to become a lover, choose your parents and your ancestors well.

GF: Choose your culture well.

SK: Right. But, of course, we aren't in a position to make that choice. So, that's saying that grace is unevenly distributed, and the capacity to love is unevenly distributed as well.

GF: What happens next in our journey toward love?

SK: Well, beginning somewhere around the age of two, and going all the way through adolescence, we are in the second stage, which I call the rebel stage. Here we are beginning to define our identity in dialogue with others. We are learning to choose for ourselves, and this entails a fair amount of opposition to what has so far been presented to us—the many rules of the adult world.

GF: What is the adolescent's life task?

SK: The task in the second stage is learning to say No. Nietzsche probably put it best, when he remarked, "I love the great naysayers, for they are the great yeasayers." Here we learn the ability to say, "No, thank you, Mother and Father, I'll do it myself." "No, thank you, culture, I'll do it myself." I see this as the beginning of the development of the capacity for transcendence. It is a very important phase in our personal development. In primitive, preliterate cultures, the individual goes right from childhood to adulthood, a transition that is marked by rites of passage for boys when they're twelve, and for girls when they first menstruate. There isn't a period where they learn to say "I'll do it my own way." Adolescence is an invention made by literate societies. The great hero in our Western culture, the Promethean hero, is the one who stands against the established order, whether it's the order of the gods or the order of society. He is the rebellious hero.

GF: Would you say that adolescence is an evolutionary route that represents a gain, a plus?

SK: Yes, I would look at it as a plus. However, it can become a minus when it becomes exaggerated. Nowadays we have a repressive sense of adolescence, because we have adolescent men and adolescent women. We have the mass media that essentially are promoting adolescent values: that one can always consume, that there are no consequences of anything, that one can endlessly try on new possibilities, that life is a game. The playing of games, of trying on different "life-styles," is perfectly appropriate in adolescence. It is in that sense something that is a spiritual plus. It is an inappropriate attitude in adults.

GF: What is the possible gain from adolescent rebelliousness?

SK: The possible payoff is that you begin to create a sense of freedom, rather than merely necessity. We look sometimes with longing at primitive peoples, envying them for the simplicity of their lives and the close-knit support network of their tribes. But if you think having your penis slit open or your clitoris removed is a great rite of passage, you are welcome to it. The good news in primitive societies was they all knew who they were. The bad news was that they were mistaken.

In our culture, adolescence or rebellion gives us the chance to be the prodigal son. It gives us a chance to go into a far country, to experience the self all the way out to the point to where it becomes alienated from its root. It gives us a chance to throw out old values and to try new ones. It is both a blessing and a danger. If you get stuck at that level of development, you're in trouble. You then become what Jung calls the *puer aeternis,* the Peter Pan kind of person, who has no commitments and responsibilities.

My whole generation was largely denied adolescent exploration. For instance, we were not permitted very much adolescent sexuality. Sex was supposed to be "responsible" and reserved until a person was married, and then in the missionary position on Friday night in the dark.

The sexual revolution has been very helpful in making the point that there is a time for frivolity and for play, and that we would make our commitments better if we recognized the appropriateness of a period of freedom and experimentation. I believe that there is an immense kind of playfulness about sensuality and sexuality that is quite appropriate to adolescent years.

I would hope that my own kids in adolescence would have some, maybe even a lot of careful sexual exploration short of intercourse, and that if intercourse became appropriate they would know enough to do that with somebody they cared about. My feeling is that then when they got to be adults they could make fewer sexual mistakes, or happily survive sexual mistakes, such as being with incompatible people.

We will never tame sexuality. Adolescents have an enormous amount of sexual energy, and there is always somebody who thinks that there must be a way of harnessing that energy. I don't believe there is. When you repress it, something happens. When you just let it flow free à la Summerhill, something else happens. All you can do is try to make young people aware of the consequences of their actions.

When adolescence is lived out, and lived out carefully and appropriately in each case, this lays the foundations for a much stronger development of eros and of compassion in later life.

GF: How do you explain that? Why would adolescent self-exploration lead to compassion?

SK: Compassion grows out of the sense that one is like the other person. Therefore, the more one knows one's own limits and appreciates the plurality and the richness within oneself, and the more one knows what's good and what's bad for one, and the larger the number of people that one can identify with, the more one will have a basis for compassion.

GF: Rebellion prepares us for the adult stage.

SK: Yes, this is an important stage too. A lot of people want to skip adulthood. (Laughter.) As a matter of fact, this was very much the style of the sixties. In our society, we have the spectacle of the dropout generation and those who try to be perpetually young, living fairy tale lives. The fact is, though, that one can't really reject something until one knows what it is that one rejects. We can't go beyond anything without going through it.

Well, the adult stage of life commences when you decide to be a part of your society, when you cease to merely reject it. Otherwise, if you continue to merely reject it, then you remain an adolescent, a naysayer, and not a very deep naysayer at that. Grown people who can't make that transition remain kids all their lives, having neither depth nor power—the disc-jockey or wise-ass kind of mentality.

Adulthood is about adopting a social role: "I'll be a rich man, poor man, beggar man, thief, doctor, lawyer, merchant, chief, and I will abide by the laws of the society. I'll now define myself by this society, and I'll be trustworthy, loyal, helpful, friendly, courteous, kind, obedient, cheerful, thrifty, brave, clean, and reverent."

The task of the adult is to become a good and responsible citizen, make a decent living, and live a moderate life, with 2.5 children, or whatever the statistics are. It's all very clear, and it's comforting.

GF: And then what happens?

SK: Well, a lot of things could happen. You could get busted out of that life of moderation by sheer success. So, people may have everything that the society said would make them happy, and yet they find they're still unhappy and restless. This is the ideal pattern: a person has tasted what's it like to be a member of a country club and to be respected for this and that. If you find that this sort of life fulfilling, good, go to sleep! (Laughter.) But if it doesn't fulfill you, then, often during what is called the midlife crisis, you are apt to wake up one morning and ask, "Is this it? Is this all there is to life?"

Failure is another cause of this waking up. Perhaps you realize that you have been failing consistently only because you didn't want to succeed in the first place. Then you ask yourself the question, "But what is it that I truly want?"

For me, this is the moment of transition from the merely cultural life to what I would call the higher life of the spirit. It initiates a new quest. It marks the great divide between people who take what Joseph Campbell described as the heroic journey and those who don't, who opt for being ordinary, normal.

GF: You call this new phase the outlaw stage.

SK: Yes. Now, there's something intrinsically selfish about this stage. Society, up until this point, has been telling you what to do and what not to do. Suddenly, you find yourself in your second innocence, as Nietzsche called it. You don't know any longer what's right and what's wrong. So, you've got to find out what you want, and who you are.

GF: How does this differ from the adolescent stage?

SK: Well, the outlaw stage is like adolescence with a bankroll. You are engaging in a new search for an identity, but beyond the experience of being an adult and all that entails. I guess the main difference is that the adolescent rebel is identified *against* something, against the parent, against the society, whereas the outlaw isn't against anybody. The outlaw simply withdraws his or her eros from the society in order to pursue the inner quest.

It's much more a falling in love with the unknown promise of the self. This quest can of course be terribly disruptive, to your job and your marriage. I think it tends to be so disruptive because our society doesn't provide a map for that sort of exploration.

There's a certain accumulated wisdom on how you get through the outlaw stage. Explore freely, at least in your emotions, if not in your actions. You can't go through the outlaw stage without opening up your dream and your fantasy life, because for the most part the extremes that we need to experience have to be experienced mostly in the imagination, not in fact. When Blake says, "The path of excess leads to the palace of wisdom," he doesn't mean: Go out and kill and rape and create mayhem; but, rather, in your imagination, allow yourself to go to the end of the world, to the end of your possibilities.

GF: Are you saying that it is in the outlaw stage that for the first time we seriously confront the question of God, the question of our relationship to the Ground of existence?

SK: No. I think that we're confronting that question all along. We're confronting it in different ways and with different symbols. Let me put it this way: in the adult stage of life the appropriate theology is literalism. Adults are pretty literal. And children can be even more so. You tell a child the story of the Garden of Eden, and he or she will draw a picture of a big chauffeur-driven limousine with a man and a woman in the back seat. When you ask for an explanation, you will be told that it's God driving Adam and Eve out of the Garden of Eden.

In the very end of our lives we're still going to think in symbols, and we're still going to tell stories and narratives about God and the hereafter. But we will hold them differently. That's what begins in the outlaw stage. We begin to see and understand our own symbolic processes at work in our mind. We begin to look at our dreams, for instance, and their rich symbolism encourages us to look at symbols in general. This puts you further away from the orthodox, but it also gives you a greater sense of community with believers of various different religions.

An adult fundamentalist Christian can only think of, say, a Hindu that he just wasn't going to make it to heaven. But the outlaw begins to see that his or her own theology is not necessarily *the* Truth but symbolic.

The same holds true of sexuality. The outlaw phase is the stage where you begin to consider incarnate sexuality. As an adult, you were probably following the adult program, twice or three times a week, with the man on top. Now you start to question yourself whether you might not want to make love ten times a week, or once a month, or be altogether celibate. You begin to know your body. The same holds true for food. You no longer simply eat what the culture prescribes for you, but you ask your body what it wants.

So, another way of defining the outlaw stage is that it is the phase where you are discovering your vocation, in a very incarnate sense. I would say that there's a nutritional vocation, a sexual vocation, or even a geographical vocation: Where do I belong? In my own case, I was seventeen years old when it became clear to me that living as I did in Wilmington, Delaware, was not appropriate for me. I felt displaced. I was always meant to be a Westerner. So, I had to get to where I belonged.

There is a great paradox involved in all this, because the more you know yourself and your boundaries and the more passion you have about your self, the more compassion you begin to develop. This is where I disagree with people like Robert Bellah who argues that we are too individualistic. We have far too little real individualism. We have mass individualism, which tells us that all real individuals wear Ralph Lauren polo clothes. What a bunch of junk! Real individuation is precisely the basis of community.

The deeper I become convinced of who this Sam Keen is and where he stands, the more I become able to listen to others and cherish their being.

The outlaw is a person who has learned to wait and fast and think, and that's the boundary between the outlaw and what I call the lover. If you can listen and wait, and if you can be silent, then you can also think and become capable of the gesture of surrender. Then you can become compassionate.

I have a quantum theory of the self, which says that after you enter the outlaw stage as an adult, you will always vacillate, or oscillate back and forth, between the outlaw and the lover. Really, they are flip sides of the same kind of development. And I think that development continues for a lifetime.

GF: This brings us to the fifth stage in your model, that of the lover.

SK: The process of becoming a lover is the process by which your boundaries, because you know where they are, can be surrendered. You can get away from yourself. You're not obsessed with yourself anymore. The more you know this, the more you become available to others, to life. In the early phases of the outlaw stage, you're not available to anything or anybody. In fact, you're rather possessed with your own self. But gradually, as you begin to be sure of that self, you become more and more available, and acquire the ability to stand still, to silence the inner dialogue in your mind, and to listen.

Becoming a lover involves rediscovering your family, and it means the creation of friendships. By the way, for me, friendship and sexuality are very different. I think when two people have a sexual relationship, this is not friendship. Friendship is a relationship where there is no sexuality, or at least there's no overt sexuality.

Becoming a lover involves loving the natural world, the political world, and even machines.

GF: Love extends to all domains of life. In *The Passionate Life,* you talked about the seven bodies of a lover, or the seven aspects of life that are embraced by the lover. The seventh body is of special interest.

SK: Well, it is the mystical body. When you know yourself, when you've been through APA, have realized your human potential, can stand on your own, and when you've learned to participate in the natural world, then there still remains the unanswered question: What's it all about? And in the wake of this question, but now from a point of view of knowing who you are, comes the knowledge that the known world is at best a gossamer veil of that which is ultimate. You sense that the world is a part of the mystery that is so deep and engulfing that you understand the limitations of your knowledge. Then there arises the comfort of not knowing, of living within the mystery of things.

GF: Why do you choose to speak of mystery rather than use the term "God"?

SK: Well, I think that "God" is one of those words we should use once a year, and then let it be surrounded by silence, because it's so immensely overused. I don't talk about God, because I think the term is vague or meaningless. I don't talk about God for exactly the opposite reason. I agree with Wittgenstein, "Of that which we cannot speak, we should remain silent." God, the mystery, is unspeakable. There are different kinds of silence, and there are different kinds of refusal to use certain words, just as I don't hug everybody or tell them I love them. I'm a Scot, after all, and we believe in reticence. (Laughter.) I especially believe in theological reticence.

I believe that theology should eventually be very humble and should communicate more by its silence. I've taught in the seminary for a long time. The image of the minister was always the image of a person with his mouth open. Theology should be the guardian of silence. It should create and make us comfortable with silence. It should be a matter of listening, not of christening some particular vocabulary or some particular institution. I feel the mystery of being and the mystery of the sacred more when I don't gossip too much about God.

GF: You once used the word "enlightenment." What do you mean by that?

SK: Oh, I must have slipped. (Laughter.) I don't like to use that word. I really use "endarkenment." You see, I believe there are two religious types. One type seeks to go toward light and gnosis; his metaphors are always those of knowledge and understanding. The other type seeks to go through darkness, and his metaphors are always those of trust. My own belief is that in the course of the spiritual process we become more and more ignorant—learned ignorance; the world becomes more and more mysterious. We allow our symbolic universe to fall apart, and then we trust. You see, we go back to the basic sense of trust, cultivated in childhood. We trust because it is dark, because we do not know. We trust because we do not see an omega point, or an end point.

Theologies of gnosis are always what I call whoring after the light. They want more light than we have. And the characteristic of it is they always avoid the problem of evil. This is obvious in the New Age spirituality, which is filled with crystals and light, and infinite possibilities of becoming this or that. Yet, the New Age spirituality is for the most part, in California, very conformist, very unthinking. It silences self-doubt, and it silences the wrestling with darkness. It plasters affirmations over all darkness and all sorrow. It is a phenomenon of early adolescence. I'm a person who would rather increase my trust than my knowledge.

GF: In your book you make the valid point that in regard to enlightenment, a person has to come to the confession "I am the body." For most people enlightenment is something that sort of descends, like the Holy Ghost in the form of a dove, and lifts them out of the body.

SK: Yes, out of the social and political world.

GF: Then, everything is devalued, everything becomes unimportant and disappears. Such radical transcendence may happen as a temporary experience. But as a life task, to me, it is rather meaningless.

SK: I agree. Those Christians who talk about incarnate spirituality have it right, I think. For them, the Christian message is that the whole glory is in the lowly stable, and that we must get down and get dirty. Don't try to escape. Well, what this is meant to convey is: Find "it" where you are. Find it in the dance of life, here and now. We're not supposed to know the whole. We cannot know the whole. To be human means to live close to the earth. This is my concept of epistemological humility. If we think we should do more than live close to the earth, then we're always longing for God's view. But I notice the people who clamor for God's view tend to proselytize immediately, and pretty soon they start making war on everybody else who has a different "God's-eye view" of things.

GF: In your book you write, "Perhaps our deepening desire is our surest guide toward the sacred." I was struck by this phrase.

SK: Well, it's stolen from Augustine. "Our hearts are restless until they rest in Thee." This restlessness of the human is only satisfied, as Huston Smith expressed it, by following the path of our bliss. Augustine said, "Love God and do what you want." There's of course the difference between surface desire and deep desire. And so, you must go deeper and deeper. In an incarnate or a creation kind of spirituality, we must believe that what we most deeply desire is the path of revelation, moving us beyond the illusion of needing things to fulfill us.

I guess a good illustration is that of addiction. Addicts think that what they want is a cigarette, a glass of whiskey, sex, or another BMW. In the moment it seems that this is their true desire, but they know very well that's not the case. If they gratify their surface desire, they obtain momentary satisfaction, but they also experience a certain kind of self-sickness, where they asks themselves, "Why am I doing what I don't really want to do?"

The journey that I've outlined from the child to the lover is in a way a journey that is deepening our trust in our own desires. It's to have the courage of your own desires.

GF: From a spiritual point of view, each stage is another episode of self-revelation. With each stage we understand a little more about what it is that we bring to our life. In the lover stage, then, there is a much clearer understanding of what it is that I as a human being truly desire.

SK: Exactly. There's such a deep understanding in the lover stage that one ceases to have many choices. In my own case, I had to come to the point in my own life where I knew I just had to get the farm and the horses that I had wanted from childhood on. The more you move toward what you really love, the more you will be compassionate, I think.

GF: . . . and the more you will increase the delight and love in others.

SK: Yes. Sometimes I think that the world is getting too danger-ous for dissatisfaction, that we have an ethical obligation to do what makes us joyful.

GF: What major task lies ahead of us?

SK: Our society has everything to deal with spiritually. It's stuck at *cakra* one.† It has to learn the lesson of possession and power and consumption. We are a society that is at the begin-ning of the end of adolescence. We are just becoming clear that we can't live out our fantasies, that there are limits, that the doctrine of progress is over, that we have to become disciplined. In a way, we are nibbling at the possibility of becoming adults.

The best thing about American society is that it has never been an adult society. It has always been boyish and girlish and full of a sense of infinite possiblity, the infinite promise of the individual. We had a great adolescence in this country. America gave the world adolescence in a way no other country did, and it was glorious. But we're now at the threshold of a new age in

---

†The Sanskrit word *cakra* means "wheel" and refers to the various psycho-energetic centers located along the spinal axis of the human body. The first cakra is situated at the anus and is traditionally connected with elimination and fear. [Ed.]

history, and the time has come to grow up.

I don't believe we're in the outlaw-lover stage as a culture. I don't believe we're going off to Nirvana. I'll be satisfied if we just become adult, if we begin to be responsible. We have to realize that we're living in a plural world, and we have to become citizens in the world. America has to stop acting like the biggest adolescent on the block.

GF: We started out with, and talked much about, love—why love?

SK: Love is the morning and the evening star. (Laughter.) Why love? It's a good question. Frequently we act as if love were the only answer. I agree very much with Paul Tillich that love, power, and justice always have to be balanced, and that there are many other virtues, like telling the truth and industriousness, that also enrich our lives. But it does seem to be the case that, as Paul says, all these other virtues amount to nothing if you don't love.

GF: In Sanskrit the most common word for love is *bhakti*. It comes from a root that means "to participate." It seems to me that this sense of participation is the key theme in your book. In a way, the five stages of life are about learning how to participate more and more inclusively.

SK: That's right. Exactly. And love is the only virtue that is inclusive of all other virtues. When Tillich talks about love, he says, "Love is the ontological drive toward the reunion of the separated." We exist for the most part in the illusion of being separate from others, and thus in a nonparticipatory state. We form this character armor around ourselves, which creates the illusion that we are separate. With that comes a great deal of despair, depression, and suffering. The path of the lover is really the dispelling of that illusion, so that you see more and more how you are a part of everything.

Frances Vaughan makes the point that our patriarchal society devalues the feminine principle, both socially and psychologically. She emphasizes the importance of re-eroticizing sex, by balancing the male and female principles within our psyches. She also wisely reminds us that in our pursuit of a more wholesome sexual life, we must not forget that the common foundation of both sex and spirituality is love and that love is the great healing force in our lives.

POLARITIES OF UNIVERSAL EXPERIENCE: SEX AND SPIRITUALITY

By Frances Vaughan, Ph.D.

The rift between God and nature would vanish if we knew how to experience nature, because what keeps them apart is not a difference of substance but a split in the mind.

— Alan Watts[1]

Sex and spirituality are universal experiences that cannot be ignored by anyone interested in human development, health, and consciousness. Every culture has rituals and taboos associated with these basic dimensions of human existence. Some attitudes toward sexuality are so widespread as to be considered almost universal. Other aspects of sexuality are perceived differently in different cultures and by different people in the same culture. For example, many spiritual disciplines in different traditions prescribe celibacy for those who would direct their attention to spiritual matters. Others suggest that sex and spirituality cannot be separated, and seeking wholeness includes them both; to deny or repress either is to split the psyche and to create conflict, tension, and suffering in human life.

PERCEPTIONS OF SEXUALITY

For many people in our society, sex is imbued with fear and guilt, desire and aversion, passion and secrecy. Stringent taboos, both secular and religious, inhibit free expression of sexual impulses in both males and females, and sexuality is often considered to be a root source of evil, being associated with temptation, sin, and degradation. Both the Old and the New Testament make it clear that sexuality is a source of trouble. St. Paul writes, "It is a good thing for a man to have nothing to do with women."[2] Marriage is traditionally the social sanction for heterosexual relationships, yet sexuality has always defied social rules and its power can be compelling, addictive, and awesome. When sex is devalued, women and nature are also devalued. Patriarchal theologies that conceive of God as masculine tend to see women as temptresses who keep men entangled with worldly desires, and spirit ensnared in matter. In psychological terms, when the evolution of consciousness is conceived as a journey of awakening from matter to mind to spirit, to be identified with matter is to be relatively unconscious. Dualistic cosmologies that presume a separation of consciousness and matter tend to value dynamic masculine aspirations toward transcendence, while devaluing the dark, mysterious feminine that gives birth to life on earth in temporal reality. Cultures that subscribe to patriarchal theologies tend to oppress women in society and suppress the receptive, feeling qualities in the individual. The feminine side of human nature therefore remains unconscious and seems to be treacherous and unpredictable. This contributes to widespread conflict and mistrust between the sexes and unnecessary suffering for both men and women.

As the agrarian societies of antiquity observed, women give birth and plant life renews itself in the womb of the earth. Sex and death were commonly associated in pagan rituals and fertility rites that celebrated the cycles of death and resurrection. Sex as sacrament was embodied in the sacred prostitute, or temple virgin, who was called a virgin because she belonged to the Goddess, not to a man. She sustained the union of masculine and feminine, heaven and earth, and thus ensured fertility and abundance for her people.[3]

One who sees herself as embodying qualities of the Goddess may be a priestess, healer, teacher, or visionary independent of the male, but procreation depends on the joining of masculine and feminine. In conventional Christianity, the only acceptable image of the feminine is the mother, and sex is permissible only for procreation in the context of marriage. Holiness is associated with innocence, virginity, and celibacy. Paradoxically, a woman is considered pure only as long as she has no sexual experience, yet she is revered only as a mother.

SYMBOLIC REPRESENTATIONS

In the Middle Ages, with the advent of romantic love, a renewed awareness of eros as divine love is connected with sexuality. In the Grail legends, King Arthur's knights go forth to seek the Holy Grail, the source of divine wisdom or gnosis, symbolized by the chalice of wine Jesus shared with his disciples at the last supper. The chalice itself is essentially a feminine symbol. The wine that is turned to blood in the sacrament of communion suggests that it is a symbol of the womb.[4] In their romantic, spiritual adventures, the Grail knights seek a connection to the feminine principle. They ride into battle in the name of love, and, according to the legend, restoration of the wasteland depends on the awakening of compassion.

In contrast, the sword is a phallic symbol par excellence; it represents the power of discriminating intellect, capable of piercing the veils of illusion as well as penetrating the human body and destroying life.[5] The sword rules the temporal world of becoming. As time eventually devours all that is born in time, a more encompassing view of reality that includes the eternal as well as the temporal must recognize the relative vulnerability of this temporal power. Essential being remains unchanged by passing shows of might and grandeur.

When the wisdom of the heart, symbolized by the Grail, and the discriminating wisdom of the mind, symbolized by the sword, are united, male and female energies are balanced and harmony is restored. As metaphors for the internal process of healing and growth toward wholeness, these images suggest the need for balancing male and female elements within the psyche and serve as catalysts for integrating these polarities of human nature.

Sexuality, including its loving, romantic, playful aspects, as well as its sordid shadow side of dominance and submission, exploitation and degradation, has always been powerfully compelling. Men and women are attracted to sexuality in all its forms. Loving sexual intimacy can be a deeply nurturing experience for both men and women. Unfortunately, from a historical perspective, few men and women have consciously experienced sexuality as an expression of love. Heroes and heroines of romantic legends and stories, beginning in the West with Tristan and Isolde, nevertheless capture the imagination and inspire a yearning for the joining of body, heart, and soul. Romantic ideals would have us believe that if two people love each other, then sex is permissible and good. Otherwise it is dangerous. Ostensibly, social rules of morality that are supposed to govern sexual conduct were designed to protect women and children from slavery and destitution. In a society where men wield the power, women need this protection. But that which protects also constricts and distorts natural, spontaneous sexuality. The sacred dimension of any human experience cannot be governed or coerced my man-made rules.

HEALING THE SPLIT

The healing process in psychotherapy often begins with honoring the feminine principle, both within ourselves and each other. Feminine wisdom and spirituality has traditionally been conveyed from generation to generation as an oral tradition. Women rarely write about their experiences in the way that men write about their ideas. Yet the sacredness of life is experienced in the human body when it is perceived as an incarnation of love, be it erotic or divine love. A heartfelt reverence for life supports appreciation of the body as a sacred vessel of life, an instrument for teaching and learning, loving and sharing. To balance logos, or intelligence, with love is to affirm the sacredness of nature and ordinary life. For many women, the erotic is a source of power, joy, and a sense of personal value.[6] Fear seems to be the major obstacle to sexual fulfillment for both men and women. Fear of intimacy, love, and vulnerability all play a part in keeping inhibitions and defenses in place.

When sexual energy is suppressed, it may be sublimated or it may surface in distorted ways. Sexual frustration has been linked to violence and aggression in both males and females. Today, after Freud's discovery of the unconscious and the sexual revolution of recent decades, sex is no longer a taboo topic, and issues of sexuality in personal relationships are widely discussed. Yet, many people still feel guilt and anxiety connected with sexual activity. Attitudes toward sexuality after centuries of repression are changing very slowly. Although the relatively recent availability of birth control has given women the opportunity for freedom of sexual expression, many are unwilling to risk that freedom. Desire for approval from male authority figures can contribute to sexual compliance in women, as well as suppression of natural inclinations. When male spiritual authorities proclaim that sexuality is acceptable only for procreation, it can become a terrible burden to women. Today, increasing numbers of women are leaving marriages that are not sexually satisfying and religious communities that require celibacy, choosing to take full responsibility for the consequences of sexual freedom.

Men and women seek love both in sexual and spiritual relationships. A deeper meaning of surrender to reality can be discovered if one seeks wholeness rather than perfection, integrating opposites rather than affirming one at the expense of another. Healthy loving relationships between men and women in pursuit of wholeness include both sex and spirituality, eros and agape. In the context of a loving relationship, sex can be a sacred act.

Whenever sex or spiritual authority is used for domination or exploitation, however, the act is no longer sacred. The problem of spiritual teachers having sex with their students in the name of spiritual development has plagued many religious movements, but it is not unique to our time. Controversial issues of sexuality seem to surface from time to time in most religious groups. Some spiritual paths maintain that those who have not fully explored sexuality cannot awaken fully to their true spiritual nature. The Tibetans, for example, think that working with sexual energy is essential for spiritual development.[7] Teachers who believe that it is essential to work with sexual energy for genuine spiritual growth may be more susceptible to sexual involvement with students, but sexual relationships are ubiquitous, and celibate communities that forbid them may find them even more troublesome than those which sanction them.

In the context of spiritual awareness, an ecstatic sexual experience may afford a taste of unitive consciousness. A moment of dissolution of ego boundaries can be a doorway to self-transcendence. The problem is that the doorway, in this case sexuality, is often confused with the state that is attained, albeit temporarily. For some practitioners of spiritual disciplines, sex becomes less compelling after gaining access through meditation to those states of consciousness that are sometimes accessed in ecstatic sexual experience.

If addictions to altered states of consciousness, either through drugs or sexual experiences, are misguided attempts to satisfy a longing for transcendence, then one must beware lest sex should become a substitute for genuine transcendence rather than a stepping stone along the way. It seems that any experience that provides an opening at one stage of the journey becomes a trap if pursued as an end in itself.

Sex and spirituality have long been split in the psyche of civilized humans, and much suffering has been endured by both men and women as a result. Yet, sex and spirituality need not be held in opposition. At the heart of both of these dimensions of human life is the universal experience of love. Healing the split in the minds of men and women who find them incompatible calls for examining beliefs, uncovering early conditioning and repressed painful memories, as well as confronting irrational fears. There is no part of nature that is not sacred when regarded with reverence and love. The natural energetic systems equated with the masculine and feminine principles are as old as creation, symbolized by the sun and the moon, the dynamic and the receptive. A transpersonal view allows us to unite these opposites within ourselves and in our relationships.[8]

Ancient Tantric practices that were designed to balance masculine and feminine energies in the body apparently used women for the benefit of male practitioners. Women may also have used men, but we hear less of this. In any event, the concept of balancing masculine and feminine polarities in the individual, in both men and women, seems to be very recent. Today, some practitioners of Tantra see men and women as equals, participating in a mutual energetic exchange that can be nurturing and healing to both.

Perception of spirit as the ground of all being suggests the necessity for balance and partnership between male and female, sex and spirituality, being and becoming, time and eternity, life and death. There are no pairs of opposites that can be severed from each other in the totality of wholeness. Healing, as a process of becoming whole, calls for the inclusion, balance, and synthesis of seeming opposites.

A CONTEMPORARY PERSPECTIVE

At present, the earth is in grave danger of becoming a wasteland and people are thirsting for connectedness, for spiritual nourishment, and contact with such feminine values as love and compassion. The sexual revolution has led many people to search for love in multiple sexual relationships. Sex without love may be temporarily satisfying, but it pales in comparison with uninhibited loving sexuality between equals. It is commonly assumed that men promise love in order to get sex, whereas women are more likely to use sex to get love. This sets the stage for endless games of withholding and manipulation, all of which are frustrating and unsatisfying in any event, and often painful and destructive.

As with other human experiences, sexuality can be either sacred or profane, depending on how it is used. As an expression of love and joining, it can become a spiritual experience. As a means of domination or manipulation, it becomes degrading and entrapping. When it is mutually satisfying, sexuality increases a sense of connectedness and awareness of shared experience, regardless of whether it is perceived as sacred or not. Sexuality as an expression of spiritual union and divine love between social equals may be unique to our time.

Sexuality can be a doorway to self-transcendence when a person is ready for it. But sexual energy, associated with the second cakra, is only one level of mutual exchange.[†] When all the cakras are open, sexual energy is not exclusively genital and can enhance awareness of energy flow in the whole body. Some men and women consciously engage in sex as a sacred ritual to increase awareness of shared divinity. However, when genital sexual energy is dominant, other more subtle forms of energy awareness may go unnoticed. As perceptual sensitivity increases with practice in concentration and quieting the mind, impulses to discharge the sexual energy may be sublimated in the service of expanding consciousness and accessing other doorways to ecstatic experience.

Erotic love, powerful though it may be, is still only one aspect of unconditional, universal love. Although sexual energy can be used in the service of spiritual development, it can also become a pitfall on the path, since it is potentially addictive and can impede other more subtle levels of awareness. To be whole human beings we must come to terms with all of human experience, and embracing the polarities of sex and spirituality is part of exploring the mystery of life in all its dimensions as an ever-expanding adventure of consciousness.

NOTES

1. A. Watts, *Nature, Man and Woman* (New York: Pantheon, 1958), 189.

2. I Cor. 7:1.

3. See N. Qualls-Corbett, *The Sacred Prostitute: Eternal Aspect of the Feminine* (Toronto, Ontario: Inner City Books, 1988)

4. See J. Bolen, "Intersection of the Timeless with Time." Paper presented at the Association for Transpersonal Psychology Annual Conference, Asilomar, Calif. August 1988.

5. See R. Eisler, *The Chalice and the Blade* (San Francisco: Harper & Row, 1987).

6. See A. Lorde, *Uses of the Erotic: The Erotic as Power* (Freedom,

---

†According to a well-known Hindu esoteric model of the human body, there are seven major psycho-energetic centers aligned along the bodily axis. These are known as the "cakras." The second cakra is situated in the genital region and is connected with sexual and eliminative functions. (Ed.)

Calif.: Crossing Press, 1978).

7. See S. Boucher, *Turning the Wheel: American Women Creating the New Buddhism* (San Francisco: Harper & Row, 1988).

8. See J. Singer, *Energies of Love: Sexuality Re-Visioned* (Garden City, N.Y.: Anchor Press, 1983).

"This Accidental Joy: Poetic Reflections" by British poet Lewis Thompson is excerpted from Thompson's posthumously published book Mirror to the Light. *The poet died of sunstroke in 1949 in the sacred city of Benares, India, his adopted homeland. His writings, which he considered to be a form of spiritual discipline (yoga), are imbued with the spirit of the highest metaphysical traditions of Hinduism. The excerpt particularly expresses Thompson's affinity for Tantra, India's sex-positive spiritual approach. His aphoristic reflections articulate the ancient doctrine that liberation (mukti) and world enjoyment (bhukti) are not incompatible. Rather, the pleasures of the senses are an aspect of the perfect bliss of the ultimate Reality. As Thompson conveys to us, sexuality divorced from the spiritual Reality is entirely destructive but it becomes a potent creative force when integrated with that Reality.*

THIS ACCIDENTAL JOY: POETIC REFLECTIONS

By Lewis Thompson

The Joy and Beauty vital desire and emotion seek are not in conjunction but in consummation, not contingent but absolute. Wholeness seeks only what already belongs to it, all its movement in Presence, the pure Dance. But all desire and satisfaction depend upon and multiply Absence, live in a mirror-world of images, endlessly multiplying never-seized reflections. Energy earthed leaves earth unchanged, makes earth the nether pole, perpetuates eternal dualism, inconclusiveness, the circling hypnosis of Necessity.

To be disturbed by our desires is to become less than the equal of our imagination: we contain all the gods.

A sense of this containing: all actual desire enjoyed within one's province, without moving, as it were—calmly, resourcefully, like a conscious dream, without modification of one's centrality. Just as thoughts no longer submitted or reacted to die away, surrender to Consciousness itself. So desire surrenders to Delight.

The whole man—this simply means entirely disinterested and spontaneous: joy, not desire.

True love is indivisible, it is always transcendent. Because it "seeketh not itself to please" it alone justifies every delight.

Yet the soul in us, because it has ever perfect Joy, never needs to *seek* for it, can only share and give.

And the technical fact remains that soul and body are not commensurate and if they are ever to become so it is the body that must surrender to a greater, timeless, and more essential delight its brief, occasional, helpless pleasure.

* * *

Sexuality must be treated like any other fact of Nature, without preference or resistance. Then alone can it find, inwardly and in event, its true place in the economy of the whole man.

In modern sexuality our ambiguous state on earth reaches a helpless desperation, a blind crying upon gods now inaccessible, the terrible suspense between two metaphysical orders, the more and more acute and exquisite oscillation across an abyss that must be *leapt.* The new order demands for the first time perfect personal integration of sexuality—the Eros is no longer to be entirely a cosmic power. That power is no longer a unifying passion helping to face death (cannibalism, Assyria, Egypt, Lamaism, Aztecs) but now a force of disintegration ever dispersing in impotent pathic crisis the condensation of the kingdom of earth.

Those who, in physiological terms, are complacent in their sexuality, can never know the power of Eros, but only those for whom he is a devouring fire, a passion which, in their seeking to exhaust it, to bring it to an impossible extremity, can only lead to death or insanity—that licks up all creation, all experience, all ideas into the color and caprice of its ingenious, cruel, ever-exigent flame.

Desire produces division, the exact opposite of concentration and Enjoyment in the present.

It is only the ego that values sexual capacity and enjoyment in themselves and it is continually their dupe.

Their oneness: the chastity in their work of Dante, Michelangelo, of the saints . . . The flaming chastity of the Christ, the Whole Man—"hard as diamond and tender as a flower."

Technically, wholeness demands integrity at each level, in every mode of experience and consciousness: and sexuality, in which the relation of the individual with others is organic, is either integral, a base, or destructive, an undermining.

The two poles of the body: brain and sex. Knowledge of good and evil sees the sweet sex as the primordial wholeness of Vigor, but can never possess the polar opposite it depends upon.

Edenic Integral Vigor is to be reborn in the Heart.
The Child, all Heart, is transparent in mind and sex.

Outside humanism, sexuality represents a powerful magical force.

Sexuality *in itself*, like everything relative, is entirely destructive. In this as in general it has a direct polar correspondence with the brain. Thought completing itself in its own sense destroys itself. It is only so far as sexuality, incapable of exceeding its limits, falls short of this, that it continues the endless process of relativities: what it perpetuates is not life, but old age and death. In itself it is a powerful expression of life, but of life divided.

Sexuality is clearly seen from its point of view as a play of Nature by which the external man is deceived and swept away and used. The whole pathos of the external man, his efforts, sufferings, ideals, depends upon the blindness of his relation with the Nature that is prior to him. Only the true man, the central being, the soul, is prior to Nature.

The sexual problem exists only so long as we have not first of all discovered how very small a part of ourselves sexuality can engage—so long as we have not perceived its limits, so long as it is still psychological, with overcharged confusion, Anguish, dreams—so long as we are still not disinterested and realistic in this sphere.

If there is everywhere integrity, wholeness, there will also be perfect harmony. The sex-force is the foundation, in the body at least, of all our energies, including the highest and most subtle.

The humanistic attempt to harmonize sex with love is unrealistic, can only succeed very rarely as a special artistic achievement. This is good and valuable only for those whose special needs or gifts are fulfilled by it.

The whole dividing and disturbing power of sexuality is in our separation of it in our minds from its spontaneous occasions. There is either an act of the whole man or there is merely a sexual act. There are either partial imaginations—lust, dreams, obsessing "perversions"—and partial fulfillments, or the enjoyment of an undivided consciousness. When the whole man and the whole woman meet there is born Luxury.

The Eros, like every other manifestation of force, is rhythmic, and only a taut string can vibrate.

At the physical level sex is entirely mechanical, entirely given, limited, predetermined, blind, untransformable, a dead-end of energy where it is caught in an overwhelming vortex of gravity. The greatest ingenuity can only exploit but cannot alter this.

The mechanical cannot be a means of expressing anything real for the whole man. But the mechanical is defined by the mind. The one solution is Wholeness, Spontaneity.

In itself, mechanically, sexual pleasure, as the Hindu scriptures say, is hardly more or other than that of scratching an itching palm: what gives it at the same time fineness, massiveness, and fascination is the subtle vital energy. But if this is supported by that physical resource it can offer in its own sphere of delight and beauty far wider, keener, and more delicate joy. To force the vital energy continually to its lowest expression for its own sake must surely coarsen the nature and leave unexplored and undeveloped the more subtle and far longer-vibrating delights that make the charm of art and of our intimate, inexpressibly delicate sense of life itself an iridescence.

The spiritual Now involves the true central being. Otherwise the "vital," betraying all to pleasure, says precisely Now, Now.

All the magical and mystical admonishments to control sexuality refer first of all to sensation, to appetite. When this element is detached the force that sexuality represents, the true nature and aim of the Eros, can recognize itself and is freed.

It can survive only in relation with the whole being, for then it is no longer subversive but the energy of life itself in its most absolute form. Its relation with all richness, grace, and beauty, the most subtle and the most magnificent, is now simple and integral: it is no longer a hunger confused by given objects but a spontaneous capacity of Enjoyment, a mode and power of life as a whole serving and fulfilling its most ultimate nature.

The bitter sobbing of Absence ravages the whole body—all the obscure and naive blood that still can serve no wisdom, that is either proud or forlorn, obstinate or tormented, rigorous or sentimental, meaninglessly solitary or meaninglessly betrayed, the servant of accident, for whom even the moon, winds, tides, and time are not beneficent gods but unknown powers, blind fate, cruelly ambiguous oracles.

Sexuality is ultimately a technical matter concerning the integrity of Energy.

But it cannot be treated thus objectively while it continues a moral or psychological problem, so long as there is inhibition against sexuality as spontaneous, undifferentiated expression of affection and delight.

* * *

In trying to treat sexuality objectively, without prejudice to the freedom, the amoralism of its own mode, and yet to integrate it with the Heart and the Intellect, we have to use seriously something whose very essence is irresponsibility, play. In fact every "seriousness" here is limitation: it is only the oneness of Play, of Poetry, *at all levels*, that can integrate it on all levels. Sexuality is a perfect symbol, the more so by its immediacy, of the intrinsic geniality of Energy, of Consciousness itself. To seek to refuse or evade it is to move in a closed circle.

Hence the stupidity, the impotence of the ascetic monk. The state of Perfect Manhood cannot be attained by a eunuch: all in the human state has to be fulfilled and justified. For the ascetic monk, the Spirit is still an abstraction and he has fallen victim to that abstraction. Though indeed we see in practice that neither the Spirit nor the gods can be cheated. People give up sexuality (outwardly, anyway, for we cannot and need not "give up" what one has understood and commanded—the very idea of "giving up" what is not one's own is blindness and presumption)—and then, since their vital force remains untransformed (they have locked away the chief key to its transformation) as it accumulates they have to drug it with tobacco or marijuana. It seems that sexual experience could be far subtler, richer, and more profitable, humbler. These people think they are beyond Tragedy, and live on an infantile distinction between "worldly" and "unworldly," according to which, irrespective of their actual individual development and experience, in which worldly men often far surpass them, they belong by definition to the superior party. As if Reality were either worldly or unworldly! They make "the path" an end. If the only complete and ultimate fulfillment is Effortless Being, ascetic monkhood makes a stage a terminus, and hence an obstacle.

What by sympathy and understanding you have not outgrown with peace and laughter do not yet "renounce": you may merely get caught in a new aspect of the ego. Only *yourself* can you renounce entirely. And you can surrender that reality only to Reality itself.

The Western sense of sin and especially of sexuality as sinful is an expression of the unspirituality for which the least thing threatens to engulf one in the world and obscure for ever one's innocence, the central inspiration to the Divine.

* * *

Sexuality cannot be *suppressed* without disturbance of the whole system of vital energy, but sexual energy can be intelligently *transformed*. This is however possible only to a transmoral realism.

The transience of all erotic joy and results is not at all an honest or sufficient reason for rejecting them; indeed for any free and disinterested nature this very transience is their purity. Only this accidental joy is not commensurate with the soul. This transience and incompleteness therefore only show that the true source and meaning of this joy lie elsewhere.

If sexuality were merely a craving for sensation it could effect no more ravages than gluttony, but it becomes a vehicle of the whole pathos of our existence. Yet even this depends upon a confusion of sensation with something else—with a disinterested and agonized love of charm, beauty, nobility which sensation never allows that agony to examine itself, to discover what is its real object. It is this disguise of the real object which gives sexuality its extraordinary resource and power, the almost infinite scope in human life of its reversions, inversions, perversions—its subtle and fatal versatility.

In its endless recurrence and at the same time the limitation by which again and again it reaches exhaustion, sexuality reaches a frontier, a crisis between limited and unlimited. It can lend itself entirely to the unlimited (the Eros), but this must entail a change of mode. No "skill in love" can achieve this, only a centering of awareness in the unlimited. This means, first of all to cease to identify awareness and experience with physical sensation, with the body. All asceticism assumes this identification. But the disentangling of experience from sensation and the perfect knowledge of sensation entailed may demand an ascesis of a very different, far more subtle and exacting kind. Only when fantasy is perfectly commanded, all ecstasies, all intoxication, is pure Spontaneous Enjoyment experienced.

* * *

Love remains ever single and absolute, the process of love an art, a play—delight and not necessity; invention, not subjection.

For some, sexuality is the most plausible form of *laisser-aller*, self-indulgence, egotism; for others the fulcrum of religious or metaphysical evasions; for some the god of a voracious private myth; for others the surrender to confusions, or a Gordian knot, of sentiment; for some a spite against the universe, a wound, the vortex of poverty. It provides a language of metaphors so vivid and far-reaching that most are used by it, many succumb to its literature, a few exploit it against God or man, fewest of all handle it freely and fulfill it under the sign of Poetry.

Perfect chastity is perfect understanding of enjoyment, perfect possession of it in oneself and therefore perfect self-possession in it. This is, no doubt, one of the meanings of the richly genial erotic sculptures of Hindu temples dedicated to the Absolute beyond all qualities.

There is only one way to be chaste if chastity is not to be negative, and that is, to love deeply.

There are as many inimitable kinds of chastity as there are flowers. Morality cannot possibly measure facts of this order.

For lovers, body or dream may mingle—contact perfected into intangibility. It may be wondered how the dualism of sexuality can still exist in the perfect oneness of realization. Perhaps, on the contrary, it is not by the last realism, the perfect oneness with Reality, of *sahaja*, effortless being, that the act of love is really itself: below this, all fail from it, are overwhelmed and carried away or else ward off the ecstasy and reduce all to abstraction, to art of habit, yet still cannot avoid it, so deep and keen is the mystery open there.

That a sex-positive orientation is not completely foreign to Christianity is demonstrated in the essay "Bio-Spiritual Approach to Sexuality" by Edwin M. McMahon and Peter A. Campbell. Both authors, who are Catholic priests, argue that for spirituality to be authentic and conducive to personal growth it must be anchored in our bodily existence. More specifically, it must proceed on the basis of what they call "bodily-felt knowing," a process by which we become aware of our own felt "organismic" meanings or certainties. Hence the subtitle "The Christian Search for a Unification Process within the Human Organism." Our bodies are invaluable resources for arriving at a more comprehensive understanding of life than is afforded by mere abstract thinking or belief. The essay faults contemporary Church authority for failing to overcome its patriarchal prejudice against an embodied spirituality and wholesome sexuality. They advocate the use of Eugene T. Gendlin's method of Focusing to get in touch again with our bodies' inherent wisdom. While their work aims primarily at a Christian audience, their fundamental ideas are valid for everyone who wishes to engage spiritual life realistically, that is, in a down-to-earth manner.

A BIO-SPIRITUAL APPROACH TO SEXUALITY: THE CHRISTIAN SEARCH FOR A UNIFICATION PROCESS WITHIN THE HUMAN ORGANISM

By Edwin M. McMahon, Ph.D
and Peter A. Campbell, Ph.D.

Sex and religion remain closely linked during these closing decades of the twentieth century. But muddled relations between them continue to provoke controversy. After two thousand years of Judaeo-Christian experience, and even longer cohabitation within Eastern religions, no single church or individual yet seems to have sorted out how or why these dynamic forces in human life go on keeping company with each other. The news media have been filled, recently, with accounts and confessions of sexual indiscretion among superstar heroes of the televangelistic brotherhood. Alleged carnal excesses practiced in certain New Age communities with a Hindu or Buddhist orientation suggest that Eastern teachers, too, appear not always totally "enlightened" in their approach to sexual/spiritual growth.[1]

Some people within the Christian community come into conflict with church teachings in areas of sexual morality. A discernible mass of former churchgoers have distanced themselves from the institution precisely because of church pronouncements regarding sexual matters—birth control, celibacy, or the status of women in the church. Our experience as two Catholic priest psychologists active in ministry for nearly twenty-five years leads us to recognize that a significant number of those drifting away from institutional churches are responsible, mature, and developing adults. They are by no means self-indulgent individuals looking for an excuse to live a licentious life. In far too many instances, these are people who are profoundly concerned about spiritual matters, and who feel totally undernourished by their church and therefore look elsewhere for resources to support their growth.

But where are the true sources of revelation, the enlightened spiritual guides who can help us mature spiritually as well as integrate our sexuality? The answers, we find, emerge from an overlooked and much neglected resource—*the wisdom and innate knowing already present within the human organism itself.*

In order to understand the unfolding of sexual integration, as well as that of spiritual wholeness, we need to appreciate the psychology of how the process of such wholeness directly evolves in a *bodily-felt* fashion. Abstract ideas, held up as goals to be attained according to norms of sexual morality or divine revelation, are never the same as the actual process of achieving these goals. The process of getting there is always more than an intention of the mind. It is an *embodied* process, and while abstract goals are relatively easy to describe, the process of embodiment is not. The actual teaching of such embodiment is too often neglected in values education. In a moment, we will describe such embodiment as a process of "congruence."

Our point in the following pages will be to emphasize that the embodied process of congruence or wholeness which animates healthy sexual integration is precisely the same psychological process that provides meaningful entry into the quest for a more profound spiritual life.

There are two areas we will look at in this essay. First, if you seek to understand and work toward a sexual ethics, then you must understand the process of wholeness or "congruence" as this unfolds within the human organism. Wholeness involves a *bodily-felt* process. It cannot be communicated as *information*. This is perhaps one of the most difficult lessons that well-intentioned educators must learn. Talking about some abstract ideal of wholeness and integration, whether sexual or spiritual, does not and can not make it happen!

The second area of consideration will be to suggest that one of the most carefully researched, continuing studies of the unification process has been carried out by Eugene T. Gendlin, at the University of Chicago in his development of "Focusing" as a resource for personal growth.[2] Focusing teaches an embodied process for bringing mental awareness and body-knowing together. This is not a system of ideas acquired through cognitive effort. Rather, it involves a special way of being present to oneself, that is, to all the inner knowing surrounding some important issue in life—mental thinking and emotions as well as the deeper, more vague "felt meanings" that animate the Focusing process. Focusing, in our view, offers a dramatically transformed perspective on sexuality and spiritual life—the latter emphasis being one that we explore through our work at the Institute for Research in Spirituality.

Before we launch into the discussion proper, we would like, briefly, to define some terms that may be useful to the reader. Bio-Spirituality is our way of describing an approach to life, religion and moral values that is consistent with the Judaeo-

Christian spiritual tradition yet at the same time includes, respects, and gives full scope to this broader process of organismic unification as it unfolds within the human body. The word "Bio-" in our description is used to direct attention toward a felt knowledge and experiencing that is always more than rational thinking alone.

The word "spiritual," in our view, refers to any bodily felt awareness that results in a surrendering into more of the truth of myself and not merely submission to the external authority of some guru, church, doctrine or moral/ethical system. It is allowing a power greater than myself to gift me with yet another step toward personal wholeness, unity between myself and other people, as well as harmony with nature and within the cosmos. This description identifies a bodily-felt process of unification as the core of spiritual development. It indicates there is a "valuing process" already at work within the human organism itself and that spiritual life as well as sexual integration depend upon the encouragement of this inner process. The fundamental distinction between "values" and "a valuing process" is central to the contribution which bio-spirituality can make to society.[3] A valuing process is grounded in the more extensive knowing that includes bodily-felt awareness. Abstract values, on the other hand, are often taught as cognitive principles of action with little or no reference to the body's knowing. The only link in many instances seems to be that such abstract principles are seen as ways to "control" undisciplined human emotions.

Two learnings that can be helpful for understanding the bio-spiritual approach might be stated as follows:

(1) It can never be emphasized enough that the "ideal" or unitive consciousness is never the same as an actual process of unification as this is experienced unfolding within our own bodies.

(2) Lasting change that will affect society behaviorally must respect how change operates in the body, not just how we change our ideas about issues.

The data necessary to articulate ethical and moral norms flows out of an integrating process within the human body, both individual and collective. The human organism itself is what carries forward the process of personal wholeness. It is a strange paradox that for all their emphasis on Incarnation and the Word Become Flesh, Christian authorities have failed to recognize and include the body's own process of moral valuing in their teachings on sexuality. We often hear eloquent "ideas" and "concepts" about the human body. But there is precious little recognition that the body itself has much to teach about sexual ethics, spiritual knowing, and the process of moral valuing. A bio-spiritual approach seeks to redress this imbalance.

This brings us to a third term that is useful for understanding the contribution of bio-spirituality. "Congruence" identifies an ability consciously to feel one's feelings physiologically and allow them to symbolize themselves accurately. The movement toward wholeness, or unification which we have briefly introduced is an unfolding of such congruence. Carl Rogers recognized the importance of congruence when developing his client-centered approach in therapy.[4] Eugene Gendlin carried this early work forward during his discovery and refinement of the Focusing process. In his more technical language, what one feels physiologically is "the experiencing process."[5] This is a bodily-felt meaning that by its nature unfolds and moves forward when not blocked. While Rogers concentrated much of his effort on clarifying the relationship between the therapist and client, Gendlin turned his attention toward the process of congruence, which he regarded as the actual engine of transformation that makes change possible. The therapeutic relationship is meant to provide a supportive context and climate within which the inner development of congruence can go forward.

Bio-spirituality, as we are developing it, carries the notion of congruence over into a far broader sense for bodily-felt knowing. This is not the place to describe our more extended meaning of the term "body." The notion is developed at greater length in our book *Bio-Spirituality: Focusing As a Way to Grow.*[6] The book outlines what we experience through the physical organism with its rational, emotional and "felt sensing" capabilities. More than that, though, it embraces the challenging biblical notions of "Body of Flesh (*sarx*) and "Body of Spirit (*soma*)." This ancient Semitic perspective offers a window on the potential for "tied-in-ness" to some Larger Body of awareness. The hebraic sense for "corporate personality" offers a striking framework within which we can situate the exciting contemporary exploration in psychology. The experience proper to bodily-felt knowing is far more comprehensive than what we imagine to be defined by the inner awareness and life of a single human organism.

Well-researched, extremely sophisticated, time-tested and above all, teachable learnings have been amassed concerning how we know in a more total organismic (rather than just emotional or mental) fashion. Focusing is an effective psychological process for getting in touch with such whole body knowing so that it can more forward and unfold. The approach helps people become aware of "felt meanings," which they carry in their bodies, and not just cognitive meanings they can think in their minds, or readily identifiable emotions like sadness or anger that they can feel. Felt meaning invariably arrives before you have any words to describe it. You experience an embodied knowing about some relationship, situation, or future occurrence that only later is known in a conceptual or rational way .

Abraham Maslow once sagely observed that "religionizing" only one part of life secularizes the rest of it.[7] Most traditional religionists tend to do just that. But a broader view has recently begun to emerge. In Maslow's view, "a whole school of psychologists now believe that 'spiritual values' are so much a part of the well-functioning organism as to be sine qua non 'defining characteristics' of it."[8] What Gendlin has done is direct attention toward the precise area of bodily-felt experiencing where the unification process unfolds in a concrete, tangible fashion. He has, as it were, put his finger on the *organismic* pulse of spiritual life, the heartbeat of unification itself—a discovery not unlike circulation of the blood in its importance to medical science.[9]

It has often been noted that religious people usually have the vocabulary of mystical experience long before they know anything about it in an embodied way. Focusing helps to make clear the difference between talk, ideas, and concepts about unity, and the actual experience itself.

The perennial attraction of both sexual and spiritual experience is that each responds to the most profound longing in human nature. It is the hunger for unification, for surrender to something greater than ourselves, to become unified within our own being, with one another, with the planet and within the cosmos. Focusing is the psychological approach we have found most useful over the last twenty years for developing a bio-spirituality. Together, bio-spirituality and Focusing direct attention toward the missing link in our struggles to grow personally, sexually, and spiritually. The human organism offers its own unfolding experience of wholeness. This is as true spiritually as it is sexually. What we all need, though, is more widespread knowledge of effective ways to benefit from such wisdom.

There are obvious challenges in the development of a bio-spirituality. As congruence matures in a church population, there is much more reliance on the accuracy, wisdom, and direction implicit within bodily-felt knowing. Inevitably, this raises conflict with church teachings that either are out of phase with the current evolution of consciousness, or worse, do not even acknowledge the value and importance of any knowing other than that necessary for orthodox adherence to a certain doctrine that is currently being questioned. The maturing of congruence in an individual or in a population means that the primal source for moral judgment and valuing resides more within the organismic knowing of an individual and less within external norms or authoritative teaching.

So often, the church confronts sincere, mature, growing people with teachings and explanations of morality that flow out of an inadequate epistemology. Authorities do not take into account the bodily-felt process of wholeness and congruence in people as this unfolds both individually and collectively. For this reason, church explanations often seem irrelevant, inadequate.

A classic example in the Catholic church, especially in the United States, was the 1968 encyclical on birth control—*Humanae Vitae.* There has been a monumental leap in bodily-felt awareness on the part of large numbers of well-intentioned, mature couples who desired to remain faithful to their church yet, at the same time, recognized that some kind of upgrading change was necessary. Church authority was zealous in its desire to preserve the primary procreative purpose of marriage. But it did this by upholding a traditional ideal rather than listening to the deepening interiorization in bodily-felt knowing, which in a common-sense way told couples they needed an effective method to space out the births of their children. Moreover, economic and other factors called for consideration so children could receive the full, loving attention required for them to grow into wholeness as well as receive the education required to survive in a technological and industrialized society.

Over the years we have observed a small number of outspoken priests, religious, laity, and theologians confronting church authorities with alternate norms in the area of sexual morality. The problem with bringing such awareness to the rest of the Christian community, including ecclesial authority, is that before Christians can have a changed perspective on some moral issues, an evolution in personal congruence needs to develop. Otherwise, the questioning simply frightens and elicits confrontation. The response to such nascent challenging to a traditional moral position is invariably the same. Church authority reacts negatively and cracks down. The more mature then leave, looking elsewhere for spiritual nourishment, while the less congruent become frightened and externally conformist. Inwardly, however, they lock in place an incongruent out-of-touchness that eventually will explode in the excesses of addictive and fundamentalist religion as well as destructive sexual behavior. It is a sad, tiresome tale told over and over again.

Having witnessed this dreary scenario repeating itself like a stuck record, the two of us decided on a different approach. Rather than becoming issue-oriented and getting mired in the effort to work out logical, theologically accurate, and scripturally sound positions that could support alternate forms of behavior and moral positions, we chose, instead, to address the problem at a far more fundamental level. We have never taken sides nor become involved in the flurry of debate over any number of moral or theological issues that have turned Christians against one another or torn the church apart. Rather, we set out systematically to discover the most effective means we could find that would help people deepen their own process of unification and growing congruence, because as this evolves the problem of alternate moral options and dogmatic positions takes care of itself. When people become convinced of an issue through faithfulness to the organic wisdom of their own bodily-felt knowing, then a clear direction eventually emerges, and they will follow it, whether church or any other authority approves, disapproves, or is indifferent to their decision. When sufficient numbers share the same experience, a community of believers is born, and that is the time in which to articulate the new direction.

Patriarchal proscriptions and taboos surround sexual activity in every major religious tradition. But the connection between male sexuality and masculine spirituality has always been problematic. The very essence of spiritual life involves openness, unification and self-surrender. Yet, as James B. Nelson observes:

> The emotionally and physically distant father, who rewards his son with love made conditional on performance expectations, contributes to a male shaped for independence but not intimacy, self-protection but not vulnerability, competition but not mutuality.[10]

Masculine spirituality, which dominates the Judaeo-Christian articulation of spiritual life, is largely shaped by just such a perspective. It is no wonder the women find little to nourish their feminine sensitivity in the combative, hard-nosed world of the patriarchal jungle.

The painful paradox, however, is that men desire closeness and intimacy just as much as women. But they don't know how to find it, and in many instances are out of touch with their own need for such closeness. Consequently, the loneliness, homophobia, and fear of death which Nelson regards as major issues to be grown through in the maturation of male sexuality equally affect any expression of masculine spirituality. But there is a silver lining in this difficult situation, one where Focusing and bio-spirituality could play a major role in the social and spiritual evolution of patriarchal religion. Nelson outlines the situation as follows:

> There are two fundamental tasks which face every infant: the establishment of gender identity and establishment of individuation—who am I as a male or as a female, and who am I as a unique individual? Because the primary nurturing parent is usually the mother (or a female mother-substitute), the processes involved in these two tasks are different for boys than they are for girls. Girls experience themselves as being like their mothers, continuous with them, and the sense of gender identity is a natural flow. On the other hand, "mothers experience their sons as a male opposite," and boys, in order to define themselves as masculine, must physically separate themselves from their mothers. As a result, male development involves a "more empathic individuation and a more defensive firming of experienced ego boundaries" (Chodorow, 1978). Male gender identity, then, becomes defined through separation and individuation, whereas that of the female is defined through attachment.
>
> Thus, if the girl is apt to be more successful in establishing her gender identity than in establishing her individuality, it is the opposite for the boy. For him, gender identity is more likely to be a lifetime project. "What does it mean to be a man?" will be a more continuing question for him than the corresponding question for the woman. And because he has established his somewhat precarious masculinity primarily through separation and individuation, intimacy may well threaten his sense of gender much more than it threatens the female's. This is accentuated because the body, now having initially established his emerging masculinity through separation, frequently has few positive clues about manhood. Because his father is more physically and emotionally distant than his mother, the clues for manhood are more likely to emerge in negative rather than in positive images: What is a boy? "Boys are not girls, they aren't sissies, they don't cry, they don't run to their mothers when they're hurt." There are many negative clues for manhood, but fewer positive ones.[11]

Part of the man's loneliness is being unable to define feelings or not even knowing how to feel them. A lack of congruence, therefore, is built right into the cultural experience and expression of male sexuality, just as many women remain out of touch with their true feelings about unrealized individuation. The women's movement and raising of a feminist perspective is doing much to develop awareness in this regard. But the problem still remains largely unresolved for men.

The implications for sexual and spiritual maturing are enormous. A masculine or feminine spirituality based upon incongruent awareness eventually will exhibit its innate flaws. Whenever bodily-felt knowing is disregarded there will be no unification process and hence a diminishment of spiritual life and sexual integration. There may be orthodoxy, there may be brilliant teachings and information about religion, there may be sublime values held up for reverence and passed on from generation to generation. But if there is no incarnational growing into wholeness within the most profound area of one's being, one's own sexual identity and one's own individuation, then a cold winter of hibernation must descend upon the flowering of spiritual life.

In the Institute for Research in Spirituality,[12] we believe that Focusing, as a teachable process easily introduced into family life, holds an outstanding promise of encouraging a bio-spiritual awakening in both sexual and spiritual maturation. It will do this not by any fresh reformulating of ancient dogmas, but simply by bringing more and more people home to the wisdom of their own developing congruence—which is a process of wholeness, of unfolding unification.

A significant aspect of our effort to make Focusing available to the coming generation is an emphasis we place on teaching children to focus. If children are taught Focusing at an early age, especially through modeling by their parents, gender identity and individuation, a direction for the maturing of healthy spiritual life, and ultimately the integration of their sexuality could be set in motion.

For the male reader: Imagine what it might have meant personally for you as a child if your own father had been your model and teacher of bodily-felt knowing. What might it have been like to be able to model yourself upon a father who was not afraid of his feelings, who could identify them, know how to be gentle with them, so that he could own even "unacceptable" feelings in a way that allowed them to change? Think of the opportunity for closeness with your own father, the non-judgmental sharing and mutual trust that might have resulted.

Moreover, what might it have been like to experience from early boyhood that it was manly and took courage to be truthful with yourself in this way, risking change and growth?

Focusing has taught us how important it is for the father to model and teach his male children Focusing, even more so than for the mother. The primary reason is that before adolescence, a body needs to identify with a self-caring, psycho-sexual, spiritual process that fosters congruence as *something appropriate for his growing masculine identity.* Then he won't later face the ambivalence of trying to decide whether Focusing is part of a feminine perspective from which he must distance himself for the sake of gender identity, if his only model and teacher has been his mother.

Moreover, for fathers to model and be in this special caring way with their sons as they struggle through difficult feelings directly addresses the problem of adolescent violence and destructiveness in boys as they search for a male identity. The youngster learns he does not have to be a "macho controller" in order to be a man. Focusing opens masculine identity to alternate forms of being male together with more humane options and ways of approaching the ambiguities of life.

When male identity moves away from the "controller model," not only will sexual integration go forward, but masculine spirituality can at last be freed to develop in a healthy fashion within the male body, individually and in community. Christian theology regards the gift of such maturing development in wholeness as an unfolding of the Body of the Whole Christ.

From a Christian perspective, the movement toward unification, which we have identified in these pages and which Focusing seeks to facilitate, is an embodied passing on of the faith, an experience of grace, a continuing incarnation and building of the new creation in the language of New Testament revelation. Within this ongoing experience of wholeness lies a power that moves the integration of both our sexuality and our spirituality forward. The hope and promise of unification for all humankind lies within our own bodies. The Kingdom of Heaven truly is "within."

NOTES

1. See Dick Anthony, Bruce Ecker, and Ken Wilber, eds., *Spiritual Choices: The Problem of Recognizing Authentic Paths to Inner Transformation* (New York: Paragon House Publishers, 1987). Cf. especially the Introduction: "The Spiritual Seeker's Dilemma," as well as 88-101.

2. See Eugene T. Gendlin, *Focusing* (New York: Bantam Books, 1981).

3. See Carl R. Rogers, "Toward a Modern Approach to Values: The Valuing Process in the Mature Person," in *The Journal of Abnormal and Social Psychology*, vol. 68, no. 2 (1964), 160-167.

4. See Carl R. Rogers, *Client-Centered Therapy* (New York: Houghton Mifflin, 1951). See also *On Becoming a Person*, (Boston: Houghton Mifflin, 1961).

5. See Eugene T. Gendlin, *Experiencing and the Creation of Meaning* (New York: MacMillan (Free Press), 1962).

6. See Peter A. Campbell and Edwin M. McMahon, *Bio-Spirituality: Focusing as a Way to Grow* (Chicago: Loyola University Press, 1985).

7. Abraham H. Maslow, *Religions, Values & Peak-Experiences*, Columbus: Ohio State University Press, 1964), 31.

8. Ibid., xiv.

9. The clearest theoretical statement of Gendlin's research on Focusing may be found in: Eugene T. Gendlin, "A Theory of Personality Change," in *New Directions in Client-Centered Therapy*, ed. by Joseph T. Hart & T. M. Tomlinson (Boston: Houghton Mifflin, 1970), 129-173.

10. James B. Nelson, *Sex Information & Education Council of the United States—SIECUS Report*, vol. 13, no. 4 (March 1985), 3.

11. Ibid., 2-3. The reference to Chodorow is taken from N. Chodorow, *The Reproduction of Mothering* (Berkeley: University of California Press, 1978), 150, 166-167.

12. The Institute for Research in Spirituality is an international organization, which offers workshops and training programs in Focusing and Spirituality throughout the United States and in Canada. An ongoing pamphlet series on various topics related to Focusing and Spirituality is available to members along with a newsletter, *Kairos*, and workshop schedule.

When we get more deeply in touch with our bodies, we find that the ensuing feeling of wholeness has the quality of love. When we feel at one with the various components that make up our particular personality and likewise when we feel at one with our environment, we discover that this feels rather like being in love. Part of this is that we seem to extend beyond our ordinary boundaries: We transcend the ego or self as which we normally experience ourselves. Thus love is ecstasy. This is the theme of the essay "The Ecstasy of Love" by reverends Arthur D. Colman and Libby Lee Colman. All too often, as the authors note, the traditional quest for ecstatic self-transcendence has excluded interpersonal relationships. The typical ascetic, yogi, or renouncer is an island unto himself (or more rarely, herself). For the ecstasy-seekers, love or ecstasy is a drug to which they are addicted. They will try to procure it again and again, and by any means. We can avert the danger of narcissism only if we keep our fellow beings in our hearts, that is, include them in our ecstasy by loving them.

THE ECSTASY OF LOVE

By Arthur D. Colman, M.D.
and Libby Lee Colman, Ph.D.

We have defined love as both a feeling and a way of relating, an emotion and a human interaction. It is conceptualized as the intersection of two dimensions of human process. One dimension contains the quest for ecstatic experiences which haunts man from the first moment he tastes the exquisite sensations of "oneness" or "wholeness." The other dimension contains the world of interpersonal relationships which dominate experience throughout life.

The dimension of ecstasy and the dimension of relationships do not intersect easily or often. Ecstatic experience may be represented by a single figure, facing the world and the self in magnificent aloneness: the burning frenzy of the possessed scholar in search of truth; the devout holy man in communion with self; the visionary prophet at one with his fantasy; even the hedonist with his multitude of sensual pleasures; none of them is with an Other. In their quest they often require teachers and guides and helpmates; but eventually they travel alone. The tradition of yoga speaks of "purification," warning again and again against the intrusion of relationships, even of the "subconscious" remnants of attachment to the "I." Most ecstatic traditions label close personal relationships an impediment in the quest toward expanding the germ of ecstasy in oneself.

It is easy to see why human relationships are excluded from the ecstatic quest. The choice between accepting ourselves as self-sufficient and reaching out to another is an eternal conflict defining each individual's balance between acceptance of existential isolation and perseverance in achieving union with others. It is as difficult to be alone as it is to be intimate. Often it seems as though the quest for ecstasy begins as an escape from the dangers of human relationship, that is, an attempt to flee the intricate tortures men and women concoct for those they know intimately.

Yet there is the potential of love, the hope of finding ecstasy in human relationships, of transcending mundane squabbles and discovering mutual joy. Whenever ecstasy is experienced in the developing closeness between two people, they speak of it as love. The intense soaring quality of "falling" in love, the unimagined pleasure of revealing the emotions of self to another, the sexual delights given and received, the serenity of being together, trusting, becoming one and separating, the mutual cosmic creation of another in pregnancy, childbirth, and parenting—to catalogue the ecstatic moments in the history of a relationship is to trace the thread of love between two people.

Love is ecstasy in a relationship. It is not an easy way to describe love, for most relationships do not support ecstatic experience. But love is undeniable. The comforts of a stable, socially appropriate relationship which satisfies the needs for dependence is not the same as ecstasy. Ecstatic moments can be temporarily forgotten or repressed. Ecstatic experience can be sought outside of relationships. But almost inevitably the stab of ecstasy is re-experienced in a new relationship with another person. Because love is so intense it will be sought again and again. Marriages and other partnerships may be jeopardized; family loyalties, even basic sexual identity, may be altered in the pursuit of ecstatic love. Entire political systems have been ravaged by the sudden rush of love affecting a critical leader or alliance. The saying that "all the world loves a lover" is patently false. Love is the enemy of order and ritual. If ecstasy can be removed from the context of a relationship and transferred to God, body, or inner vision, then impulses toward disorder have been brought under control. Society breathes more freely.

Love is as threatening for the individual as for the culture. Relationships offer far more than ecstasy. They offer security, a stable base from which to pursue other life goals. They offer the opportunity to mitigate the ever present sense of isolation. And more perversely, relationships offer a place to indulge in the endless fantasies that are the unfinished part of every childhood, the scripts, the games, the past pleasures that can be recapitulated in a variety of disguises. It is difficult to set such pleasures aside even when the total form of the relationship is a nightmare. The risk is great since even the most pathological liaisons may serve the quest. The sadist who is beaten by another to the accompaniment of his own autistic fantasies is structuring a distorted human dyad to serve a hidden need. The ecstasy of pain/pleasure is only a peripheral aspect of a relationship. The hand that holds the whip is interchangeable. This way of relating with others strains even the most non-demanding definitions of human interactions. Yet once an ecstatic orientation is fixed, it is incredibly difficult to change directions. It is like asking the dedicated yogi to abandon his discipline or the monk who has found God to enter a human relationship.

Human love is not an easy Way to find fulfillment. It is a Way, but not the only way.

All ecstatic traditions require an enduring commitment. Love is no exception. It may be the most rigorous of all because it requires more than self-discipline. It requires trust in the fidelity of another. It is like meditating on an unfixed point, a pattern which may move or change or disintegrate at any moment. It is like meditating on a poem in composition; it is as unstable as the novice's ability to fix his attention. It is like trying to lose his sense of "I" on a seesaw with another. It is like trying to encompass the universe when the universe walks and talks and makes love. It is like trying to lose oneself in an orgasm when the Other may withdraw unsatisfied. Love offers little hope of fulfillment and yet it is the standard of all ecstasies and all ecstatic traditions.

In the beginning, the infant does not know of his own existence as something separate and apart from the world around him. It is only gradually that his merger with totality is replaced by a merger with his mother and later the people in his environment. The infant experiences intense pleasure, even ecstasy, before his relationships with others are forged. That experience is identityless, pleasure experienced as a part merged with a whole. It goes beyond one's animal origins to a total union with the universe. Here is the model for ecstasy with loss of "I," for total union, for the final liberation. It is sleep without dreams, with no vestige of differentiation, a time and a consciousness before the egg and sperm divided, before life began.

The ecstasy of love derives from a later pre-relational state, the infant's experience of his own merger with another human. Within the extraordinary emotions provided by the original symbiotic dyad lies the kernel of the love experience. In this dyad a pre-emergent "I" glimpses his core human identity as more than an object and evolved his first assumptions about personhood and relating.

Love is revelling in humanness. It pulls us back from the molecular stream and calls attention to our special place in the universe. It differs from other forms of ecstasy in which personhood is yet another encumbrance, another layer to shed on the way toward the ultimate nothingness which is unity with everything. Its aim is the most total awareness of our special place in the universe of matter. Its form is the dyad because there is no more profound way to acknowledge our human bonds. The ecstasy of love is the final assertion of being human.

This essay caused great controversy when it first appeared in Utne Reader *in 1985. Glancing back to the history of ancient Sumer, Egypt, and Greece, Deena Metzger notes that women were celebrated as a doorway to the Divine — a doorway that was swiftly closed with the rise of the patriarchies. She states that the ancient prostitutes were not whores but priestesses, or "vamps." In her essay, she explores ways out of the current antisexual stance of our contemporary society, dominated as it is by the largely body- and sex-negative values of the Judeo-Christian tradition. Her plea is for the restoration of eros. Her thoughts on the holy prostitute are, however, not applicable to women only, and are certainly not restricted to feminists. Rather, men and women alike must rediscover the sacredness of sexuality and "revamp" (that is, refurbish) their outlook on life to include the sexual and the spiritual dimensions.*

RE-VAMPING THE WORLD: ON THE RETURN OF THE HOLY PROSTITUTE

By Deena Metzger, Ph.D.

Once upon a time, in Sumeria, in Mesopotamia, in Egypt, and in Greece, there were no whorehouses, no brothels. In that time, in those countries, there were instead the Temples of the Sacred Prostitutes. In these temples, men were cleansed, not sullied, morality was restored, not desecrated, sexuality was not perverted, but divine.

The original whore was a priestess, the conduit to the divine, the one through whose body one entered the sacred arena and was restored. Warriors, soldiers, soiled by combat within the world of men, came to the Holy Prostitute, the *Quedishtu*, literally meaning "the undefiled one," in order to be cleansed and reunited with the divine. The Quedishtu or Quadesh is associated with a variety of goddesses including Hathor, Ishtar, Anath, Astarte, Asherah, etc. It is interesting to note, according to Patricia Monaghan in *The Book of Goddesses and Heroines*, that Astarte originally meant "She of the Womb," but appears in the Old Testament as Ashtoreth, meaning "Shameful thing." Despite scripture and orthodox thought, war was seen as separating men from the divine, and one had to be reconnected in order to be able to re-enter society. The body, the sexual act, was the means for re-entry. As the body was the means, so inevitably pleasure was an accompaniment, but the essential attribute of sexuality, in this context, was prayer.

In Pergamon, Turkey, I saw the remains of the Temple of the Holy Prostitutes on the Sacred Way, alongside the other temples, palaces, and public buildings. Whatever rites we imagine took place in these other buildings, it is common whether we elevate them as do neo-pagans or condemn them as do Judeo-Christians to associate the Holy Prostitutes with orgies and debauchery. But it is possible that neither view is correct, as each tends to inflate the physical activity and ignore or impugn the spiritual component. Our materialist preoccupation with form blinds us to the content.

But it is no wonder that from the beginning, the first patriarchs, the priests of Judea and Israel, the prophets of Jehovah, all condemned the holy prostitutes and the worship of Asherah, Astarte, Anath, and the other goddesses. Until the time of these priests, the women were one doorway to the divine.

If the priests wished to insert themselves between the people and the divine, they had to remove women from that role. So it was not that sexuality was originally considered sinful per se, or that women's sexuality threatened property and progeny, it was also that in order for the priests to have power, woman had to be replaced as a road to the divine; this gate had to be closed. And it was, we can speculate, to this end that the terrible misogyny that we all suffer was instituted.

Women had been the essential link to the three worlds. Through the mother one came into this world; through the Mysteries, the rites of Demeter or Isis, one entered the underworld; and through the Holy Prostitute one came to God. Access was personal and unconditional. It was not sufficient for a new priesthood to supplant the women. In the days of the *Quedishtu* every woman served the divine as Holy Prostitute, often for as long as a year. This was contradictory to the hegemony that a priesthood required.

For the sake of power, it is often necessary to set the world upside down. Therefore the priests asserted that the sacred way was depraved, that the way to the divine was the way to perdition. Reversals such as this are not uncommon. Incoming religions often co-opt, then reverse, existing spiritual beliefs and practices. So Hades, the spiritual center of Greek paganism, became Hell. The descent into Hades, the core of the Eleusinian mysteries and a spiritually required initiation for anyone who was concerned with soul, was likened to suffering and perdition. Where once Pindar had written, "Thrice Blessed are those who have seen these Mysteries for they know the end of life and the beginning," later Dante was to inscribe, "Abandon all hope, ye who enter here." Similarly, Dionysus, the god of life, became Satan, as Adonis, the consort of Aphrodite, became Christ. Mary Magdalene the Holy Prostitute was converted and transformed, Aphrodite became Eve became the Virgin Mary. The reversals were complete. Psyche's (soul's) journey toward individuation became almost impossible as Aphrodite, the mother of Eros, no longer existed to beckon the Self.

Three of the essential roads to the three worlds were blocked or debased. God did not die in Nietzsche's time but centuries earlier with the subversion of the priestesses and the secularization and degradation of the holy body.

This essay is about seduction, about vamping, about eros — an attempt to restore a tradition, to reinstitute a way of seeing the world. It is not only about restoring practices, it is first about restoring the consciousness from which those practices may derive.

What was the impact of the suppression of the Holy Prostitute on the world? We are not concerned here with the deprivation of consciousness implicit in that suppression. All the practices that honored the way of the woman ceased. The Eleusinian mysteries, which had provided immortality, were suppressed; the mysteries of the Cabeiri, designed specifically to redeem those with blood on their hands, were suppressed; procreation was infused with anxiety and guilt; fertility festivals which had provided a link between earth and spirit were condemned. When the priests separated the body from the divine, they separated the divine from nature, and thereby created the mind/body split. The world was secularized. We can only speculate as to the consequences, though we must assume there were consequences when men returned from war without the ability to clean the blood from their hands, when the physical, quotidian community between the divine and the people was not reconvened. It was not woman per se that was attacked, but the divine who was exiled. Perhaps the world as we have come to know it, impersonal, abstract, detached, brutish, was engendered in that division.

In a sacred universe, the prostitute is a holy woman, a priestess. In a secular universe, the prostitute is a whore. In this distinction is the agony of our lives.

The question is: how do we relate to this today, as women, as feminists? Is there a way we can re-sanctify society, become the priestesses again, put ourselves in the service of the divine and eros? As we re-vision, can we re-vamp as well?

Vamp: A woman who sets out to charm or captivate by the use of sexual attractiveness.

Re-vamp: To mend, repair, renovate, refurbish, or restore.

In 1978, I wrote a novel, *The Woman Who Slept With Men to Take the War Out of Them*, about Holy Prostitutes . . . . In the novel, a woman whose name is Ada walks down the street of an occupied village from the cemetery, passing her own house, to the General's house, which she enters without a word to lie down unashamed on his bed. She does this with the full cognizance that she is committing a political act. Later in the novel, Grace, a prostitute in an old-age home, reminisces:

> "Still so sweet the men who came. We didn't allow whips. No rough stuff. And when they left—little lambs. Do you think the wives sent us a basket at Christmas time with a little homemade jam, for

thanks?

Always used to say those men would have torn the entire town apart on Saturday night if not for us. I thought we should have gotten a commendation from the marshall's office. I told that to the chief of police straight out. We were the best investment in law and order they ever made."

What does it mean to revamp a society? It means that we must become vamps again, sexual-spiritual beings, that we must act out of eros. This means that we must first alter ourselves in the most fundamental ways. We cannot become the means for the resanctification of society unless we are willing to become the priestesses once more who serve the divine not in theory and empty practice, but from our very nature. It means that we must identify with eros no matter what the seeming consequences to ourselves. Even if it seems foolish, inexpedient, even if it makes us vulnerable. It means that we cannot be distracted from this task by pleasure, power, lusts, or anger. It requires a sincere rededication.

It is, however, exactly this rededication to the principles of the feminine which is so problematic. The feminine has been so devalued and degraded, has so little power in the world, we have suffered so much loss of opportunity, have been so oppressed, that it is difficult, if not sometimes seemingly impossible, to continue to enact the feminine in the world without feeling as if we are opening ourselves to further violation. So we are caught in a terrible paradox. To feel powerful, to acquire some gain, we must learn the very masculine modes which oppress us and which are about to destroy the world. In either case we seem to participate in our own destruction. But if we utilize the feminine, it is possible that the planet will survive, and also the species, and that eventually we will thrive, and without the feminine and eros everything is irretrievably lost.

And so women must all become Holy Prostitutes again.

When contemporary Feminism was established sufficiently to offer real hope and possibility, women who had formerly considered themselves atheists turned to spiritual matters. The Goddess and goddesses were reinvoked. There was an extraordinary interest in spirituality, myth, rite, ceremony. The spiritual instinct buried in a secular universe erupted.

As part of this new spiritual order, we must engage in two heresies. The second is to re-sanctify the body; the first even more difficult task is to return to the very early, neolithic, pagan, matriarchal perception of the sacred universe itself. But to overthrow secular thought may be the heretical act of the century. That is why we are in so much psychic pain.

Susan Griffin writes the following in the last chapter, entitled "Eros," of *Pornography and Silence*:

> *"The psyche is simply world.* And if I let myself love, let myself touch, enter my own pleasure and longing, enter the body of another, the darkness, let the dark parts of my body speak, tongue into mouth, in the body's language, as I enter a part of me I believed was real begins to die, I descend into matter, I know I am at the heart of myself, I cry out in ecstasy. *For in love, we surrender our uniqueness and become world."*

If we become world through love, then love is essentially a political act. If we become world reaching to the divine, then love is essentially a spiritual act which redeems the world.

How then do we become Holy Prostitutes? How do we materialize without literalizing her? How do we bring her essence into being? How do we restore the temple? How do we change not only behavior but our consciousness as well?

To become the Holy Prostitute is to be willing to endure the agony of consciousness required of the heretic. It is the willingness and ability to hold one world view when the majority hold another. It is to commit oneself to eros, bonding, connection, when the world values thanatos, separation, detachment. The Holy Prostitute was Everywoman and she made herself available in the service of the divine especially to those outside the province of the divine. The contemporary Holy Prostitute must be willing to try to bring the sacred to the one who is defiled; she must be the one who will take in "the other"—the one who makes love with "the other" in order for him to be reconnected to the community. She carries the belief that "the other" does not want to remain an outsider.

These ideas are old and familiar, easy to say, so difficult to enact. Yet when they are transformed from idea to belief within ourselves, transformation outside ourselves follows.

Recently, I have been doing some work which I call Personal Disarmament. I ask individuals to consider themselves a nation state and to impose upon themselves those conditions they would like to impose upon the country. In this exercise they must identify their enemies, their armies, defense and offense systems, secret weapons, etc. Then after this self-scrutiny, I ask them to publicly commit at least a single act of personal disarmament to initiate the change to a peaceful world. It seems to me that our militarism and defensiveness are signs of our inner fear and aggression. I believe that ultimately it will be easier for us to disarm as a nation if we are disarmed as individuals.

The same scrutiny is essential to the issue at hand. If we built brothel adjuncts to our temples and sent our young girls there at 18, it would be ludicrous, it would change nothing: nothing can change as long as we devalue the feminine, denigrate the body and disbelieve in a sacred universe. Certainly the sexual revolution has proven this, for it has changed nothing. So it is not sex we are after at all, but something far deeper.

The task is to accept the body as spiritual, and sexuality and erotic love as spiritual disciplines, to believe that eros is pragmatic, to honor the feminine even where it is dishonored or disadvantaged. These, then, are some of the questions I think it is appropriate for us to ask ourselves:

Whom do I close myself against?
When do I not have time for love or eros?
When do I find eros inconvenient, burdensome, or
    inexpedient?
When do I find eros dangerous to me?
When do I indulge the erotic charge of guilt?
Where do I respond to, accept, provoke the idea of sin?
When do I use sexuality to distract rather than to
    commune?
When do I reject eros because I am rejected?
When do I abuse the body?
How do I reinforce the mind/body split?
When and how do I denigrate the feminine?
When do I refuse the divine?
When do I pretend to believe in it?
When do I accept the divine only when it serves me?
How often do I acquiesce to the "real world?"

Recently, in a guided meditation, I was confronted by a large, luminous woman, approximately eight feet tall, clearly an image of a goddess, though I had never encountered a goddess figure in any of my own meditations. Her hair was light itself. As she came close to me, I was filled both with awe at her beauty and terror at her presence. If I were to take her into me, I knew my life would be altered, I would have to give up many of the masculine models I had adopted in order to negotiate successfully in the world. The woman was powerful, but her power was of receptivity, resonance, magnetism, radiance. She had the power of eros; she drew me to her. As she appeared, I was reminded of a statement by a friend. "When it comes to the bell," Dianna Linden said, "we all want to be the clapper, we don't want to be the body; but it is the body which sings." Still, when she appeared, I consciously experienced the terror of the feminine I had so often read and heard about. I was afraid of my own nature. At that moment, I committed myself to risking heresy, to converting, whatever the personal cost, to the feminine.

So though I have written about, thought about it, and tried to act accordingly, I must admit that I have not been able to fully put on the robe of the Holy Prostitute. This fills me with sadness, and also awe at the difficulty of the task. But I do commit myself; she is the woman I aspire to be.

The shadow of nuclear war, the fear of planetary devastation may provoke people to premature action. My friend Stephen Nachmanovich asked, "Why do things get worse when we try to fix them?" In the '60s, Daniel Berrigan said, "Don't just do something, stand there." Action devoid of consciousness is useless, even dangerous. Consciousness, however, leads inevitably to right action. To come to consciousness takes an interminably long time. To bring a society to consciousness may seem to take eons. But our circumstances are so dire, we must not risk unconscious action. The stakes are too high. We must allow whatever time it takes to re-establish the consciousness of the Sacred Prostitute. We must allow ourselves whatever time it takes to restore eros.

"Erotic Love," is an excerpt from George Leonard's book Adventures in Monogamy. *As Leonard explains, true erotic love is ecstatic and as such involves the stripping down of the ego-personality. Another way of putting it is: Deeply committed erotic love is a form of surrender. It is also a form of intense interpersonal reaching-out. It is a bridge between the gender islands of males and females.*

EROTIC LOVE AS SURRENDER

By George Leonard

Love is the News without which there can be no news, no perception, no life.

For me, the erotic encounter is ecstatic in the dictionary sense of the word. It takes me out of my set position, my stasis. It permits me the unique freedom of stripping away every mask, every facade that I usually present to the world, and of existing for a while in that state of pure being where there is no expectation and no judgment. The act of love, at best, is an unveiling. Layer after layer of custom and appearance are stripped away. First goes clothing, then every other marker of status and position: job, title, honors, monetary worth. Propriety must also go, and with it pride. My freedom lies precisely in surrender, in my willingness to relinquish even my hard-won personality (*persona*, Greek for "mask"), my image of who I am in the world and what I should be—my ego. If I am willing to travel this far and expect nothing, then nothing can go wrong. There are no "sexual problems," no "sexual solutions." There is no technique. I am as a god; whatever happens happens.

And it is in this state of surrender, of not-trying, that my full erotic potential is realized. For I am now willing to lose everything and find nothing. All that has maintained me in the ordinary world is of no use here—grammar, syntax, sensory acuity. Even differences of gender fade away in the climactic rhythm of our joining. I am not male, my love is not female. We are one, one entity. Through the tumult of love, we have arrived at a radiant stillness, the center of the dance.

At this point, there is a choice that lies beyond conscious choice, predisposed by trust, commitment and passion: to travel even beyond space and time and enter a sublime darkness. Seeing nothing, hearing nothing, I am totally connected with my love, and, through her, to all of existence. What was veiled is unveiled, what was hidden is revealed; beneath all appearance, beyond all customary distinctions, there is a deeper self that wears no mask. In the darkness, there is an illumination. In love, I have found nothing and all things.

It's not always like that. If erotic love is extraordinary, it is also commonplace. There are occasions when the act of love simply soothes and nurtures. There are times when a caring love, half-asleep, may simply lend his or her body to a more aroused partner as a gesture of friendly love. There are also episodes of pure genital lust, exuberant carnal joy. Not everyone can find a lifelong, committed erotic relationship, but everyone can be caring rather than mechanical, giving rather than manipulative. Love has many names and many faces and is not in short supply. Every erotic act offers the possibility of a loving human interaction. To deny or fail to appreciate the commonplace is to reduce the possibility of transcending it. I have also learned over the years that living organisms are not machines, that erotic arousal is not a predictable, mechanical phenomenon. Love is like the weather: unpredictably cyclical. A sudden, unforeseen fall of desire doesn't necessarily mean rejection or the end of a relationship. It is probably only a change in the weather of love. To try to force arousal during a dry spell or to give up and seek "sex" elsewhere is to shut out the cloudburst of passion that in all likelihood will follow (though no one can say just when). To wait patiently, to ride lightly with the rhythms of life, is no failure of will or action. For even during a lull of physical passion, the light of our joining is in my lover's eyes. Under every conceivable sky, we remain connected—to one another and to all things.

That erotic connection will hold me to my lover and to life for as long as I live. I will seek responsibility because joining my body with hers is the ultimate responsibility. I will be trusting because trust is the other side of surrender, and the deeper connection is impossible without surrender. I will commit myself to her without demanding possession because the mere thought of owning her makes her an object, an *It*. I will open myself to the unpredictable, the mysterious, sensing a sort of poetic physics of love. In the quantum world, the more we know about the position of an elementary particle, the less we know about its momentum. In love, I think, the more we try to pin a lover down, the less momentum, the less movement and excitement, we experience. I will not try to pin my lover down. Danger, uncertainty, and a touch of the forbidden add to the thrill of our every moment together. In all the primates, including humans, the presence of a sexual rival increases the flow of sex hormones. But I need no contrived danger. No rival for her love is required to increase my excitement. For I know that death is my inexorable rival. Sooner or later death will separate us. In this realm of being, we must say good-bye. Perhaps more than anything else, our full awareness of death's capriciousness and inevitability makes our love both poignant and profound.

It is the glory and grace of erotic love that it offers each of us the opportunity of passionate connection with another and, through that, of a larger connectedness. The erotic urge draws us toward creation, toward the condition of potent nothingness from which all existence unfolds. To make love is ultimately to affirm life, new families, new generations. In the light of truly personal erotic love, war is no longer abstract, a matter of cold statistics ("only 100 million deaths"), but rather a matter of immediate personal concern. The possible destruction of life on earth is no longer *out there* but here, in this place and this time: the possible destruction of our love, of all love.

I believe that creative, deeply committed erotic love can serve as a healing force in a dangerous world. It shatters any ideology that fails to distinguish lives from ideas. It leads us to experiences in which it is not necessary to take a drug, commit a crime, or go to war in order to feel fully awake and alive. It connects us to other people and to all the earth and perhaps to the stars as well.

And if erotic love is too important to be repressed, it is also too important to be devalued, for to devalue love is to devalue life itself. I want my children and their children to live in a world in which the depersonalization and trivialization of the erotic is no longer rationalized and glorified. I would like someday soon to celebrate the end of "sex" and the beginnings of a radically repersonalized, fully erotic society.

Our current situation is perilous. As always, the game is a close one. But I believe—in some way we must all believe—that love will prevail, that love eventually will join us in a family as wide as all humankind that can laugh together, weep together, and share the common ecstasy.

PART TWO
Sexuality in a Spiritual Context

In the essay "Sexuality as Sacrament: The options of Spiritual Eroticism and Celibacy," Georg Feuerstein shows how conventional religion considers sexuality to be a constant threat to our spiritual welfare. All the great religions recommend sexual self-restraint, if not celibacy. But there are also sex-positive traditions like Tantrism and Taoism that proffer an erotic spirituality. They acknowledge that we have genitals but seek to put them to a higher use — the transmutation of genital sexuality into erotic ecstasy revealing the Mystery of sexuality and life.

SEXUALITY AS SACRAMENT: THE OPTIONS OF SPIRITUAL EROTICISM AND CELIBACY

By Georg Feuerstein, M.Litt.

There are two undeniable biological facts. First, we are born with genitals. Second, when stimulated our genitals give us considerable pleasure. These two facts have been a perennial preoccupation of religious authorities as well as political authorities. Both authorities are, for their own reasons, forever concerned about orderly life. Sexual passion has typically been viewed as a potential danger to the established order. Sex, so the story goes, makes us irrational, and the irrational is a threat to organized religion and the state. Hence the sexual drive or libido must be repressed and channeled.

As Freud argued so vociferously, the history of human civilization is the history of sexual repression, the subjugation of instinctual life to the discipline of the self-controlled personality, or the conversion of what he styled the "pleasure principle" into the "reality principle." According to Freud, human civilization is impossible without the repression of the libido. For, the redirected ("sublimated") libido is the foundation of religion, philosophy, and art.

However, as the Sexual Revolution has taught us, the clerical or political suppression of our sexual instinct is a direct threat to our growth as human beings: We have the right to be sexual. In this respect, Heloise is a more convincing voice than her erstwhile lover Abelard. For Abelard's religious ardor and dogmatic defense of chastity, one suspects, have their origin in the violation he suffered at the hands of Heliose's revengeful family, who cruelly castrated him.

Even when she was made abbess of the Convent of Paraclete, Heloise's passion for Abelard remained greater than her enthusiasm for a pious life, or even her love for God. In one of her rebellious letters to her former paramour, she wrote with exemplary self-honesty:

> They praise my chastity, not knowing how false I am . . . I burn with all the flames kindled in me by the ardours of the flesh . . . The amorous pleasures we have tasted together are so sweet to me that I cannot bring myself to detest them, nor even to drive them from my memory.[1]

The only reason why Heloise had entered the convent at all was to obey Abelard's wish, not so much God's. Her tragic story encapsulates the conflict between conventional religion and the life of passion and desire (eros), which includes sexual self-expression. Notwithstanding Abelard's persistent effort to redirect Heloise's passionate feelings toward higher goals, her unfulfilled erotic life effectively blocked her spiritual maturation. Abelard, one of the most brilliant theologians of early medieval Europe, rechanneled his own passion into aggressive intellectual labor, which in the end led to his condemnation by Rome.

Mere repression of the sexual impulse only leads to neurosis and psychosis. This is true on both the individual and the social level. As Alex Comfort, a contemporary apostle of sexual liberty, expressed it:

> In spite of their overt anti-sexual bias, or more correctly, perhaps, beacuse of it, centralized urban societies produce a heightened emotional tension that leads to a state of persistent, because often unsatisfied, sexual excitement. The dissatisfaction of the public with its personal experiences of sexuality is expressed in art and entertainment as an intensive preoccupation with romantic love, with sexual success and with virility.[2]

Of course, with the right to be sexual comes a great deal of responsibility. Sexuality is not confined to tingling sensations in our genitals. It is not merely a neurological happening in the brain either. Rather, it is an aspect of the totality of our being human. Therefore it also involves the dimension of action. As Karol Wojtyla, who is better known as Pope John Paul II, reminded us, it is in our active life that we can exercise self-determination, and that this is precisely "the point at which human freedom and the sex urge meet."[3]

> The sexual urge can transcend the determinism of the natural order by an act of love. For this very reason manifestations of the sexual urge in man [and woman] must be evaluated on the plane of love, and any act which orginates from it forms a link in the chain of responsibility, responsibility for love. All this is possible because, psychologically, the sexual urge does not fully determine human behaviour but leaves room for the free exercise of the will.[4]

Religious authorities have never been able to deny the fact that our bodies sprout genitals. Yet they have traditionally paid an inordinate amount of attention to what we are supposed to do with them, usually by way of insisting on extreme constraint. Seldom has this demand been coupled with sound advice on how to live a chaste life without falling prey to sexual neuroses.

According to one school of thought, which has been highly influential in the past, genitals are exclusively for procreation.

When we do not desire offspring we should, it is argued, simply forget about the existence of our reproductive organs. In fact, after having sired or given birth to two or three children, we should never again involve ourselves with the debasing activity of sex. The great ideal of this way of viewing life is extreme celibacy, the renunciation of all sexual activity.

A second, less radical opinion acknowledges the fact that few people will, unless forced, choose to be celibate forever. This second camp of religious authority also emphasizes the procreative function of sex, but in addition permits people to be sexually active beyond the immediate purpose of giving birth. According to this view, sex is to be regulated in terms of style and frequency. This seems to embody a more viable attitude, and in the following it will become clear why.

Within this more moderate group of opinion we find a broad range of approaches. At one end of the spectrum is the view that sexual activity is not really desirable beyond procreation but people, weak as they are, cannot be obliged to practice celibacy. At the other end of the spectrum are the body- and sex-positive schools of Eastern esotericism, such as Tantra and Taoism.

In opposition to what is often believed about these Oriental approaches, they do not endorse the pursuit of pleasure for its own sake. Thus, Tantra is definitely not hedonism. Tantric exercises are not primarily about feeling good, though feeling good is certainly not considered a sin either. Tantra and other comparable traditions are primarily about transcending the ego and realizing the larger Whole, whether it be called Universal Self or God.

These schools do not deny pleasure. What they ask us to do, however, is to deepen pleasure, until we find the transcendental bliss in it. Conventional pleasure, they argue, is always attendant with a degree of pain, partly because it is finite and varyingly intense and partly because when enjoyed in excess it can lead to physical and psychic suffering. By contrast, the transcendental bliss (ananda), as experienced in the state of ecstatic self-transcendence, is complete in itself and is utterly satisfying to our whole being. It signals the end of all psychic suffering. Whereas in the wake of pleasure, displeasure is sure to follow, bliss has no shadow side. It always nourishes and sustains our being.

Before I say more about this body-positive orientation, I will first look at the opinion favoring celibacy, and what this means.

THE SECRETS OF CELIBACY

As is well known, the official Catholic dogma on sexuality reflects a largely body- and sex-negative orientation. But sex-negativity is present also in non-Catholic denominations. Hence Christianity, with some legitimacy, has been called an antisexual religion. It has not always been thus, however. When we read through the Old Testament, for instance, we find no trace of sex having been looked upon as evil. Otherwise Solomon's sensuous *Song of Songs*, which has embarrassed generations of prudish Christians, could never have been included in this sacred collection.

The ancient Hebrews believed that God had charged them with the sacred obligation of filling the earth with progeny. To them, sex was a procreational duty. The Hebrews did, however, have fairly strict rules about sexual behavior, and transgressions were handled rather severely according to the age-old law of "an eye for an eye."

The appearance of Jesus of Nazareth brought about an important change. Although he endorsed the sexual mores of the Hebrews, he at the same time introduced a new attitude of forgiveness. The classic story is about the woman, a notorious "sinner," who broke into an intimate gathering of the apostles. She let her tears flow freely over Jesus' feet, and then she wiped his feet dry with her hair. This caused a certain amount of eyebrow-raising, but Jesus praised the woman highly for the love she bore for him, and forgave her the many sins she had committed during her unregenerate life.

As for Jesus' own sexual life, he is generally thought to have been celibate. But the fact is that the New Testament makes no statement about his marital status or sexual preferences whatsoever. That nothing is said about a wife need not necessarily mean that Jesus was unmarried. In fact, a few historians have suggested that, given ancient Jewish social mores, it is highly likely that he and all or most of his twelve disciples were married.

It was Paul of Tarsus, on whose ideas the Church chose to build itself, who seems to have felt problematic about women and sexuality. He discouraged marriage, and he himself was unmarried. In his seventh letter to the Corinthians, he wrote "I should like everyone to be like me." What he meant was that he preferred his flock to be celibate like himself. In his view, it is best for a man not to touch a woman, but since sex is a perpetual danger, man and woman should be joined in holy matrimony. By implication, marriage was for those who didn't have a strong enough character to practice celibacy. Paul explicitly did not regard marriage as sinful, but it was "second best" for him and presumably for most of his fellow Christians. Consequently, marriage was entered with a certain amount of subliminal guilt—hardly a basis for happiness in a relationship that was supposed to last a lifetime. But, then, happiness was thought to be reserved for the hereafter.

Paul believed he had a very good reason for recommending celibacy as a person's first choice. He preached that Christ's establishment of the Kingdom of God on earth was imminent and that, therefore, no children should be brought into the world. History proved him wrong.

The greatest antisexual authority within Christendom was, however, not the apostle Paul but St. Augustine (354-430 C.E.). He also happened to be the most talented and influential of all Church teachers. His theology dominated Christianity for over a thousand years. In his earlier life, Augustine was greatly troubled by temptations of the flesh. He had at least two love affairs, one of which produced a child. His conversion to Christianity had not a little to do with his desire to be finished with sexuality, but it didn't quite turn out that way.

Augustine, a learned man, had imbibed the dualistic metaphysics of Gnosticism, which made a sharp split between body and spirit. In the light of this "pagan" teaching, he came to consider all forms of sex as sinful. He spoke of the guilt connected with procreation. As he saw it, marital sex was a lesser sin, which could be forgiven. Nevertheless, Augustine maintained that upon resurrection, men and women would retain their sexual characteristics. But he believed that the female genitals would then be "part of a new beauty, which will not excite the lust of the beholder . . . but will arouse the praises of God."[5]

Augustine regarded concupiscence, or what we call "sexiness" today, as the great temptation on the spiritual path. He firmly believed that Adam's fallen nature is transmitted biologically through sexual procreation. He saw in lust a direct expression of Adam's corruption, which had led to the Fall. We are born corrupt, sinful, and guilty. Augustine's teachings succeeded in souring sex for generations of Christians, who could engage in the sexual act only by piling guilt feelings upon their originally "sinful" nature.

The early Christian community was exposed to traditions like Gnosticism, which devalued worldly existence in favor of the life of the otherworldly spirit. The old story of Adam and Eve's eviction from Paradise was interpreted in explicitly sexual terms. It was thought that sex was in fact a punishment for the betrayal of God in the Garden of Eden. Consequently, the renunciation of the sexual impulse was the only way people could redeem themselves in the eyes of God.

The same kind of reasoning led to the doctrine of the Virgin Birth. The New Testament simply states that Mary was a virgin until she gave birth to a son. This was soon reinterpreted to mean that she remained a virgin even after the birth of Jesus. Since Jesus the Christ could not possibly have been born through natural intercourse using the "sinful" vaginal passage, his conception must have been a miracle. His mother, Mary, was obviously a virgin who had never been tainted by any sexual thought, desire, or act. To ensure her absolute immaculateness, she came to be held as having been herself born free from sin.

After emperor Constantine put an end to the centuries-long persecution of Christians by making Christianity the religion of the Roman empire in 312 C.E., there was a great rush toward monasticism. Christians who wanted to follow the apostolic life in earnest now formed small communities or went into the desert. By their own choice, they lived as celibates.

The word *celibacy* comes from the Latin *coelebs*, meaning single, alone. Originally, it was applied to unmarried men and women. Later it came to be used for men and women who pursued religious life either on their own or in the relative seclusion of a monastic community, and who practiced chastity. In those early times, women sought celibacy not so much because sex was an ambiguous area of Christian moral life, which it definitely was, but because married women had little chance of pursuing their spiritual aspirations. Men had similar reasons for renouncing the pleasures (and problems) of the flesh.

The motives may well have been somewhat different during the Middle Ages, where Church dogma firmly ruled against sexual pleasure, and neither men nor women could possibly expect much personal satisfaction from guilt-ridden, hasty intercourse. They gave up sex for agape, the selfless, soul-ennobling love.

Some medieval women developed a tremendous capacity for transferring their sexual impulses to the religious and mystical realm. As theologian Dody Donnelly succinctly put it: "God makes love, as all the mystics can testify."[6] The close relationship between mystical experience and orgasm is well documented in the history of religion. Almost three decades ago, the British writer Marghanita Laski surveyed secular and sacred experiences of ecstasy in literature and in contemporary social life. She found that nearly half the respondents to a questionnaire mentioned sexual love as a trigger for ecstatic experiences they had had. These were ordinary, "secular" men and women. Laski dryly concluded, among other things, that "it is now possible to dispose of the theory that ecstasy is largely if not wholly a phenomenon of sexual repression."[7]

Mechthilde of Magdeburg, a thirteenth-century German nun, alarmed her superiors by expressing her erotic feelings for Jesus in her diaries. She invited others to rendezvous with Jesus on the "couch of love," where he would cool their passion. She was not alone in her passionate sentiments, but the Church was hardly ready for such an erotic spirituality. Yet this bridal mysticism foreshadowed the rebellion against Church dogma during the Renaissance and the Reformation. Today, more feminist-oriented nuns reject the idea of becoming the bride of Christ, because they see in it another version of male chauvinism.

In the Middle Ages, the Christian laity was asked to practice celibacy but predictably failed to live up to this ideal, as it had failed in the preceding millennium. No excuses were accepted from the clergy, however. This irked earthy people like Martin Luther, who considered compulsory celibacy a "handiwork of the Devil." He defied the Church and at the age of forty-two married a twenty-seven-year old woman, who had been a nun for fourteen years. Other reformers, like Calvin and Zwingly, attacked Rome's stance on clerical celibacy as well. Yet, none of them really advanced our understanding of sexuality in relation to spiritual life. For them, sex was still second best to celibacy.

In response to the Reformation, the Catholic Church convened the Council of Trent over a period of eighteen years, from 1545 to 1563 C.E. But again very little progress was made. All sexual activity outside of marriage continued to be considered sinful, and marital sex was looked upon as a last resort: In the spirit of Paul, married folk were asked to resist their sexual impulses as much as possible, before yielding to the demands of the flesh. An open invitation to repression and guilt.

Today, celibacy is generally, though as we will see not

universally, looked upon as an oddity by the public. As Rose-
mary Radford Ruether put it, "Asceticism does not have a good
press in the twentieth century."[8] And asceticism is widely
confused with sex-phobia and body-hatred. Hannah Ward, a
Franciscan sister, recalled an incident that happened to one of
her fellow sisters. During a coach journey, a young girl kept
looking at her curiously. She asked her mother what "it" was,
who explained to her that the habited figure was a nun. The
girl's curiosity was only piqued, however. She turned to the
sister herself, peering between the seats, politely asking her:
"Excuse me, do you have breasts?"[9]

The little girl's innocent question was of course justified,
because the nun's habit was invented precisely to conceal
sexual characteristics. Moreover, her question is one that crops
up, in different forms, in many an adult mind when confronted
with a habited nun. Did she become a nun because she had
sexual problems? And is she sexually active despite her vow of
celibacy? The last question is particularly appropriate, given the
recent public confessions as found, for instance, in the book
Lesbian Nuns: Breaking Silence.[10]

Our consumer society is clearly far removed from the
traditional ideal of asceticism. In our unease with the ascetical
lifestyle, we like to point to the excesses and morbid manifestations in the history of asceticism. We may remember St. Benedict
(c. 500 C.E.) who, when he was sorely tempted by a vision of a
woman, threw himself into briars and nettles until his skin was
badly torn and he was bleeding profusely. Origen (c. 200 C.E.),
another respected Church Father and Neoplatonist, castrated
himself to meet the ideal of an antisexual Christianity.

But such acts of desperation were never what asceticism
was supposed to be about, at least not according to the more
enlightened points of view. Thus, St. Anthony emerged from the
desert after twenty years of fasting and ordeal neither emaciated
nor broken-spirited but, according to the testimony of Athana-
sius, filled with spiritual radiance and physically healthy.

Despite the widespread misunderstanding about celibacy
and asceticism, both have clearly become a post-Sexual Revolution choice for a growing number of people. They are discovering
celibacy as a means of dealing with our sex-drenched society,
the constant bombardment by sexual signals through the mass
media and advertising, as well as the sexual stress in interpersonal relations. They freely choose to renounce sex for a given
period of time—from several months to several years—or decide

to adopt it as their permanent lifestyle. For these neo-celibates, sex "is an idea whose time has passed," as George Leonard put it.[11]

Dr. Stuart Sovatsky, a contributor to this volume and director of the Kundalini Clinic in San Francisco, is someone who has been celibate for many years. His recent book, entitled *Passions of Innocence*, is a clarion call in favor of celibacy.[12] His sensitive work points to the hidden wonders of celibacy, without prettifying anything. In many ways he advocates a purist model of celibacy, but his work is not lacking in compassion. For instance, he is very clear that celibacy should not include masturbation. Rather, the whole idea is to preserve and transmute the sexual energy, not release it through orgasm. Sovatsky is, however, also adamant that celibacy has its time and place and that it should never be forced.

On the other hand, "soft" celibacy, or celibacy that involves moderate sexual self-manipulation, is an option for some people, including Christians. This is borne out by the long essay on masturbation penned by brothers David Schulz and Dominic S. Raphael (a pseudonym) and contained in the present anthology. These two priests condone the practice and deem current Church dogma on masturbation to be cruelly out of date. The work that liberated many readers from masturbatory guilt was, as noted in the Introduction, the two *Kinsey Reports*, published in 1948 and 1953 respectively.

The classic work that first unashamedly recommended masturbation for physical health and psychic balance was Betty Dodson's *Liberating Masturbation*, published in 1974. Five years later, Manfred F. DeMartino edited the anthology entitled *Human Auto-Erotic Practices*, and in 1981 Margo Woods issued her down-to-earth and oft-times frivolous book *Masturbation, Tantra and Self Love*. As the title suggests, this work seeks to put masturbation into a quasi-spiritual or quasi-Tantric context. For Woods, masturbation is a "meditation" whose object is not to achieve orgasm, which "ends the play," but to generate and harness psycho-physiological energy. This is also the goal of Tantra, though it is set more sharply against a backdrop of radical self-transcendence. Still, Woods does advocate the value of a loving heart, which tempers some of her other recommendations that might be felt to encourage narcissism. She wrote:

> When the heart is open, when love is flowing, the possible evils of a strong sexual drive are eliminated because the heart wishes no one ill. It knows what other people need, it listens, it wishes them

only good. It is stronger than the sexual drive and directs it towards the highest good.[13]

Thus far I have focused on celibacy in the Christian context, and have said little about this practice in other religions, even though it has been an integral part of many religious traditions. In all traditions, celibacy is thought to enhance a person's ability to contact the sacred, to get in touch with the great Mystery. But Christianity has failed to explain how this should be so, other than in general moral terms. However, Hinduism, Buddhism, and Taoism have developed specific teachings that describe the underlying esoteric process of celibate "sublimation."

Yoga students, for instance, will be familiar with the Sanskrit expression *brahmacarya*, which is the age-old ideal of celibacy within the Hindu tradition. I will single out this practice for special treatment, because it is surrounded by a rather sophisticated understanding of what we may call the "bio-spiritual mechanism" of celibate sublimation. Such knowledge seems useful even to those who do not wish to live a long-term celibate life.

The word *brahmacarya* means "brahmic conduct." This can be interpreted as meaning the conduct of a brahmin, a member of the priestly class of Hindu society, or the conduct that is in consonance with the *brahman*, the Absolute or Universal Reality. The *brahman* is conceived as beyond space and time and hence beyond all differentiation, including gender distinctions. It is sexless. The *brahmacarin* or *brahmacarini*, that is, the male or female person practicing brahmacarya, seeks to emulate the sexless nature of the Absolute. In so doing, it is said, he or she acquires the "same form" as the Absolute, or Divine. In other words, he or she becomes enlightened, freed from the limitations of the ego-personality.

It is clear from the classical descriptions of the brahmacarin or brahmacarini that he or she is no weakling. On the contrary, brahmacarya, or chastity, generates great psychophysical power. The Hindus understood, earlier and better than anyone else, that the preservation of the sexual energy can, if rightly done, serve as rich fuel for the spiritual process. The body has a hidden mechanism for converting sexual energy into something that is both more subtle and more potent, and that can act as a force for breaking open the gateway to the unitive or ecstatic consciousness.

Without knowledge of this esoteric process, the student of spirituality is like a blind person. Therefore it is important that the spiritual practitioner should understand what is happening in the laboratory of the body as a result of the preservation and regulation of the sexual energy (to whatever degree).

According to the classical accounts, whenever the male semen is emitted, it involves a loss of valuable energy. We can understand this as a loss of hormones that might otherwise be utilized in the chemistry of the body to nourish organs, notably the brain. Mantak Chia, a contemporary Taoist teacher, remarked about this:

> Ordinarily discharge of the seminal fluid completes the act of love. As soon as the fluid is spent, the body strains to replace it. The faster sperm is used, the more the body is forced to produce. Quite obviously, production of this nutritionally rich and psychically superpotent substance requires an enormous amount of raw materials. The reproductive glands receive these raw materials from the blood stream. In its turn, the blood withdraws the precious elements from every part of the body, liver, kidney, spleen, etc., including the brain. Every organ pays heavy tribute to the glands that produce the sexual seed. Because a single drop of semen houses such prodigious life energies, frequent loss of fluid depletes the body systems of their most precious nutrients and speeds the inevitable physical decline into old age. Retaining the seed within the body is the first step to reversing this cycle in which the male pays an unnecessarily stiff price for sexual satisfaction.[14]

But the Taoist and Yogic authorities insist that there is something more fundamental involved here. They claim that semen, which is continually generated by the gonads, invigorates our psycho-mental life through the agency of subtle energy. The Hindus call this energy *ojas*. This ojas is thought to rise from the sexual center to the brain. It is the product of a process of continuous transmutation that occurs in the genitals when the semen is preserved.

Although the traditional works on Yoga are more concerned with the male practitioner than the female yogini, ojas is a force that is not unique to men. Women, too, can preserve their sexual charge and transmute it for higher purposes.

In some extraordinary states of consciousness, this spontaneously happening alchemical process can actually be seen in inner vision. The late Gopi Krishna, an adept from Kashmir whose works on Kundalini-Yoga are widely read, offered this description:

There can be no doubt whatsoever that the incessant, easily perceptible, rapid movement at the base of my spine . . . was an indication of the fact that . . . a hidden organ had begun to function all of a sudden in the hitherto innocent-looking region, converting the reproductive fluid into a radiant vital essence of high potency which, racing along the nerve fibres as well as the spinal canal, nourished the brain and the organs with a rejuvenating substance out of reach in any other way.[15]

Gopi Krishna speculated that a new psycho-somatic center was in the process of forming in his brain as a result of his accidental awakening of the "serpent-power," or *kundalini-shakti.* This kundalini is conceived as being normally latent in the human body. Upon its arousal it completely revolutionizes the chemistry of the body, leading to psychic states and, ultimately, enlightenment. According to Gopi Krishna's understanding, this newly forming center in his brain was drawing energy from the genital region.

There is no scientific evidence for what Gopi Krishna saw happening in his own body, but this does not necessarily say anything about Gopi Krishna or his experience. More likely, it merely reflects the bias and ignorance of contemporary science. What Gopi Krishna has shared with us in his books has been known for centuries in India, Tibet, China, and elsewhere— wherever men and women have dedicated their lives to exploring the vast regions of consciousness.

Next I will turn to the second school of thought, which believes not in the total renunciation of sexuality but in its controlled use.

THE MIDDLE PATH OF REGULATING THE SEXUAL DRIVE

Between the path of lifelong celibacy and the worldy path of unbridled pleasure-seeking lies the middle way of regulated sexuality, or sexuality as spiritual practice. Most of us are what in traditional societies like India are called "householders." Few of us are equipped by biological predisposition, character, or circumstance to live successful lives as lifelong celibates. If we had to adopt celibacy, we could do so only by repressing the sexual drive.

But sexual repression is worse than sexual overdrive. Both, of course, are forms of avoiding the Larger Reality, the higher Self. Sexual repression, however, turns people into sour-faced misanthropes who spread their unhappiness like a virus.

It is perhaps better to be on the self-indulgent side than to lock one's feelings up inside and punish everyone else for one's "forbidden" urges and thoughts.

Perhaps the most important point to understand about sexuality is that the sexual drive is a particular form or aspect of the life-force in the body. So long as we look upon the sexual drive as a thing of its own, independent of the total economy of the body's psycho-physical energy, we tend to perceive sexual problems too narrowly.

In old-fashioned terms, sex cannot be separated from eros. Eros stands for our sensual delight, or passions. Unfortunately, "erotic" today means mostly "sexually arousing." But in its original meaning, the word "erotic" had a much broader connotation. Eros is the kind of passionate love that seeks to include, to participate, and in its negative aspects, to possess.

Our society is overly sexual but withered in its erotic sensibilities. As Sam Keen, author of *The Passionate Life*,[16] expressed it to me, we need to relearn loving, not abstractly and only platonically, but bodily, sensually, passionately. Such love has to begin with trust in our bodily existence, and it is always an embrace of our embodiment and the embodiment of others.

In practical terms, what this means is that instead of zeroing in on our sexual problems and sexual concerns, we should simply cultivate our erotic life as a whole and become passionate men and women—passionate about what we do, feel, think, and say; passionate about our commitment to each other, our work, our friends, colleagues, neighbors, fellow citizens, human beings far and wide, animals, trees, the environment.

Once we give our lives this new erotic focus, many of our sexual "problems" will evaporate. If you have a toothache and keep thinking about it, the pain will drive you crazy. However, if you simply put your attention on something else—listen to soothing music or watch an absorbing movie, the pain mysteriously vanishes, or at least recedes into the background of your consciousness.

The trouble is we have made a fetish out of sex. We are obsessed with sex and feel complicated about having it and about not having it. We confuse eros with lascivious eroticism. However, a similar correction needs to happen relative to the concept of agape. In Christian hands, this idea has been interpreted to signify a loftily idealistic love that aspires to be perfect and disregards the body and its lowly needs. Properly understood, agape is self-transcending love, which by no means negates erotic or passionate love but integrates it into a larger reality of being human. The American psychiatrist Gerald G. May acknowledged this when he made the following astute observation:

> Spiritual passion and erotic passion are so similar that people often find themselves using one as a substitute for the other. The problem is that either way, the substitutions never quite seem to be right.
> It has long been recognized that religious novices seeking celibacy because of sexual fears often do not do well in religious life. To transfer erotic energy directly into spiritual outlets requires great maturity, if indeed it can be done at all. To attempt this because of fears or fixations inevitably deepens one's confusion at both psychological and spiritual levels. To seek satisfaction of one's spiritual passion through genitality is just as destructive.
> Making these distinctions should not encourage one to compartmentalize love excessively . . . Eroticism is in the last analysis a manifestation of the energy of divine love that has been differentiated into a certain form . . . The world does fall away in the ecstasy of erotic love. It falls away at the moment of orgasm and at many other moments of total preoccupation with one's lover. In contrast, the ecstasy of agapic love is characterized by an awesome joining with all the rest of the world, becoming a part of it. In an erotic "high," the world disappears in love. In the spiritual "high," the world appears in love.[18]

For a good many people, sex has become their "ultimate concern," in theologian Paul Tillich's phrase. They confuse genitality with eroticism and, in some cases, even with agapic love. Another way of saying that we are unerotic in this sense is that we are largely unable to "contemplate desire." This is how the contemporary spiritual teacher Da Free John put it in his wise and challenging work *Love of the Two-Armed Form:*

> The satisfaction of desire is always so urgent for ordinary people. The usual man must suddenly satisfy himself and become empty. He cannot tolerate the prolongation of desire itself . . . Thus, desire is a problem . . . . In order to become an uncommon man or woman, we must be able to enjoy desire itself . . . In Communion with God the stimulations and fascinations of ordinary things vanish, so that ultimately you desire or love to the most absolute degree, and yet you do not at the same time suffer the slightest capacity to be emptied or satisfied.[19]

To paraphrase the above paragraph: When we have a desire we want to see it fulfilled—immediately. The instant gratification of our sexual desires merely leads to depletion, followed by the need to repeat the experience again and again. For the most part, our behavior is unthinking, automatic. We don't know any better and expect instant gratification all the time. We are consumers, especially in our sexual life.

Teresa Bielecki, now known as Mother Tessa, is the cofounder of the Spiritual Life Institute in Colorado. In an interview with Rick Fields, she remarked:

> People feel that every time they experience desire, they have to act on it. There are other ways to act on it besides genitally. We can laugh, and recognize ourselves as sexual animals. Different people will deal with it differently. The old cold shower and exercise option is always good. Sometimes you need not think about it at all. Simply distract yourself. And sometimes you need to work with it very consciously. You take it to prayer.[20]

When asked whether celibate mysticism is not merely repressed sexuality, Bielecki responded by quoting the British philosopher E. I. Watkin: "Mysticism is not disguised sex; sex is disguised mysticism." She explained:

> This is the heart of living a celibate life. The deepest hunger in every person is the hunger for God. Sexuality is an expression of that, which is why men and women fall in love with one another and why sexuality is given to us.[21]

When we have learned to postpone the fulfillment of our sexual desires even a little bit, we find that our body fills with the glow of anticipation. Sexual energy is a powerful force. If we can learn to store it rather than squander it every time our genitals announce their tumid existence to us, we magnify our erotic potential, heighten our awareness, and render our body radiant.

Then, when we get together with our loved one, we approach him or her with a bodily fullness that transforms the encounter from a quick tumble of genital sensations to a luscious enjoyment of each other's being, in body and in spirit. Then lovemaking becomes actual loving participation in the other's psycho-physical presence. Obviously, this is not something that is likely to occur in a casual sexual encounter, which usually has more to do with stimulating each other's genitals to the point of orgasm, followed by a cigarette and platitudes.

So, what should we do when the sexual monster rears its ugly head? Well, first of all, we must understand that the sexual drive is not in the least ugly. It is part of our being embodied. It is as natural as any other bodily function. There is nothing obscene about it, and all the bad feelings we might possibly have are simply learned responses. They are inappropriate responses, and so we need not be concerned about them at all. As children we were taught about the bogeyman. He scared us, until we found out that he did not exist. The sexual monster is a similar kind of fictional character. We can safely laugh at the fact that we once believed in it, but we do not allow it to rule our life.

Second, we must simply accept that we are feeling sexual. In fact, we must allow ourselves to really feel those feelings in our body. Instead of immediately creating a problem for ourselves by dreaming up ways of gratifying the sexual urge, we can simply sit with those feelings for a while and welcome them like a good friend. In that case, we simply notice the excitement in our genitals and the surrounding area, and understand that we do not have to do anything about those sensations, other than accept and notice them as fully as we can. Generally, what happens then is that the sexual excitement spreads as a warm tingling sensation over other parts of the body and ceases to be troubling.

The Rumanian spiritual teacher Omraam Mikhael Aivanhov told the story of a pretty young girl who confessed to him that wherever she looked she saw the male genitals.[22] She was immensely burdened by this, having been brought up as a good Catholic. He calmly advised her that instead of thinking she was obsessed and that the image was horribly disgusting, she should simply accept what she was seeing, and more than that, to think of it as a wonderful and mysterious display.

He wisely suggested to her not to dwell too long on the image, but to enquire into the mystery behind it: "How intelligent! How did Nature know how to make such a magnificent image!" This, he said, would open her to a new dimension, beyond the image that so troubled her. The young girl left, immensely relieved and happy.

Third, we can assist this process of sexual diffusion by proper breathing. Breathing is probably the most important practice discovered by yogins, shamans, and mystics. It is the most direct way of regulating the body's life-force. Breathing is like the outer shell of the subtle psycho-somatic energy called *prana* in Hinduism and *ch'i* in Taoism.

Fourth, we need to understand ourselves. What are our most profound goals? If we truly—*truly*—aspire to a life devoted to spiritual growth, we will have to accept a measure of discipline, including sexual discipline. We need not necessarily become celibates, but we will have to cultivate new attitudes toward everything, including our attitude toward sexual "consumption." If, however, we do not find in our heart of hearts that we are motivated by such a noble goal, and instead want to live a life dedicated to other concerns, our sexual discipline can be correspondingly lax. But even then we will have to become aware of our typical patterns and learn to negotiate them rightly.

The serious spiritual aspirant will have to seriously consider his or her sexuality and introduce a degree of discipline, without repressing himself or herself. The great ideal of a body-positive spirituality is to transmute the sexual energy, without squashing it and oneself, and to use it in order to intensify one's consciousness and one's erotic capacity.

In certain traditions, like Tantrism and Taoism, the idea is to actively conduct the sexual energy into the body as a whole, especially toward the crown of the head where an important psychic center is located. The transmuted sexual energy is thought to break open the door to the higher Self, the Atman, beyond the ego-personality. It is the winged dragon that can help us soar to greater heights, or that can devour us if we are not wise. Sexuality is a tremendous force.

To quote Omraam Mikhael Aivanhov again:

> Think of the human being as a building with fifty, a hundred, or even a thousand floors; you need a very high pressure to get the water up to the people living on the top floor. Men and women must know and use this [sexual] tension to feed and water the cells of their brains, for the Cosmic Intelligence has constructed a special network to channel this energy right up to the brain.[23]

He added graphically:

> Only idiotic puritans fight against this energy, and they are always hurled to the ground and crushed by it, because they are fighting against a divine principle.[24]

This is what we have to discover: that sex is more than orgasm produced by genital friction. It is a possible sacrament, a way of experiencing, and living in, the erotic Mystery that embraces all of us.

NOTES

1. Cited in S. Lilar, *Aspects of Love in Western Society* (London: Panther Books, 1965), 87.

2. A. Comfort, *Sex in Society* (Secaucus, N.J.: Citadel Press, 1975), 53.

3. K. Wojtyla, *Love and Responsibility* (London: Fount Paperbacks, 1982), 47.

4. Ibid., 50.

5. David Knowles, ed., *Augustine: The City of God* (Harmondsworth, England: Penguin Books, 1972), 1057.

6. D. H. Donnelly, *Radical Love: An Approach to Sexual Spirituality* (Minneapolis, Minn.: Winston Press, 1984), 76.

7. M. Laski, *Ecstasy: A Study of Some Secular and Religious Experiences* (London: Cresset Press, 1965), 146.

8. R. R. Ruether, "Asceticism and Feminism: Strange Bedmates?", in L. Hurcombe, ed., *Sex and God* (New York/London: Routledge & Kegan Paul, 1987), 229.

9. H. Ward, "The Lion in the Marble: Choosing Celibacy as a Nun," *op. cit.*, 72.

10. R. Curb and N. Manahan, eds., *Lesbian Nuns: Breaking Silence* (Tallahassee, Fl.: Naiad Press, 1985).

11. G. Leonard, *The End of Sex* (Los Angeles: J. P. Tarcher, 1983), 12.

12. See S. Sovatsky, *Passions of Innocence: Tantric Celibacy and Other Erotic Mysteries* (New York: Bantam Books, 1989).

13. M. Woods, *Masturbation, Tantra and Self Love* (San Diego, Calif.: Mho and Mho Works, 1981), 103.

14. M. Chia, written with Michael Winn, *Taoist Secrets of Love: Cultivating Male Sexual Energy* (New York: Aurora Press, 1984), 21.

15. G. Krishna, *Kundalini: Evolutionary Energy in Man* (London: Robinson & Watkins, 1971), 163.

16. See S. Keen, *The Passionate Life* (San Francisco: Harper & Row, 1983).

17. G. Leonard, op. cit., 214.

18. G. G. May, *Will and Spirit: A Contemplative Psychology* (San Francisco: Harper & Row, 1982), 154-155.

19. Da Free John, *Love of the Two-Armed Form* (Middletown, Calif.: Dawn Horse Press, 1978), 319-322.

20. Cited in Rick Fields, "Celibacy and Religious Passion: An Interview with Teresa Bielecki," *The Sun*, no. 157 (1988), 7.

21. Ibid., 7.

22. See Omraam Mikhael Aivanhov, *Sexual Force or the Winged Dragon* (Frejus, France: Prosveta, 1984), 34ff.

23. Ibid., 130-131.

24. Ibid., 132.

How can we spiritualize our intimate sexual relationships? This question is discussed in practical detail in the contribution "Sexual Communion" by Da Free John (Da Love-Ananda). This essay consists of selections from Da Free John's work Love of the Two-Armed Form, *which is remarkable both for its wise point of view and its comprehensiveness. He is an American spiritual teacher who has studied sexuality intensively because he recognized early on that most seekers fail to mature spiritually as a result of their emotional-sexual problems. He understands the spiritual process as being a readaptation from mere ego-fulfillment and pleasure to ego-transcending discipline and bliss. An integral part of this lifelong process is the gradual conversion of lovemaking into what he calls "sexual communion." In sexual communion, the focus in not on genital gratification but on self-surrender in intimacy with one's partner. The fruit of sexual communion is not orgasm — though orgasm should not be strenuously prevented either — but bliss, or whole-body ecstasy.*

By Da Free John (Da Love-Ananda)

I. THE ESSENCE OF THE PROCESS OF SEXUAL COMMUNION

The primary function of the process of sexual communion is to establish or consciously support a direct relationship of mutual Communion (or mutual surrender) between the nervous system (epitomized at the heart and extended throughout the body) and the All-Pervading Current of Life (which is prior and senior to the body-mind).

Secondary to this primary function or process is the bodily conservation and internal or whole bodily conductivity of bio-chemical energy (including hormonal or glandular secretions, such as the seminal fluid).

And the instrument for this total process, in both its primary and secondary aspects, is the functional and relational surrender of the body-mind, via (1) the direct physical and even verbal communication of love-feeling and sexual desire between the partners (both during and apart from times of sexual inter-course) and (2) the release of sexual tensions, in the genitals, the heart and lungs, the brain, and even everywhere in the body, which are produced by the erotic power of sexual stimulation, and which, if not transcended or released to the whole and entire body-mind, would tend to produce the degenerative or-gasm (which separates the nervous system, and, therefore, the body-mind as a whole, from Life and discharges or eliminates, to a critical degree, biochemical energy and vital secretions).

II. THE CONSCIOUS EXERCISE OF SEXUALITY

The conventional genital orgasm or discharge may and, in the earlier stage of one's adaptation to the process of sexual com-munion, even should be permitted on occasion. If one practices sexual communion in the manner described in these essays, continuous sexual play may, on any occasion, be prolonged for as much as an hour or even several hours. And it may, at least in the earlier stages of one's spiritual practice, be engaged with considerable frequency, if all positive factors are present. (In general, however, sexual intimacy should be occasional, allowing for periods of ordinariness or simple, loving contact. These periods also allow time for the intense accumulations of Bio-Energy to normalize. Frequent sexual intimacy tends to create a pattern of obsessive desiring, unless both individuals are able to make full use of the awakened energies through a highly developed life of service and spiritual practice.)

As a result of this "yoga of sexuality" a great and profound degree of Life-Force and super-chemistry is likely to be accumulated. The Energy and clarity realized in the conscious exercise of sexuality, through love-desire, should be used to intensify one's whole life of service, "bodily prayer," meditation, and study, as well as all other ordinary activities. However, if more energy is accumulated than we can pleasurably use in an harmonious life of spiritual and human practices, then the intensity will produce profound internal heat, which may tend to produce obsessive desire for sexual release.

Therefore, the individual who is beginning to adapt to the process of sexual communion must measure the intensity he or she bears in this practice. If health is good and stable, and the sense of bodily and sexual intensity has recently seemed to be excessive or tending to become obsessive, then the genital discharge can be permitted during the next occasion of love play. However, the genital discharge should never be casually and regularly indulged. It should, even at the beginning of adaptation to the process of sexual communion, appear no more than once a week in the most active individuals. Over time, the frequency of actual genital crisis should decrease to no more than once or twice per month, and the genital discharge should, in general, become subject to regular, natural, spontaneous control.

Even so, on any occasion where genital discharge is permitted, it should be exercised in precisely the same manner as the pre-genital crisis is exercised in this conservative or regenerative approach to sexual play. That is, it should be associated with relaxation into full feeling of the pervasive Energy, and exhalation with the feeling that the Energy is spreading from the genitals, pervading the entire body, one's lover, and the world to Infinity.

There is also a middle ground in this. It is a matter of how closely one allows oneself to approach actual genital discharge. Normally, one should exhale and permeate the entire body just as the sense of the crisis originates. At other times, one can go a little further, even to the point just prior to the actual discharge. In that case, it is recommended that the male lover withdraw the penis, rest all motion, and relax, feeling-intending that the genital spasm will not occur. He may also press the genital region between the testicles and the perineum with the fingers of one hand. (The ejaculatory fluid will not be completely conserved by such means. A portion of it will enter the bladder in any case.)

Thus, over time, both male and female individuals should adapt to regular and naturally conservative participation in the cycles of motion, feeling, breathing, and transference of attention from the local stimulation of the genitals to the whole body ecstasy in love. The general recommendation is to practice the exhalation-permeation exercise prior to actual genital discharge as a regular rule. Then, occasionally, depending on one's general condition, the conventional orgasm may be more closely approached or even actually permitted, but, in any case, the conscious exercise of the exhaled and permeating breath should be engaged.

III. BREATH, FEELING, AND ORGASM

There are two principal moments of the application of the breath cycle in sexual communion: one before the crisis of orgasm and one at the threshold or coincident with the crisis of orgasm.

1. The application of the breath cycle previous to the crisis is the primary and mature form of the use of breath. The genital play, engaged with open feeling as well as complete and whole bodily attention, awakens or stimulates the Life-Force and living chemistry of the entire bodily being. The process of sexual communion is one in which that stimulated or "excess" Life-Force and biochemistry are conserved rather than eliminated. Thus, what is added to the living bodily being through polarized sexual play is retained and also circulated in the bodily system, to serve regenerative or rejuvenative purposes.

Therefore, the application of the breath cycle previous to the crisis of orgasm is most important, since it effectively regains the balance of the bodily process, and thereby prevents the eliminative crisis of the orgasm. The genital play itself not only stimulates the Life-Force and biochemistry, in both partners, but it also tends toward a temporary bodily imbalance, in the direction of the expansive and "right-sided" states. There-fore, by virtue of this imbalance, the bodily conditions tend to approach the instant of eliminative spasm or discharge, in order to regain the balance of the left (the passive or contractive) and right (the active or expansive).

But the conventional or eliminative orgasm in fact elimi-nates both Life-Force and biochemistry, as if these were bodily wastes. Hence, the conventional orgasm is ultimately degenera-tive and enervating, particularly when practiced frequently over time or by those who are relatively devitalized or otherwise beyond the time of early youth.

The process of sexual communion is the way of sexual union. It involves emotional and mental responsibility, true intimacy, relational commitment, regulation of occasion through the monitoring of mutual love-desire, and regenerative or reju-venative responsibility for the total physiology of the sexual play. And the central and senior function in this process is the breath cycle.

The breath cycle is made to incarnate the entire bodily being as a whole or single Force in the play of true sexual communion. The breath cycle is the function through which each partner should organize sensitivity to the entire play. The breath cycle is thus not only the medium of chemical ingestion and elimination of the air, but the cycle of reception and release, or rhythmic coordination of the physical body, the Life-Force, and the full force of free or unobstructed emotion (or love–feeling) and attention.

Thus, during the entire course of any occasion of sexual communion, each partner periodically comes to a moment of profound intensification of life and feeling—a sense of imbal-ance which, if permitted to continue, would produce the crisis of orgasm. Each partner must be sensitive, through intentional and emotional play with his or her lover, to this sense of imbalance or impending crisis. As often as it occurs, the individ-ual should inhale fully and relax deeply all over the body. Then exhale fully, relaxing deeply all over the body. This should be done one or more times, until a generalized feeling of fullness, balance, and natural control over orgasm is enjoyed. Then the play may resume as before. By this practice the crisis of orgasm may be prevented or detained indefinitely. (The whole matter is not one of frustration of orgasm but of undermining its necessity through the continuous return to a condition of bodily balance, fullness, integrity of feeling, and mental freedom from recoil on self through concepts, images, or exclusive sensuality.

2. The application of the breath cycle at the threshold or coincident with the crisis of orgasm is the secondary form of the use of breath in sexual communion, and it is most commonly practiced by individuals who are only beginning to adapt and mature in this process of sexual communion. It is more of an emergency matter, since the eliminative spasm of the genitals has in that case already begun to be indulged. Whenever the critical imbalance of the bodily being is allowed to be prolonged (in either the contractive or the expansive mode), enervation is the eventual result. In the case of genital stimulation, prolonged expansive excitation leads to orgasm. But it should be clear that such orgasm is, when casually indulged, more of a disease, or a symptom of imbalance, than it is a "natural" bodily event. Thus, the event of such eliminative orgasm should be controlled through right application of feeling, through the breath cycle, previous to orgasm. Occasionally, the crisis may be approached and even permitted, but if that event is to serve a positive, regenerative, loving, and nonseparative effect, there must be responsible application of feeling, attention, and Life, via the cycle of the breath as well as other physiological means.

Thus, on occasions of loving sexual communion, the crisis of orgasm should be either prevented or delayed in the manner previously described (i.e., the primary application of the breath cycle). If, after prolonged embrace, the genital orgasm is to be permitted or approached, the moment of the rising crisis should be met, via the breath, in such a way that (as in the primary application of the breath cycle) the whole bodily balance, fullness, relaxation, and loving polarization between the lovers is quickly regained.

In the case of the application of the breath cycle previous to the crisis of orgasm, the inhalation was to be engaged first and primarily. However, in the case where the crisis is immediate, inhalation or infilling will only tend to promote the eliminative spasm in both male and female. Therefore, on occasions when the crisis of orgasm is approaching or inevitable, there must first and primarily be the exercise of full exhalation, with the sense of releasing and relaxing the intensified and local genital Energy to the entire body. When the sense of fullness, balance, and natural control over orgasm returns, then infilling and relaxing via inhalation may be done.

In the case of such application of the breath at the point of crisis, the genital discharge generally does in fact occur to one or another degree. But the primary Force of orgasm, as well as the biochemical secretion, internal or external, of both male and female, will, by right application of the cycle of breath and whole bodily feeling-relaxation, be to a high degree conserved. Thus, the regenerative use or application of the intensified Life-Force and biochemistry of sexual play may also occur on the random occasion of genital orgasm. Through right application, the orgasm is converted—the bodily balance is restored in the instant of the crisis—and far less of Life and chemistry and mutual feeling intimacy is lost in the process. Such orgasm becomes whole bodily orgasm or regenerative orgasm. Over time, the individual learns, bodily, how the thrill of orgasm may become a conservative whole body thrill rather than a necessarily degenerative moment of pleasure gotten by elimination of chemistry and Life via the genitals, or the heart, solar plexus, and vital or lower body region in general.

In the response that should develop as the routine at the point of the crisis of orgasm, the exhaled breath and release of both tension and attention in the genital region may also be followed by a period in which the exhaled breath is held out. During that period there should be whole bodily relaxation of sexual tension, feeling, and sensation. When it is felt that the involuntary urge to genital orgasm is essentially at rest, then the inhalation may be resumed.

If too long a period passes or must pass before relaxation of the genital spasm occurs, then the breath cycle may be resumed, but only short and shallow inhalations should be engaged, in order to prevent the intensification of genital pressure and the general state of bodily tension and attention that would tend to produce conventional orgasm.

Until there is complete rest from the tendency to genital spasm, repeat the cycle of inhalation (shallow) and exhalation (full and held out as long as is comfortable). When there is relaxation into whole bodily Fullness and natural sexual attention, then the motions and play of sexual communion may resume.

If, however, there is an individual or mutual preference for genital separation, then the lovers should simply rest with one another in close bodily embrace, with or without genital contact, until an appropriate moment to depart from one another lovingly.

Ecstatic states and orgasm are similar insofar as both involve a temporary lifting of our ego-boundaries. Sex can sometimes — and possibly more often than we tend to realize — tend to ecstatic states. In her contribution "Spiritual Breakthroughs in Sex," therapist Dell Sokol writes about her own experience as well as the experiences of a number of other spiritual practitioners for whom love-making suddenly became an ecstatic adventure.

SPIRITUAL BREAKTHROUGHS IN SEX

By Dell Sokol, Ph.D.

PERSONAL FLASHBACK

My emotional-sexual history began in a small Texas town steeped in Fundamentalist convictions. I supposed that sex was something only married people did, and in the dark. Sex was taboo for single females and the risks seemed great: pregnancy, disease, and disgrace. I was aware that an unspoken, but entirely different, attitude was held toward men. For the males in my community, disease may have been a moderate concern, but pregnancy and disgrace were not problems. When I was ten years old, my mother was visited by a mature single woman in town who described her support for sexual freedom by stating: "All old maids should be able to have a baby with no questions asked." My mother was amused by this liberated view, while for me it was a glimpse into another world.

The beginnings of sexual activity in my late teens was accompanied by guilt and fear, even though I was by then living in far more liberal California. I somehow survived my upbringing with the notion that sex was something forbidden yet pleasurable and desirable. The guilt and fear became subtle inhibitions after marriage. I had great difficulty in accommodating what had been forbidden for years. Even sudden approval and acceptability did not change this. I began to realize that I was living out a widespread cultural bias. As E. Whitmont observed:

> At a genealogical congress at the beginning of the century the question was seriously debated as to whether women do or do not have any sexual feelings. And indeed the overwhelming consensus of the learned pundits was that the good woman does not have any sexual feelings. Psychologically at least, women had to be bland and innocuous in order to be good.[1]

That this attitude is by no means behind us was made clear by Gabriel Mandel in his introduction to F. Ricci's book *Tantra: Rites of Love;* he remarked:

> To this day, there is no European (read Westerner) of normal upbringing who can approach an erotic picture without experiencing a vague sense of guilt or morbid curiosity. This sense of guilt

afflicts the individual with a neurosis that in turn is aggravated by the morbid curiosity, so that the erotic picture accentuates his psycho-physical impotence rather than arousing his organic capacity.[2]

Subtle and not so subtle inhibition took the place of spontaneity and playful abandon in my marriage. Sexuality always seemed to hold more promise and mystery than I had realized. A divorce was followed by a brief period of what I would have then termed "sexual freedom." However, it took the form more of rebellion than freedom and was characterized by anger and confusion. A stable relationship subsequently led to a deeper enjoyment of sexuality that was in general realized with the help of alcohol to relieve inhibition. I became aware of this only after the fact. At the time I did not consider myself sexually inhibited; nor did anyone with whom I had a relationship.

This awareness arose only when a spiritual discipline eliminated my intake of alcohol. My inhibitions became even more evident to me when I started to participate in emotional/ sexual considerations based on the teaching of the Western spiritual teacher Da Free John. His students explored in extended groups their emotional-sexual histories and also considered the legitimizing of erotic practices. There was a growing awareness that tantric sexual practices could not successfully and authentically be engaged until inhibition could be naturally released. These sexual considerations and practices were taken up only after several years of spiritual discipline, which included two to three hours of meditation daily, conscious exercising each morning, yoga practice each evening, breathing exercises for ten minutes each evening, a strict lacto-vegetarian diet, as well as daily study, and service.

There were also periods of voluntary celibacy ranging from six weeks to six months. This sexual regimen was taken up in order to determine whether celibacy was a natural and desirable state. It was not known at the beginning of each period how long the celibate condition would last.

I learned that, in the beginning, the process of meditation is largely defined by the bondage of attention to one's emotional-sexual character. In fact, it is this overdetermination that is to be observed, understood, and transcended. In any period of meditation, the ease and ability to observe, understand, and transcend whatever is arising in consciousness allows meditation to deepen. This process is not a technique or an ego-based effort but rather is based on an intelligent openness to the presence and argument of the teacher. I have found in my own practice that my insight into my emotional-sexual structure was greatly facilitated during these periods of celibacy. I doubt if these insights could have been gained in any other way.

In twelve years of study with Da Free John, I have had extensive instruction and monitoring of meditation. I have been taught to respect and enjoy the visions, experiences, altered states of bliss and ecstasy that arise in meditation. At the same time, I have been taught not to seek them or cling to them. I do not confuse them with "truth," but regard them as the burning off of karmic mind-garbage.

During those periods of intense discipline, in the first ten or fifteen minutes of meditation, the room would fill with radiant light, either red, gold, or white. That light radiated from everything in the room. A feeling of great peace filled my body, and soon I was unable to hold my eyes open, although I remained alert to any noise or sensory change in the immediate environment. I would become aware of a force of energy moving up the spine, the spine becoming hot, and the energy exploding out of the top of the crown in a fiery white or red eruption. Initially there might have been a burning pain at the top of the head, but subsequently this would become indescribable ecstasy each time the ascending energy burst through the crown. I would remain in that ecstatic state for a period of thirty or forty minutes, then gradually return to the bliss state, and finally to the sensory world of relaxed awareness.

Within the context of meditation, a synchronicity exists between the spiritual teacher and the student. The spiritual teacher *does* one's meditation, indeed, *is* one's meditation. It has been my experience that Da Free John is a source of spiritual transmission, which is always available to me. My ability to receive his transmission depends on my availability to the process and my openness to his spiritual influence.

During that period of intense meditation, about five years ago, I also began to experience kundalini manifestations during sexual encounters. There were spontaneous gestures of the hands and arms, and a very high singing sound would emit from the back of my throat. I also experienced rushes of heat and energy up my spine, and visions of light and color. My lover would sometimes appear to me in different forms.

Toward the conclusion of that time of emotional/sexual consideration, about four years ago, we took up a specific sexual practice. My husband and I adopted a discipline that required genital contact without orgasm for ninety minutes to three hours every other night for three weeks. This practice was preceded by a ritual that included burning incense and candles, anointing with holy water and ash, "recognition" of each lover by the other. This was considered to be a sacramental occasion as well as a joyful and playful experience. Heightened attention to the lover was considered essential.

During those three weeks, I was in a state of euphoria most of the time. As a result of this foundation practice and opportunity, a wonderful and mysterious event occurred spontaneously during sexual activity. The particular experience I will describe occured during the third encounter of this practice. This occasion was accompanied by electronic music. I remember being strongly aware of the music at one point prior to the experience.

My lover and I had been together in sexual encounter for more than an hour. Up to this time, I had experienced manifestations of kundalini such as spontaneous movements, a high humming sound in the throat, the rushes of energy up the spine, and visions of light and color. The energy that usually focuses in the genital area had spread to every cell of my body. Now there was an exquisite, calm bliss and total loss of the condition of my normal self-sense. I experienced engulfing overwhelming bliss. When I touched my lover's hand, I was that. No separation existed from anything that arose in consciousness. A large bright orange scorpion appeared. It was very beautiful, and I was that also. Scorpio is my astrological sign.

A huge, indigo spider appeared with tiny hairs on its legs, sparkling like diamonds. How can I make the spider sound beautiful? Yet it was beautiful, and I was that too. This vision of a spider has taken on significance for me in the years following the event. At the time it occurred, I was mindless and attached no sign or symbol to the event. However, from time to time, I continued to consider this spider. I came to see the spider as a symbol of transformation.

I now intuit the spider to be the devouring Mother Goddess, yet there was no fear. The fundamental tantric realization is that the world is pervaded by the Divine Goddess, honored in the tantric traditions as the ultimate Condition of nature and consciousness. Therefore, this realization "overcomes the distinction (or duality) of clean and unclean, sacred and profane, and breaks (his) bondage to a world artifically fragmented. He affirms in a radical way the underlying unity of the phenomenal world, the identity of Shakti with the whole creation. Heroically, he triumphs over it, controls and masters it. By affirming the essential worth of the forbidden, he causes the forbidden to lose its power to pollute, to degrade, to bind."[3] In the state of nonduality there is no distinction between the devouring Mother Goddess and the Mother Goddess in her giving, serving form. Hence there is no fear.

A galaxy of stars spun endlessly through the universe, and I was that. The rapture exceeded any pleasure, joy, ecstasy, or bliss that I had ever experienced or imagined. This was the most prolonged and intense bliss I have ever known. Individuality dissolved into the primordial infinite joy.

There was a complete loss of the condition of the skin-bound body-mind. There was no 'I' or 'self'. The most significant aspect of the state of unity was this transcending of the self-sense. There was not a 'union' of 'I' with lover, or 'I' with the scorpion, spider, or galaxy. Rather, there was only undifferentiated unity and consciousness as all that.

My husband was aware that something extraordinary was going on even though I did not speak. After some time, the level of consciousness began to change. Gradually I felt once again my separation. With that separation came profound sadness. I wept. During that experience of non-duality, I had no sense of time. Later, my husband estimated the length of the experience to have been about fifteen minutes. I could remember that I had felt an incredible joyous rapture of undifferentiated unity, of being everything, from the hand of another to a galaxy. The state of non-separation seemed to be my natural condition. Now I felt only the sadness of the separate self, a seemingly "unnatural" state.

Any language I may use to describe the experience can only be a faint outline, as opposed to the full depth of what actually happened. To me it was a demonstration of possibility, a confirmation that the state of non-duality or undifferentiated unity may be realized through this body-mind. I was graced with a glimpse of that possibility. Anyone who is seriously involved in spiritual practice is also from time to time involved in doubt. I had an intellectual "belief" in nonduality. I believed not in one God but that there is only God. What was an intellectual belief is now whole-body knowing.

I had adopted conscious sexual practice as a discipline without any pre-conceived goals or expectations. I had not expected to realize this state of nonduality in my life. I had always assumed that only a saint, a sage, or a spiritual adept would be blessed with such a realization.

Did the experience change my life? I believe that no experience is the means to salvation. Visions and phenomena of yogic energy must not be confused with God-realization, which is perfect and permanent self-transcendence, although they may lead to insight and understanding, as well as a greater commitment to the spiritual process. My life had greatly changed prior to this experience, through years of meditation and discipline. The experience was an awakening, an affirmation of the Divine breaking through the ego boundaries.

I was determined to investigate the experience and bring it fully into consciousness. At the same time, I was aware of my reluctance to confess the full ramification, because of the implicit demand to live a life that was based on that realization, and because of the possibility of disbelief and even ridicule from anyone I might have shared this with, except my husband. The ultimate taboo is not sexual freedom or death. The ultimate taboo is ecstatic self-transcendence.

The experience confirmed to me the truth pointed to by my teacher: There is a state of prior happiness, and we are actively preventing it. We egoically add to that perfect condition, and those additions are obstructions that interfere with our innate happiness. That condition is not something to be attained; rather, it is available in any moment when one is able to connect with it by relaxing into it. The sexual discipline gave me the time, space, and incident to become that superb state.

I believe that sex is at times sacred, and at other times lustful, playful, serious, joyful, humorous, anxious, angry, and, between those who are free to responsibly choose a sexual relationship, entirely good. The misuse of sex through violence or coercion has arisen because of three thousand years of patriarchial, anti-sexual, anti-ecstatic indoctrination, via religion and the secular state in all its forms. I also believe that if all the religions of humanity were permeated with the knowledge and experience of the Goddess with both male and female aspects encompassing the Godhead, our attitudes would be sex-positive, and sex would be free, joyful, and sacred.

A balance is required for every human being, between the male and the female forces, which are the challenging and the nurturing forces respectively. Each influence demands respect, or the body becomes unbalanced, less than the whole body. Exclusive worship of either Goddess or male God is not the answer. Rather, in this time and place, an infusion of both aspects permits full expression of our true sexual character, with God and Goddess in a playful, ecstatic dance of love, until that too is transcended.

When I experienced this transcendental state in sexuality, I felt it was important and saw it as confirmation of initiation. Although the experience was not a problem for me, it was in some ways a puzzle, a curiosity, and posed questions for me. I felt a need to integrate the experience into my life.

Given my own characteristics, I chose partly meditation and partly academic research as a balanced approach to integration. I had witnessed a profound connection between spirituality and sexuality. I wanted to understand this connection more fully. My intention was to bring the experience fully into consciousness through study and my research as a doctoral candidate in clinical psychology. In this way, I felt I could assume responsibility for this gift.

As part of my doctoral research, I and a male collaborator interviewed in some depth four men and four women who had had experiences similar to my own. The four men and three of the women experienced the transcendental state with their respective marriage partners. One woman's transcendental state was experienced in the form of an initiation with her teacher. The following includes verbatim responses of several of these interviewees with minor editing. The names are fictitious to preserve anonymity.

RUTH'S ACCOUNT

(Ruth is a woman in her early thirties, who has been married for seven years with no children. She has been a member of her present spiritual community for thirteen years. She is a renunciate, serving her church. She has been initiated into the middle level of practice. Ruth began by relating the first instance of a transcendental sexual experience in 1979.)

My husband and I were making love, and I had a very powerful cervical orgasm. When I have that kind of orgasm, I generally scream very loudly . . . It's like a loss of the sense of being encapsulated as a body, losing a certain sense of the subjectivity you walk around with ordinarily. I remember at the end of our love-making—I don't remember if my husband had withdrawn completely or not—we were gazing at one another, still lying together. Maybe he was sitting up and I was lying down, and we were looking into one another's eyes. Nothing was said between us . . .

There was an energy field. The energy between us was communicated between the eyes, and made me begin to cry. We were both obviously feeling the same thing, without any words being spoken. It was as though we recognized one another, not merely from the objective point of view, but as though we were one entity, or one field. There was no obstruction or delineation between us. My heart felt like it had burst open. I was weeping at the heart-communion or love that I felt for him. That would basically describe the incident.

The one thing I felt, just like after having an orgasm, was total bodily surrender, an openness . . . I felt in my heart area, the region above the solar plexus, and in the solar plexus, but particularly in the heart area . . . There wasn't a sense of uptightness or energy being contained or isolated, obstructed. Everything was flowing, moving. I think there might have been some sorrow associated with it as well.

This open sensation I am describing to you doesn't happen too much to me now, but earlier on, when I began to have these more powerful orgasms, it felt as though my whole body would open up to . . . a universal field.

And then the closing down of the body-mind would occur, and I would feel the loss of that sense of communion, or oneness, openness, without any individual identity, and just resume my ordinary perception of things. That's when the sorrow would set in.

At times I would feel my husband become [identical to] my teacher. I wasn't making love to him anymore, I was making love to my teacher. Not just the teacher in physical form, but what I identify as him: as a being, and as an energy presence, and heart communication. It was as though my whole body was being enveloped by what is greater than I perceive myself to be.

Now sometimes when we would make love, just in the earlier days, there would be a lot of sorrow, because that has always tended to be my characteristic emotional contraction. When we would make love it would get me back in touch with that. Sometimes when we would make love, even without having an orgasm, although sometimes after the orgasm, I would just plain old feel sorrowful, and cry about that. I was not crying because of the communion felt, but because of what the deep penetration stimulated in me, and also perhaps because of the loss of life associated with orgasm. There were two different things occurring. One time it was noticing plain old sorrow, and the other time it was noticing it wasn't sorrow, but rather loss of the sense of self.

(Ruth was asked to elaborate on the feeling of loss of self-sense.)

I was very vulnerable, very airy, light. The whole body was breathing, in a certain sense. I was perceiving through the heart, not just through the eyes. It was like the feeling being, or etheric being, was in resonance with my husband's etheric being. Somehow this alignment occurred, and we were not just limited to the flesh body. I have had that experience before—it occurs whenever I fall into my feeling rather than perceiving via my head.

It occurs when I perceive from the heart region, as feeling occurs there. It is trusting this part of the body—the solar plexus and the heart. It's almost like seeing, if I can use that word, because it's allowing my feeling to be my eyes, rather than seeing with my eyes alone. In terms of the breath, the whole body was breathed, being lived. There wasn't any effort. There wasn't any thought about myself.

The same experience happened one other time. It's not as vivid to me. This was just a few years ago. I don't remember the year or where I was living. It was a very similar kind of incident. I remember the energy connection again between our eyes, and the tears that sprang forth. And I recognized it to be the same thing that we had shared together. Neither of us obviously knew what it was, except it was nothing we had anything to do with, nothing we could try to recreate. This was something that seems to occur through our mutual submission to one another and our loving.

I've likened it to something where all sense of familiarity is abandoned, not by choice, but it's just gone. It's a true moment of total ignorance, of just not knowing who your partner is, or anything about him, or any offensiveness you might register about him, or any complaint you might have—none of that even arises. You don't think, "Boy, what a great time we just had."

You are just being the whole body in love, without anything being categorized. It's being the whole body, becoming ignorant, allowing the body to just be. I don't know if I'm describing the feeling for you. It's total submission.

It was blissful and very ecstatic. It was not gleeful—I wasn't lying there smiling. You let down your guard and there's no sense of self-consciousness. You're just free—you know how you are with your lover.

But there's always that moment where you look at each other, and its, "Oh yeah, there he is," kind of the face you still put on. Even though you're totally intimate when you're making love, there's still some kind of face we retain.

But the loss of all self-consciousness, toe to crown, is another way to describe the initial experience. You are so vulnerable, in touch with what it feels like to drop everything, and then you resume this feeling of being limited or separate from everything else. But for a moment, just to experience the loss of all that is very blissful, and I wonder what it is that I do that prevents me from feeling that in all moments.

(The interviewer asked Ruth if the energy was concentrated in any part of the body. She responded with insight into the potential for pain or hurt if she couldn't relax bodily into the movement of energy within her.)

It would go up my spine, and a lot of heat would go up my spine. My whole face and head, the top of my head, would become very hot, heated from the energy. It was like literal rushes going up my spine to my brain. And it was a real demand for me to relax my vagina and my cervix. I felt if I didn't relax, it would hurt, but if I did relax, the whole conductivity would begin to occur.

It was like a thrill or waves of energy. I felt exhilarated in my body. I guess you could say it was wave upon wave of blissful sensation, but I had remained totally surrendered, relaxed bodily. If I tensed up, it would interrupt it. If I remained relaxed, I would basically be screaming very loudly throughout the experience, and it could go on and on. It would not be limited to just fifteen seconds, as long as my husband could sustain his penetration. This one time it was prolonged, and we were both befuddled by it.

I think some sorrow would arise. Once I submitted or felt through the sorrow, it felt blissful. Bliss is not necessarily an emotion, but it's associated with happiness. I didn't feel "happy," but it was an extraordinary state, more than my ordinary state of happiness.

(At this point in the interview, Ruth reflected on her spiritual practice, which involved a commitment to the self-generated discipline of daily sexual practice for a prolonged period of time each day. She described the effects on her and her husband with

such phrases as "blown out," "burned out," and "cleaned out.")

Everything is stimulated, every nerve in the body is being amped or overloaded. One time we both said that maybe we should talk to someone about it to see what we were getting in touch with. Was there something we should be doing with it? Should we be avoiding this? I talked to a few women about it who were also practicing this discipline of making love every day. You would feel an impasse where you did not want to transcend yourself.

But with my husband penetrating me [vaginally] from behind, I finally realized I could transcend myself. I could go beyond this limitation I thought was just always going to be there. I could completely surrender to him and to this process.

(Ruth was asked to clarify the different types of energy she was feeling. The previous energy had been an energy field. This energy was associated with movement along the spinal axis.)

It's a different energy. This energy is associated with the spine. It's associated with the whole body, but I particularly notice its concentration up the spine and the heat rushing up the spine into the brain core. The other experience had more to do with the heart. The energy was concentrated at the heart, or basically it began in the eyes and in the area of the third eye, or ajna-cakra, and then it would travel down into the heart and open. There would be this sense of ignorance and of profound and deep love for my husband, but also of him not being limited to who I perceived him to be . . . There was none of that occurring.

(In conclusion, Ruth spoke about her husband's practice of conservation of orgasm, and her own experience with bypassing orgasm.)

A lot of time we would both be screaming because my orgasm would precipitate his. But over the years he has toned that down because it would wipe him out too much. He has learned to conserve orgasm or just become more quiet if he did have an orgasm, so as not to lose all of his vital strength through that release.

One time I also bypassed the orgasm, and I felt it as regenerative, felt the energy actually did turn upward. But again it was not something that I could recreate. I don't know how I did it, or if I did it—it just happened. I thought, "Gee, that was great, how do I do it again?" It's occurrence was totally graceful, just a moment where I stepped out of the way of being eager to release my energy.

SARA'S ACCOUNT

(Sara is a thirty-eight-year-old woman. She has been a member of the present spiritual community for eleven years. Sara has been married eight years and has no children. She is a renunciate who serves her church full time and has been initiated into an advanced level of practice. She related a transcendental sexual experience that occurred when she and her husband were away from home.)

It was nice out. It was warm. Everyone in the house had gone to bed. There wasn't anything extraordinary that we had done by way of preparing, of anticipating that we were going to make love. What seemed magnified that day was a certain kind of attention to each other, a kind of loving feeling toward each other, most specifically toward each other's qualities. More than that, there was the feeling of connection to something greater that I felt through Robert that day, and I felt him allowing me to do that. That's what I think was key, very conscious, though neither of us said anything about it.

We had been married six or seven years, and you become sensitive to the psychic tone, the energy that is going on between you every day. It was just a subtle recognition, noticing the fact that he and I were allowing each other to be a kind of window to the spirit world, to the reality that is greater, to the domain of feeling.

(Sara was asked if she had done any kind of religious or devotional practice just prior to going to bed.)

We would meditate twice a day, but I don't think we meditated right before going to bed. I remember we had spent some time in the living room of this house . . . I made up the bed. It had a very cozy feeling to it, very soft and surrounded, very nestlike. We enjoyed that a lot, and I think that just enhanced the feeling of intimacy between us.

We began to make love. Somehow I felt this opening, simultaneously physically and spiritually, as he began to penetrate me. I felt it almost immediately. I find this is fairly typical of these occasions when we have a very transcendent experience. The experience of opening tends to be there right from the beginning . . . I think it has very much to do with my availability, my sensitivity. In other words, if I am psychically closed, even if I am physically open and sexually aroused, that's not really the foundation for the transcendent experience. It is the spiritual preparation or disposition [that matters], and already that sensitivity to, or intuition of, the greater reality is really, really there. That somehow gets awakened as my body becomes awakened. It occurs simultaneously.

I recall something that happened that evening. There were these phases of subjectivity. During the process of making love, there was more or less self-consciousness, and the self-consciousness is the part that is felt to be the contraction in the body. As a spiritual practitioner, what I do in the midst of that is simply acknowledge it: I notice that I am being subjective. For instance, I'm thinking to myself, "Is this going to be one of those?" Or I'm wondering if my husband's feeling what I'm feeling or if I'm just noticing something with my mind, noticing that I'm doing that. That noticing is taking place somewhere other than the mind . . . The noticing of the mental activity, subjectivity, thinking, verbal thoughts occurs in the heart, the pre-mind.

The very beginning is often very mindless. Shortly thereafter it's similar to meditation. Then suddenly the contraction becomes obvious. I notice at the same time that I'm contracting, that I'm withdrawing because I'm putting attention on myself. This is a very familiar process, though, and because it is familiar I can relax.

On this particular occasion that's what occurred, and this opening felt enormous. It wasn't even physical anymore. It felt like my pelvis literally became like a funnel of energy, just widening and receiving this incredible force of energy into it. But it wasn't just the thrust of what I felt coming into me. It was the energy that was much greater. There was not a lot of extreme movement. But paradoxically there was this etheric pleasure and awakening, this kind of etheric arousal, as well as actual hormonal, physical, fleshy arousal. So it was both at the same time.

And I knew what was happening, and I knew at that point that it was blowing my mind, because I could feel the force of my teacher. All of a sudden the cork was taken off the energy in me.

And it started flowing out of me to Robert. All of that energy is what I recognize as the influence of my teacher. That is the way I recognize him, by that certain feeling of his presence, or actual power. And it's not just rushing or flooding through my body, because the sense I had of my body was extremely expanded.

I think the only sense of form that was left came from the movement. It was just a sensation I was aware of but what I felt myself to be was not that. I didn't feel myself to be the body . . . I felt myself to be radiance, tangible radiance and bliss. It was the two of us, and so my sense of what I was was completely inclusive of him. It became one energy, one comingling force of love.

(When asked whether she was aware of her body or her husband's body, Sara answered that she became one with bliss.)

I haven't thought about this incident for a long time . . . In that ecstasy the self was curiously diffused and not really distinct. All there was was energy that was somehow being generated between the two of us, but I no longer had any perception of the two of us. It was just what was happening and I was that.

(The interviewer asked Sara to describe other aspects that preceded the peak of the experience. Sara pointed to her heart and responded.)

It would be basically a growing sense of love. It very much comes from here, and that particular night that was also very true. Whenever something like this happens, it's only when the love is really a foundation. The love is the energy, is the force that becomes what I just described. It takes over. It become the reality. Totally. It expands from the heart and moves throughout the whole body until you don't know it's the body. It is just that feeling, that love, but it has become energy.

I would describe it as the Shakti, the Mother, the female force, which is not personal to me. So it didn't start in me when it came through me. It started somewhere up here, or somewhere down here. I don't know completely. Sometimes it feels like it's coming through the top of my head, sometimes it feels like it's coming up. But it goes through the body and out. I would feel my hands go out and my legs become completely like, almost like stuck in a toaster.

(At this point, Sara used the gesture of stiff arms and splayed hands, attempting to demonstrate an intense energy. The gesture was similar to a classical Hindu mudra. She used the humorous cartoon metaphor of receiving a very high energy shock from an electric toaster.)

I go in to a kind of mudra, with a lot of sounds that seemed to come from very deep. There are a lot of strong exhalations and pranayama [spontaneous breath-control] . . . It's really hard to describe. But what is actually happening at the level of feeling and energy is, paradoxically, not the body, even though it's associated with the body.

(Sara discussed her environment and stated that the love-making went on for forty-five minutes or more. Nothing specific had been done to create a mood.)

Just pure happiness. It's like the culmination of the surrender because the whole thing is happening to a point of surrender, totally opening and submitting in the most positive sense of that, just opening myself completely to that love and to the love of my husband, receiving completely and giving all my energy, all my attention, all my love in that moment, [being] totally there . . . The process is psychically and physically submitting and allowing that force to grow and to be conducted between us.

There is bodily bliss because everything opens. When the muscular stress is released actively, there is just total selfless happiness, ecstasy, and a kind of primal knowing that this is the truth.

Then at a certain point the mind's eye itself becomes the radiance . . . There is literally light in the head. There is a specific kind of conductivity that the teacher teaches and that I practiced for a very long time, so it almost happens to me naturally when there is a certain kind of genital arousal. I relax and breathe and release the energy up the spine, up the body into the head, and the head becomes a very sensuous organ then, and this is felt as light absolutely.

I knew it was absolutely an extraordinary time, that it was just because of the sort of peak magnification of all the elements of sex—the physical, the love, the psychic, the spirit force, the light, all of it. It was all there, and our awareness of those things moved through those things. It was an extraordinarily full, human, and spiritual occasion. It was very revelatory. It revealed that this is the human reality: to share that ecstasy. It affected me for days.

(The interviewer asked Sara about the transition from the transcendental state back to the ordinary state. She indicated that the transition was gradual over a period of days.)

Something occurs. You realize that you've lost it. It's not so much that you notice that it's actually gone, but that it's a memory. You notice that your are remembering it.

(Sara was asked if this experience occurred at other times.)

Oh yes, many times. Some of the most extraordinary times. For instance, recently we made love. It wasn't long, maybe twenty minutes of actual contact. We hardly moved at all, and I could not believe the ecstasy. This is a phenomenon that has occurred repeatedly, but not predictably, where my husband will be inside me and the movement is not even particularly what creates the bliss. It is just energy.

I remember trying to practice what my teacher teaches about sex for about three to four years after we were married, and I could not figure out what the hell he was talking about! I could not understand how anything could be better than orgasm. I would try. We would make love, and I would try to bypass the orgasm as he taught, and every time I would say "Fuck this" and just go for an orgasm. And I remember laughing afterward, saying "Sorry, but I just don't get it."

And then it just changed. I don't remember exactly when it changed, but I think what happened was I gradually relaxed my effort about it.

Actually there was an experience, now that I think about it, which did actually cause a transformation. I don't know if I can talk about it because it involved kind of an unusual circumstance. I'm not sure. Well, let's put it this way. It involved a circumstance that was not with Robert but with a woman. We were using a vibrator, and she had it on my clitoris probably for half an hour. It was a really intense, big, heavy vibrator. Something happened in the midst of that because when she first started I was afraid because of the pain I always experienced when my clitoris was touched too hard or too much. And I felt that pain, and I felt that around that pain was this contraction.

I wondered what would happen if I relaxed the contraction. So I relaxed the contraction, and the pain changed, until it was only pleasure on a purely physical level, and all of a sudden . . . that's when I first experienced the most vivid, obvious vision of the current of energy in the body. And it was the first time that I actually felt the Goddess force, the Shakti, as a being, not just as energy, come through me . . .

I was her, I mean my body just became a corpse. It was just a box. The feeling was simply forced, the overwhelm of the nervous system . . . The intensity of the stimulation of the nervous system and hormones produced an actual effect . . . It wasn't psychological, it was intuitive. There was a shift—maybe that's psychological—there was a shift in my sense of my being. I was still noticing this, but I was not noticing it as I am now sitting here noticing the room.

All that was left of the noticing was just the noticing function. It wasn't Sara noticing it. It was the noticing function, awareness itself, but what was happening was a being coming through me. It almost felt like somebody actually coming in . . . It was definitely a possession.

There were two of us, and she was revealing an aspect of existence that could be known bodily, and it was energy in the body and the heart. It was a wild, wild crazy woman, wild eyed. I felt my eyes bugging out of my head and my tongue sticking out of my mouth and my hands like this . . . and I started speaking in tongues also, which completely blew my mind. As soon as the vibrator was taken off, . . . that was it.

But this changed my experience of sexuality forever . . . It blew up this kind of thing that you have about sex, the good feeling you get from sexual experience, or try to get. It broke that because it was so obviously about submission. It wasn't about me trying to do something. It was about me not doing something, but rather receiving it or allowing it, rather than doing and creating and making.

(When asked whether she had an orgasm, Sara responded:)

It was continuous, uninterrupted . . . This was definitely something else, which I've not really experienced completely like that ever again.

(Sara was next asked whether any psychic changes resulted.)

Oh yes, definitely. From the standpoint of spiritual practice it's always full of insight, a sort of insight that comes afterward, about how I shut down from the ecstasy in my usual state, because it's obvious that the ecstasy is inherent feeling at the body [level], of my being . . . and also naturally it would affect my meditation. I would be in a much more relaxed and receptive disposition physically, emotionally, and psychically when I sit down to meditate . . .

I don't know what this has to do with anything, but meditation becomes extremely sexual, whole bodily, playing with all those hormones. Very often in my meditation there is a stage as it's deepening where it goes through something like love play in a very hormonal sense. I feel the heat and change of energy and so forth, and then it just cools out. That's when deep meditation begins.

It's definitely bliss into ecstasy because the bliss is something that I feel in the body. The ecstasy is something where the body is gone. Energy goes up. It's communion. It's love. It's transcendent, the energy feeling, transcended, even the light I'm talking about in meditation, and gone just into light.

. . . When my meditation gets very deep it affects my sexual life, because when we lie down together I'm already available, although that direction is not predictable, whereas sexuality very directly will affect my meditation. Meditation doesn't always have the predictable sort of effect because there's so much complexity in the relationship. Even when I'm having a deep meditation, I can be completely uptight . . . That's the ecstasy part really, the loss of the self-sense, separate, mindless.

MARTHA'S ACCOUNT

(Martha is a 46-year-old divorced mother of two grown children by her first marriage. She lives as a single woman in a large communal house with a group of people who choose to live together in order to share expenses. She is not presently involved in a formal spiritual practice.

The experience she described occurred five years ago with her husband of nine months. At the time, both she and her husband had been involved in a spiritual community for about eight months. Each day she worked with sacred elements and performed religious worship. They lived in a house in the mountains that overlooked a river and wooded area. She emphasized the beauty of the surroundings. Following her description of the setting, Martha stated that her intention on that occasion was to merge with her lover, to the point of actually becoming one.)

I wanted to totally merge with him, to really become one, where we wouldn't be thinking about satisfaction or whether we were going to have an orgasm, or if it was enough foreplay, or anything whatsoever, but just to love. One morning we were sitting there, as we would, against the wall on our bed just looking out the window, with my husband having his arm around me.

We started making love, and it was such feeling of depth. For some reason, everything came together where I was totally relaxed and he was totally relaxed, and we didn't feel like we had to be anywhere, to get anywhere. We were just in the moment. As it progressed finally into coitus, I started feeling deeper and deeper and deeper, and finally I began to feel as if I was falling. The image that comes to me was like when you see a spaceman falling into space. I was free-floating, tumbling in space.

All of a sudden I saw a ball around me. I saw planets, and I was definitely not on Earth anymore. I was in outer space, totally in outer space. I knew I wasn't in my body. There was a sudden knowing that I had left it back there. I don't know where he was, because he wasn't tumbling with me. It was just me. There was nothingness, and yet it wasn't like emptiness.

I felt very full, very warm, but not like warm outside a body, just warm through, and the air around me was warm, and it wasn't so separate and got less and less separate as time went on. First there was the feeling of plunging and then falling, and then floating and tumbling, and then seeing what was around me, the planets, and then becoming aware that I wasn't in the body. This happened very quickly . . . .

It doesn't seem there was an emotion. It was not apart from happiness, but it wasn't me experiencing happiness. It wasn't happiness as I know it usually. I felt not apart from the things I was seeing. I felt we were all made of the same stuff. It was all the same. My body was no different than a star, planet, or comet, or particle. It was cellular, I guess, if cells can have an emotion. It was being in touch with the cells of everything. It was life. It was being alive. There was no beginning or end. It was timeless.

(Martha seemed to be having difficulty finding words to describe an emotion. The interviewer asked her if it seemed peaceful, strange, blissful, or ecstatic, and she responded:)

Very peaceful, very restful. It was ecstatic, it really was.

(Martha was unable to tell how long the experience lasted. She subsequently shared the experience with her lover. He had noticed that something special was happening. He felt "really wonderful," but also seemed jealous. During the experience, she had had no awareness of him at all. Her first memory was of him holding her.)

Suddenly I was in his arms, and it was exceptionally delicious and close. There was feeling of the joining of bodies. It was like: "What is my skin?" And then, "Where does his skin begin?" It was wonderful. My love for him felt so deep, really deep, heart to heart.

It has taken a lot of superficial notions out of my head about what love is about . . . It's a lot more than whether I like his features or his qualities. I always want that again. I want to have a relationship with somebody where I'm totally relaxed about not wanting it to end, where we are really in relationship . . . and I can totally let go again. . .

(At the time of this interview, Martha had set aside her spiritual practices, which had provided the framework for her ability to go deeply into the relationship. She was asked to recall what was going on in her life at the time of the experience and to describe her spiritual practice.)

I was doing a lot of religious ritual. I was taking care of temples. I was working with sacred elements, sacred places, training priests. That was my life—wake up in the morning and do a *puja* [sacramental rite].

(Martha was asked to describe here feelings in the days following the experience. She responded in terms of an ability to "see" energy.)

I could see more. I could see the life in everything, and that state lasted for a couple of days. I could see the energy, life-energy, in grass, trees—everything was kind of shimmering . . . And yet I felt extremely ordinary, very, very ordinary. I felt like there was nothing extraordinary about seeing.

RAMSEY'S ACCOUNT

(At twenty-eight years of age, Ramsey was the youngest inter-viewee. He became a spiritual seeker in his early twenties. He has been married eight years, and has been initiated into the beginning level of tantric practice. He has been a member of his particular spiritual community for eight years.)

It was a Sunday afternoon, around five o'clock. The sun was beginning to drop. It was kind of a peaceful feeling in the room. Claire and I were just resting with one another, holding one another, and I began to feel my heart break. I felt how mys-terious it was that I was holding this other being in my arms. I felt completely connected to her. I felt her heart. I felt the mystery of our meeting together.

Very slowly and relaxed, we began to love one another. I didn't really feel it was me—it was more like I was part of a divine dance that was being orchestrated by relaxing into it.

We made love very, very gently and softly for about an hour and a half. I was feeling this cord of energy going up and down my frontal line, and I began to breathe her energy through my body. I literally would breathe her. I would inhale and feel like I was breathing in her life force. And I would touch her heart, her navel, her forehead, and I would feel like I was touching her life energies.

(Ramsey described an ongoing discussion which he had been having with several of his male friends about his personality characteristics. He said that this discussion had brought him to the point of "vulnerability." He felt that this self-knowledge was part of a process that was allowing the transcendental experi-ence to occur.)

To be just in touch with that was bringing me into more of a wounded-heart position, which allowed me in an incredible way to connect to Claire. For the past three weeks we've been moved to just rest with one another and just feel that heart-breaking wound. I would feel waves of sorrow, but thoroughly enjoyable feelings of the poignancy of our condition, how vulner-able we were.

It didn't feel like it was generated from my own egoic sense. It was more of an etheric [sense], it was outside of my body, surrounding my body. It was an energy movement. It felt like a presence, a sense in which this play was happening. This kind of archetype of love, symbol of love, was happening within this presence, this very still, rested presence.

It was totally joyful. It was like incarnating the deepest feelings of love in the heart, and through gestures and love touching. It just felt like it wasn't egoically centered. It was nothing I could conceive of—it was greater than that. I couldn't grasp what was going on. It was a greater process. In some sense it feels totally natural, and in another sense it feels completely powerful. There is no problem in it. There's no self-conscious-ness in it . . .

There was no orgasm. It was orgasmic, but it wasn't leading to orgasm. I mean, I would touch her and the touch would be orgasmic. I would do it so gently and so fully and my attention was so present in the moment of touch that it wasn't leading anywhere. It was its own gesture.

Ninety percent of our contact is not orgasmic. Orgasm diminishes the feeling at my heart. It's a great feeling when it happens, but it somehow diminishes the energy. I've come not to enjoy that aftereffect. It makes me sleepy and dull. I'd rather just remain with the energy.

There were moments where through Claire's sheer re-sponse I would bodily begin to feel that there might be a point of orgasm beginning to occur because she would just be pulling so much from me. Once she gets that excited, it's overwhelming. At that point, I would just relax and breathe and maybe withdraw a little bit, just relax and feel her more.

Then when I felt my body maintain some equanimity, where the energy was more polarized outward again, I would continue again. That would happen a couple of times.

(The interviewer asked Ramsey if he had an intuition that this experience was going to be something special.)

It's happened many times. When I meditate, there is a similar polarization that occurs. It is a particular form of wonder and happiness in love play because you are connecting to another heart, another living current. So it's very dynamic. But it's a similar process, so I'm familiar with it. It's like surrender to it. It isn't a mind, it's generated prior to mind. There is just that sense of connectedness, and seeing her is a heart connection . . .

In those moments I feel that I am loving all women. It's like she's all women. It's like we all have this Goddess, and she is all

Goddesses and all women.

(Ramsey was asked to compare this transcendental experience with his experience of meditation.)

I think the difference with meditation is the bodily surrender to the Life that is living and breathing us. And it is based on the intuition that there is actually such a presence that pervades things. You can absolutely allow the tensions in your body to relax, and you can let your body go, let it dissolve in this being. This process that I engage with my wife is a similar thing, except what I find in that engagement is another heart, another being, an energy. I can only say I just feel it in my heart. I feel the vulnerability of this person, the vulnerability of myself, yet universal qualities. I make a psychic connection to life in a way that is different than when I meditate.

It is a natural relaxation, like I'm relaxing past my body, allowing my body to relax, so it doesn't gather up my attention. It lets my attention become diffuse and come in contact with energies that are not only of this body, but are surrounding it, pervading it, allowing the sense of self to relax. And when you do that in the company of one with whom you are intimate, that's a complete mystery. How do you describe it?

You could call it an intensified sense of being. It is delicious, wonderful, miraculous. It throws me into a sense of wonder that anything is. You could look at this woman whom you love . . . What is she? It is a complete mystery, and the heart just feels.

(Ramsey was asked if he felt that he could be in this state during any sexual encounter, or during any moment of life.)

You can't seek it or duplicate it through your own devices . . . It's not that you could experience it with everyone, but that there are laws of relationship that need somehow to be conformed to in order to really regularly experience this. I feel that absolutely this experience could be had in every moment of life. There's a law to it, probably called self-yielding, or giving up, or as a dear friend calls it, "a sacrifice, or heart wound."

(Ramsey was asked to describe the condition of his body during the experience.)

I would literally feel the vital [solar plexus] like an eye opening and closing. When it is closed it hurts. But if I allow myself to just feel the hurt of that closure, allow myself to rest in the body, even though it hurts (and through breathing and just accepting my bodily state in the moment), I begin to connect to the muscle that is tight. If I'm trying to change my bodily state, it keeps tightening. If I somehow accept the bodily state and just keep feeling, just commit myself to just feeling it anyway, I find it begins to relax spontaneously. I begin to feel more energy there.

Sometimes it cracks open. I feel air, I feel energy, I feel light, where normally, 99 percent of the time, I feel a cramp. And recognizing that has changed my life, because it has allowed me to recognize that when my mind is very active, it is usually that area that is very tight. And so instead of dealing with all those thoughts that are going on in the mind, I usually go directly to that area and feel it. Usually it is painful. I allow myself to just continue to feel it and continue to breathe. I remain in relationship to it, and at some point I feel it does begin to relax. And then I find the real enjoyment, because when it opens I feel great. I feel already happy, nothing I need to do.

(The interviewer asked if the process Ramsey described would be occurring during sexuality.)

Definitely. The energies intensify because there are two people. There seems to be a doubling of energy, the person's life energy that you are coming into direct contact with. I felt like I was breathing her in. I was literally breathing her into my body. I don't know what that is. I am conducting it into my own body, and at the same time I am also giving it to her, giving my bodily energy, the energy that I am to her . . . There is a state in which you feel that you don't care what is going to happen—you could die, you could live . . . It's so good you'd be willing to go in that moment. There's the feeling you could just surrender to whatever it's going to be because you're connected to what's wonderful . . . .

Bliss is a moment of real pleasure in the body. But ecstasy is almost like you're beyond it. I think that a lot of these sexual experiences that I'm describing are blissful experiences and an intuition of ecstasy, but not fully rounded in ecstasy. It is not really being outside of myself, but intuiting what that position is.

JAMES'S ACCOUNT

(James is a businessman in his mid-thirties. He was married for five years and has one child. He was a student with his teacher for eight years. He and his wife were subsequently divorced, and he has set aside his spiritual practice to concentrate on his career.

James' transcendental experience involved himself, his wife, and the conception of their daughter. This interview is representative of several contributors who were not included in the final research but who reported an intuition of the moment of conception of their children.

The setting of James' transcendental experience was an ordinary suburban house that he had just rented. However, for James this house, and in particular their bedroom, took on added significance eight months after the transcendental experience occurred. At that time James and his wife, who was by then eight months pregnant, offered their house as a temporary residence for their spiritual teacher. Their teacher occupied the same bedroom that they shared. For James this gesture of housing his teacher was doubly significant because his teacher was also awaiting the birth of a daughter.

James described his experience as basically identical to a transcendental state that had occurred previously.)

Suddenly we were relating more to each other as light bodies. The room filled with light. I could see light inches from my hands. In fact, I don't even think I had my eyes open the whole time. It was so psychic. Just a whole different level of connection. At one point I felt completely taken over. It wasn't real anymore. I felt completely possessed, taken over, animated, by the spirit.

(It is significant for James that his own name is similar to his teacher's name. He reported that in the midst of this spirit possession, he spoke out loud about his identity with his teacher, repeating the names as if they were the same. The interviewer asked him what it felt bodily to be someone else.)

I was just expanded beyond myself and into the room and the space surrounding. It wasn't like two physical bodies at all. If there was any vision at all, it was just light bodies. I remember a psychic vision, just skeletal light bodies coming out. That's how I felt myself. I didn't feel any limit to my own skin body. [I felt] well extended beyond that, into the room and connected with her, direct.

[There was] just a sense of enjoyment, laughter. Laughter was the overriding characteristic of the whole thing. When I was saying I was my teacher, I was laughing hysterically, literally. It's great. There was an overlay of energy that we were tapping into. I felt somehow that energy [was] his. I had no similar experiences or intuitions. This was the first real indication I had of the teaching and the teacher.

(James was asked if he felt that there was commonality of movement and mood with his sexual partner.)

Absolutely. She knew exactly what was going on with me, and I knew exactly what was going on with her. We were truly one, both ecstatic. She knew. She drew me into her space. I don't know how it happened. It was extraordinary for her, also, something she has told me never happened before or since . . .

We had been making use of the practices whereby the energy is used to bypass orgasm. Between us there was no difference. That kind of light energy we experienced, strong visualizations of light . . . whether she gave it to me, or I gave it to her, I don't know. It's just that together we experienced, or released, ourselves beyond ourselves, and I have in the middle of all this onrushing of light the precise intuition that we have conceived a child. I just knew it, and it was okay. Six weeks later she said she was pregnant. I knew it was going to come. It was a secret we carried around for a while, definitely a blessing.

(When James returned to his house the bedroom was set aside as a meditation room in honor of his teacher. James and his wife moved into an adjoining room. Shortly after, their daughter was delivered at home, in the bedroom next to the meditation room.)

We have this photograph that shows the baby coming out of the womb and being thrown up onto the body of the mother. The picture clearly shows a swatch of light, just bright, yellow light. It's a glow, not movement. You might not think anything of it, but we knew the circumstance nine months earlier.

STAN'S ACCOUNT

(Stan is an artist and teacher in his early thirties. He has been married for eight years. At the time of his transcendental experience, he and his wife were living in a communal household that included two other couples.

Stan was in the process of changing his life from being at a middle level of commitment and practice with his spiritual teacher to now pursuing the development of his artistic career. Stan admitted to being a person who was very susceptible to the life current. By this he meant that he experienced frequent occurrences of a mystical nature, or movements of energy within his body, including experiences of lights and explosions in his brain core.

Stan began by describing his movement into another dimension during a sexual encounter.)

The one I remember most was once when we were making love. I am very susceptible to the life current, and I could feel it moving up the spine and then moving into the head. That was where it tended locate, in the head.

Then I was moved into another dimension altogether, where I visited an ashram with Swami Nityananda. In his company, I entered into a blissful state that felt like it lifted me out of the body that I was in. I didn't feel in that moment connected in any sexual way. The sexual connection was still there, maintained, but transcended through this other association with this spiritual master. He wasn't even my spiritual master. But still he was just as good.

I remember when I returned to my senses, my experience of my relationship with my wife was one of communion, [rather] than just desire in the sense of fulfillment, so that the embrace was prolonged in a different way. That was one of the earlier incidents.

(Stan was asked to describe the transcendental nature of the experience.)

It has a sense of a blissful location, especially in the head. But it also is extended into the whole body, so the whole body seems to be pervaded [by], or lifted out of, its ordinary sense of self and suspended in pleasurable head-to-toe experience or energy.

(The interview moved to a discussion of the details of the experience. Stan was asked if that sexual encounter ended in orgasm.)

Not on that occasion. It was an extended sexual encounter without the physical orgasm. It tends to be the case, I feel, that when I move into a more transcendental awareness in the midst of the experience that the orgasm does not occur unless I intend it. The pleasure is more important than the actual climax. The energy was already ascending up through the spine.

It's like a current and it actually ascends. It moves through all the different centers in the spine and has a sense of moving out from the spine as well as to the rest of the body. Also, it has a rushing movement. Finally it seems to locate somewhere in the head and even beyond that.

The difference I feel is that the orgasm seems to be concentrated in the genital area, whereas this is much more an extended feeling of participation. Once the orgasm starts happening, it's inevitable. This is more like it can continue through different cycles of its own movement.

(The interviewer inquired if Stan's wife was aware of this transcendental condition.)

I tend in those moments to assume that . . . it would be obvious to her that I was not related in a conventional way. She seemed sensitive to that and didn't try to interrupt it in any way. There was a relaxed atmosphere. There was no pressure to do anything.

(The interview concluded with Stan responding to whether or not he felt this had been an initiatory experience.)

Yes, I think it was. It occurred in a sexual moment and is now extended into ordinary moments. I valued it fondly. Later I saw some footage of Nityananda in his ashram, and I remember feeling it was familiar. And I felt I knew what his condition was. I could feel that he was a supreme being, just saturated with bliss. I was familiar with it, and I remembered that I had already had that kind of experience with him.

NOTES

1. E. Whitmont, *Return of the Goddess* (New York: Crossroad, 1982), 124.

2. F. Ricci, *Tantra: Rites of Love* (New York: Rizzoli International, 1979), 8.

3. D. Kinsley, *The Sword and the Flute* (Berkeley: University of California Press, 1975), 112.

This interview with psychologist Julie Henderson is entitled "The Lover Within," which is also the title of her book. She speaks vividly and honestly about her own past frustration with what she describes as "rubbing bodies together," that is, ordinary love-making without sacramental implications. She emerges as a strong advocate for a Tantra-style spirituality, recommending that we pursue spiritual orgasm rather than sensory orgasm, or pleasure in Being rather than pleasure in "having" sex, which is the distinction highlighted by Jean Lanier. For Henderson, conventional sex reduces the pleasure or delight in Being to genital sensations by which we focus on ourselves. She too argues strongly that true spirituality involves sensitivity to one's partner, true intimacy, and the cultivation of relationship.

THE LOVER WITHIN

An Interview with Julie Henderson, Ph.D

GF: Who or what is the Lover within?

JH: I suppose I would answer that question very differently, depending on who I was talking to. To some people I might say that the Lover within is our own personal experience of Aliveness moving within us. But then I would go beyond that to say that it's not personal, or not only personal, that we feel Life moving within this location, within this body-mind, but that this location is always changing, always in movement. The boundaries of the self are learned, and we can also learn to release them. In learning to form them and to release them we are immediately engaged in surrender, which is most of the time an ecstatic process. Therefore the experience of Aliveness, or Life, or the Divine, or Being—the words are not so important—is one of releasing or giving up, over and over, whatever we think we are.

To the degree that we maintain a sense of location, then, there are currents flowing through and around this location, and some of that energy we experience as personal, and some of it as impersonal. The long-run process, as I experience it, I describe in terms of noticing where we are withholding ourselves from that flow and of releasing any contraction that arises in resistance to it.

Thirteen years ago, I still understood this resistance primarily as a matter of somatic, muscular contractions and also as the emotional contractions that follow. It became progressively clear to me that you can dissolve muscular contraction and also learn to be more emotionally expressive. At that point you become aware of energetic patterns; some of those are clearly contractive and can be dissolved as well. Then you begin, after a while, to be able to feel the substance of mind in movement, and many of those movements are contractive, and you dissolve those.

Most of last year I went through quite a crisis, which had been in the making for years. It struck me with full force that the assumption that I was a human being was merely another contraction. The implications of that were pretty scarey; I didn't want to know that sort of thing.

GF: What were those implications for you at the time?

JH: Well, at that time the implications, in a neurotic sense, were that if I gave up that assumption there would be no one left to take care of this body-mind. I got past that one. (Laughter.) Now it just feels like mind is making movements within mind, and some of those are pretty sticky, and we tend to get identified with them. By and large I am engaged in dissolving any contraction that creates a sense of disconnection between this body-mind and the rest of what is. I suppose you can call that spiritual. For me personally, this arises as an inevitable progression out of work that didn't start out to be spiritual at all.

I was originally involved in body work. And I came to somatics in an effort, not very conscious, to support my own embodiment, because going up and out the back door is easy as hell for me. As Ram Dass puts it, one can always go off to La-La Land, nothing to it. Of course, other people may have a hard time going off to La-La Land, and maybe they need to learn how to do that, but for me the invitation and the loving challenge is to embody that Life or Being, not to think about it or even feel it, or move charge around in exciting ways, but to be that Life without obstruction.

I would say that we are all here to embody what is, but most of the time we are in wild flight from knowledge of that. I don't know too many people who are really committed to consciously embodying whatever they intuit they are. Until last year, I myself didn't have a really clear idea that this could be an actual practice. In retrospect I would say that even after I had been practicing bioenergetic analysis for four or five years, I had perhaps come down into the viscera but not into the bones. My present work is to be present as Consciousness in and as the body, transforming its condition but not being bound by it.

GF: Why did you choose to speak of the Lover within? The title of your book is very poetic, almost romantic. It reminds one more of Kabir than somatics.

JH: I can't remember exactly, but that was the phrase that I used myself to describe what it was like when I first let Life touch me. It was like a lover's touch.

GF: Every writer has a certain kind of person in mind. In my experience, it's usually a person just like me. (Laughter.) Who did you write your book for? Did you have mostly women in mind?

JH: Not at all. But I did have people like me in mind. I wrote my book for people who, in their sexual life, were not persuaded by merely rubbing bodies together, that is, who felt that if there was no energetic exchange, it might as well not be happening. That point of view, or aspect of sexual experience, had never been addressed in any of the books on sexual functioning that I had come across.

GF: That's really surprising, considering all of Reich's writings.

JH: In Reichian or neo-Reichian work there is an enormous emphasis on proper genital functioning, and particularly on being able to have an orgasm. And orgasm is seen as a whole-body, pulsatory event. But I came to realize that there is a point at which, once that level of functioning is established, there is another movement of charge that happens during sexual embrace. That is an upward movement, which happens spontaneously. It doesn't have to be fought for. Rather, it occurs when surrender is the intention. Then ordinary genital orgasm is no longer the point. I even found myself saying things like: There is a constant, persistent, universal orgiastic Condition that you can participate in at any time. All you have to do is align yourself with it and let go. Now that's way over Bailey's barn from the point of view of a Reichian.

GF: Your approach is obviously not merely about increasing sexual pleasure. Nevertheless, some critics may feel that you are simply playing into the hands of pleasure seekers, the New Age narcissists, who will use even their partners to enhance their own selfish pursuits.

JH: Well, as I hope is clear in the book, my primary concern was most fundamentally to induce in people a direct experience of Being. I generally chose not to speak of this directly. As I said in the back of my book, this is an old trick. The pleasure in Being is often reduced to, or isolated in, sexual activity because we're frightened. A primary concern was and still is for me to communicate to people that they can feel orgiastic, or ecstatic, at any time and anywhere, if only they are willing.

Having experienced over too many years what it's like to have my body borrowed, I don't think a person could actually learn to do the exercises in my book and remain as narcissistic as he or she started out. I really don't think so.

GF: Some people who have an interest in spiritual practice also have a problem with sexuality. Now that they are also meditating, they may feel very confused or awkward about sex.

JH: Or angry.

GF: Yes. At any rate, they feel complicated about sex. How would you address their question about integrating their spiritual aspirations with the sexual drive?

JH: I would say: Forget about calling it sex! Are you willing to surrender what you are into the Divine Ground? Then surrendered physical union is one of the clearest arenas to practice that greater union and surrender. And if they feel "no good at it," then I would ask them: What is it you like? Do you want to feel pleasure in Being? Are you willing to support feeling pleasure in Being, even if it doesn't have anything to do with sex in the beginning, or maybe never? It is possible that you may never be any "good" at genital sexuality. The question is: Is that okay with you, so long as you are orgiastic? Are you willing to be orgiastic without being sexual? They believe that if they can't get the multiple orgasms that *Playboy* is talking about, they're never going to feel good, they're never going to be in harmony. This is, of course, quite ridiculous. But that philosophy is ground in like glass; it hurts people.

GF: Would you say that when you started out on this particular path you came much more from a materialistic point of view? Did you, perhaps, feel that your inner life could be manipulated to the point where you would have experiences that were blissful, ecstatic, or orgasmic? And now you tend more toward the view that this bliss is already there, and it is more a matter of letting go of inner obstructions so that you can realize that which is already the case?

JH: That sounds a little bit extreme. I certainly was engaged, at that time, in dissolving contraction, but I guess I didn't yet have as strong a foundation of trust as I do now. I had dissolved many, many layers of trying to manipulate my reality, other people's reality, make this happen, make that happen, and certainly had come to the point of voluntary ecstatic release, but I would say, an element of manipulation was still there. I still thought that somehow I could effect my own happiness. It is different now. To the extent to which there is an 'I' left at all, there's a sense in which this location, this body-mind, moves into harmony with Life. I look at this all as a matter of levels of contraction coming into awareness and being dissolved with more or less resistance.

GF In your book you make the point that our boundaries, our energy boundaries, are all artificial.

JH: Learned.

GF: We create, posit them. If that's the case, and given your feeling sense that the bliss that arrives when you surrender is the ever-present "ground condition" of our lives, why do you say the "Lover within"? Within where?

JH: Well, I wouldn't put it like that now, although I just might because it sounds nice. To the extent that we experience ourselves as localized selves, there will be a sense that there is a fine, virtually transparent membrane, and that there is a Lover within and without, who shakes that membrane.

GF: A wonderful image. Now, a physicist of the classical, pre-quantum persuasion might object to your use of the word "energy" in connection with sexuality.

JH: It is probably as well to say that I don't limit aliveness to sexuality. In fact, when a client comes to see me and starts out saying, "I've got this sexual problem," I simply ignore the words. What is it that he or she is actually experiencing? For instance, one woman came to me and told me that she comes almost to orgasm and then nothing happens. I asked myself, What does she mean by "almost" orgasm? If that were truly the case, and she simply stopped trying in that moment, and instead were to take a deep breath and relax, she would certainly experience something she would enjoy very much.

GF: In other words: What's the problem?

JH: Exactly, what is the problem with having or not having an orgasm? In my own case, all the brouhaha in the fifties and sixties that I went through about not being okay sexually was primarily because the sexual charge was already moving up, and I kept trying to move it down because I thought there was something wrong with me if it didn't move down. I had enormous resources at my disposal, but in terms of allowing the fruition of my own pleasure in Being, there wasn't a vocabulary or an orientation available to me at the time. There wasn't anybody to tell me, "Oh, no, this is fine, this is fine. Your instinct is terrific.

Allow the charge to move up. Simply allow it to keep moving."
People feel like it's not okay what's happening to them. They
often don't know how to allow themselves to experience the
pleasure that is intrinsic in Being.

GF: Or the displeasure connected with human existence.

JH: That's true. To be embodied is to be vulnerable. Suffering is
real. There is, however, a profound difference between misery
and suffering. In fact, a lot of the teaching I do is about how we
create misery in order not to know how we're suffering. As I use
the words, misery is what we experience when we become
fascinated with our circumstances and insist on a certain
outcome; suffering is the intense sensation of life operating on
us, unfolding us and re-shaping us—the conscious diamond
being cut. The attitude of surrender embraces this also.

GF You regard the body as an energy system. What does this
mean?

JH: I look on the body as the corporeal expression of patterns of
mind, of attitude. This particular orientation arises again out of
my background in somatics, where body and mind are approached as two aspects of a single system. I experience that
matter really is highly compressed and elaborately shaped
energy, that energy is equally highly compressed and elaborately shaped Consciousness, and that they're not different.
They are experientially different, but not different in kind, and
that as the contractions are addressed and released, the embodied being is experienced as less and less dense. So, I really don't
conceive or experience them as separate, although English is a
pig when it comes to trying to talk about things like that.

There's a footnote somewhere in my book that I added on
after I had read about how energy is, after all, not absolutely
conserved. I was wild with excitement, and called up a friend of
mine in New York who is a nuclear physicist. I asked him why he
had't told me of this finding. He said, "Oh, it doesn't mean
anything." I said, "What are you talking about? Of course, it
means something!" He responded, "Well, it almost never happens." "But . . . but . . . but," I said to him, "it 'almost never'
happens that matter isn't conserved, and look at the changes
that have come out of that!"

So, it *almost never* happens that energy isn't conserved!
But it does happen in certain extreme situations, and it's very

important that it can happen at all. In fact, the implications are staggering. My experiential knowing at the moment is that energy is condensed consciousness, just as matter is condensed energy. I experience that directly. It's not conceptual. Perhaps there is a brilliant young physicist somewhere out there who has already worked out the mathematics for this.

GF: According to all spiritual traditions of the world, consciousness is innately blissful. Would you agree that the condition of joy, delight, or bliss that is realized through your practice of surrender is simply something that occurs to you or in you or as you.

JH: These are good prepositions. Maybe that's the progression.

GF: Do you cultivate the attitude of surrender also in regard to things or events that are not blissful? Do you recommend to people to stop worrying about things when they aren't blissful, when they're simply in pain, when feelings of grief occur, or other similar feelings that are very deep?

JH: Like virtually everybody I know, for a long, long time I was concerned with enforcing happiness. I was going to wrest it from nature, make myself be happy. Then, as it became clear to me that I could, through changes in my breathing and movement, feel anything at all—not merely an imitation but the real thing with a whole physiological response—I made another startling discovery: I began to notice that there was resistance in me to having that freedom, that there was a part of me that was willfully contractive.

Thus, even though I knew I could be happy, I would create misery because I felt I didn't have what I wanted. And I gradually began, with the help especially of my colleague Daniel Weber, to be able to experience all of this soap opera, all of this willful creation of misery, as an avoidance of what I now call suffering, which is the direct experience of life reshaping itself toward greater awareness and spaciousness.

GF: Suffering as the experience of change, and even of growth?

JH: Yes, the inevitable unfolding of conscious substance. And change is painful, but only to the degree that there are adhesions, attachments, as they say, in the spiritual traditions, only to the extent that we are not surrendered. I feel a great deal of sympathy, or maybe even compassion, for what it's like to be an embodied being. It's hard to be surrendered enough and to change fast enough that there aren't sensations of ripping. But to the degree that one can reside in surrender, the sensations of transformation may be intense but not inevitably painful. It takes an enormous amount of trust, though. At the age of forty-six, I can say I almost really trust this process. I have a lot of faith in the capacity of life to come up with something I haven't surrendered through yet. (Laughter.)

GF: In some of your exercises, or descriptions of exercises, you ask people to intend love. Can you say something about this?

JH: Yes. Sometime in 1985, a friend gave me a set of the three volumes by Longchenpa, called *Kindly Bent to Ease Us*. In them I encountered for the first time the Buddhist concept of the "four great catalysts"—love, joy, compassion, and peace of mind. I read that wherever I was able to bring one or more of these four forces to bear, they would alter what was happening internally and externally. So I began to explore this more deliberately. I did so in the context of research I assisted with at the Human Interaction Laboratory of the Langley Porter Neuropsychiatric Institute, where I was particularly concerned with the question of how one feels what one feels. I studied how patterns of movement, breath, and sound are the emotions that they express. I began to examine the patterns of movement, breath, and sound that were love, joy, compassion, and peace of mind, and I started to teach how to embody those.

Remarkably, it wasn't until a few months ago that I heard these great "catalysts" discussed as the *bodhicitta*, the awakened will toward enlightenment. Now, intention is not a matter of simply willing something in the egoic sense. I understand it as an organismic, whole-body agreement to allow a movement, an act, a way of being. In this sense, we intend heart beat, lung movement, swallowing, all the pulsations of life. Also in this sense, we intend what we feel and how we are. By and large, intention is preconscious for most people. And so intending love or any of the other "catalytic" conditions is the same thing for me as fostering their embodiment, and we do that to whatever degree that we can.

GF: How can you explain intending love to a person who, say, comes straight out of the business world where almost everything is about cutting each other's throats rather than loving each other, and who really has no background in what loving might mean?

JH: Well, I would begin by asking such a person whether he wants to be loving? If the answer is Yes, I would go on to ask him what it means to him to love someone.

GF: He might say: Pat my dog on the head and bring my wife a bunch of flowers occasionally.

JH: If that were his reply, I would ask him whether these are actions that somebody told him to do. I would ask him: What are the sensations that arise in you as you describe something as an act of love, like bringing flowers? In this way I would lead him very gradually into an awareness of that particular aspect of his embodiment, which might take six months to a year, depending on how . . .

GF: . . . emotionally constipated he was.

JH: Right.

GF: So, it would be a matter of simply getting them to feel what they are already feeling but aren't allowing themselves to feel or to express.

JH: And to feel okay about it, to feel safe with it, to recognize that they can be vulnerable and still potent. In fact, that they can be more potent if they are willing to be vulnerable at the same time.

GF: Toward the end of your book you say that unconditional love is found through moving toward the energy of that which is. What do you mean by unconditional?

JH: Oh, well, let's come back to somatics. In a practical sense, I mean the movement that is accompanied by the maximum release of contraction that's possible within consciousness in that moment. This last year, for instance, I've spent a lot of time exploring the specific practicalities of alignment. In basic bio-energetic and biodynamic practice there are a good many techniques that are used, more or less crassly, to induce vibration. The intention behind that is that the vibration allows energy to move through the tissues, which helps to release contraction. However, it's clear that if the body is brought into alignment with itself, with the earth, with what is, then there will be a spontaneous pulsation, which may be a visible vibration or not. That pulsation enables us at any given moment to release at least some of the contractions of which we are aware. That is surrender. When we do that, other contractions come into our awareness, and then we have a challenge to our capacity to release them. To the degree that we are committed to that process, we are in continual surrender. We may not be very good at it, but what matters is our intention, or the degree of unconditionality that we bring to that movement.

So, practically speaking, how much of yourself is withheld? That withholding can only be done by contraction, whether it's a contraction of mind or a contraction of energy, or a contraction of the body. If I ever write another book, I will definitely be saying a lot about the practicalities of alignment. Sexual union is the mudra, the "gesture" of alignment, or surrender. When two bodies come into alignment with each other, surrender to pulsation, and abide ecstatically as that: that is, for me at least, the most direct way to practice at the highest available level of charge and one profound way of going beyond the narcissistic exploitation of Being.

GF: What happens when, say, a woman wants to practice this sexual yoga but her partner has no interest in it?

JH: I guess, then it becomes a matter of clarification. There are things that a person can do alone. There is, however, a danger involved, which is the same danger as when a marriage partner is learning to be assertive. If there is dissension in the relationship already, any move toward independence will create more dissension. So, the first question is really whether that person, male or female, is willing to risk the relationship in order to come to greater harmony, risk the relationship to enliven the relationship. And if they're not, they should stop right away, because that's precisely what is involved.

A partner who is not interested is a partner who is not interested. Partners may not be interested primarily because they're afraid, and under certain protected situations they might learn to be more interested. But there are people who are simply so self-involved that they don't give a damn about their partners. Then the question arises whether, if you have a spiritual intention, you are restraining your own practice of love by living with somebody who doesn't want to love and grow.

GF: Some people, of course, may feel that if they can't love the person who is nearest to them, even though he or she rejects what they stand for, then what good is their quest for love and spiritual growth anyway.

JH: I would say, if you can really do that, you also don't need anyone's help or to ask any questions about what to do. But if you're just pretending, that will be no good to anybody. You're just martyrizing and creating more contraction in yourself.

GF: Okay, let's assume that the husband isn't a total dolt and loves and cares for his wife but somehow is intimidated by her spiritual aspirations. Essentially he is ignorant, but he is willing to learn.

JH: Well, first he can read my book and have a tantrum, and say what the hell is she talking about. What I come back to again and again when talking with individuals and couples, but especially couples, is this: Are you willing to feel pleasure? Are you willing to feel pleasure with each other? It doesn't matter whether you're going for a walk in the country, fixing a pizza, or making love. Are you willing to feel good in the presence of your wife or husband? Are you willing to let him or her know that you feel good? Are you willing to share and exchange the sensations and the energy of that feeling good? Are you willing to make gestures and sounds that express that feeling? Are you willing to let each of you see and hear the visible, audible manifestation of your pleasure and well-being. If people are willing to do that, it's cut and dried. You just teach them how.

The real difficulty is with people who are so frightened or so injured that they really do expect to be punished if they feel good. Now, what I mean by feeling good is whole-body pleasure, the surrendered pulsatory condition of the body-mind. Oftentimes people have to start out with very much less than that, though. Sometimes couples have reached a deadlock in their relationship, and so the first thing to do is get them out of the lock. Here the key questions, as I said, is: Are you willing to feel good with each other? Are you willing to feel good with each other even if the other person doesn't change and you don't get what you want either right away or maybe never? Are you willing to feel good with your partner right now? Often they will end up holding hands, ecstatic, and then they get scared by their own happiness.

A lot of times people are not willing to feel pleasure, and that becomes the point of departure in therapy. You start by exploring their resistance: What great demon is going to come out of the closet and eat you up if you feel good? In our culture, it's considered in very poor taste to be visibly happy.

GF: To be ecstatic. They lock you up, right?

JH: That used to be one of my great fears, my paranoid terrors. I was afraid that I would become so ecstatic that I would run down the street singing, and they'd lock me up. It hasn't happened. At any rate, in my teaching work I always come back to as basic a position as I can. The main question is always: *Are you willing?*

GF: Your book *The Lover Within* is important for the beginning stages of spiritual life, when a person starts his or her journey of embodiment. There is, however, more to spiritual practice than is covered in your book. I know that you have been influenced by Tibetan teachers, and have recently started to practice "Consort Yoga" very seriously.

JH: Right. *The Lover Within* prepares you for the next level. When you have mastered the exercises in that book, then you have the option to actually engage in sexual spiritual practice. And if you don't have the capacities awakened by those exercises, then you basically can't proceed with Consort Yoga. At least that's how I look at it now.

A lot of what my partner and I do involves the surrendered, mutual, present embodiment of love on one hand, and the capacity for spontaneous alignment, for pulsation, for feeling the great mudra or "gesture" of Being, on the other. If you don't have the basic skills, you just can't do that. You may have a terrific good time and a good intention, but that's not what spiritual sexual practice is about.

GF: Do you set up your sexual moments as a ritual, sacred occasion? Do you have any preliminaries, like lighting incense or otherwise preparing the room?

JH: No. In my experience, we're so aware of each other energetically that it's like a simultaneous continuing form of worship or *puja*. We are always in preparation for union. Often we make love after a more formal meditative practice, but not always. There simply is a mutual impulse to embrace.

GF: What Da Free John calls "love-desire."

JH: Yes, mutual ecstatic celebration of Being beyond the personal self.

GF: I noticed that you were actually referring to Da Free John's bulky volume *Love of the Two-Armed Form* in your book . . .

JH: . . . I think he has mostly influenced me through the chapter on spiritual sexuality in *The Dawn Horse Testament*, which I find really quite graceful.

GF: Are you yourself still doing any of the practices mentioned in your book?

JH: Oh, well, it depends on which ones. Some of the more basic energetic exercises I do all the time, modifying how I am in the world. Otherwise I do them only when I teach and model them. Anyway, I'm not doing them like pushups.

GF: What does your own practice consist in at this point—apart from the daily gesture of surrender, that is?

JH: My own practice involves teaching, which is always a matter of learning. As formal practice I do an enormous amount of what I call "connection," or "finding," I guess often through a form of guru yoga, such as by using the picture of somebody who has a lot of juice for me. I sit with it and create space for *that* to arise in *this* place. I open inwardly to receive the Beloved. The preparations and sensations are the same that I bring to preparation for lovemaking with my consort. That's probably the most obvious formal thing that I do.

I also do two particular Tibetan practices that I could easily describe in somatic terms as having to do with radical restructuring. I do *chöd* and the practice of "dissolving the six *lokas*," or worlds. What these exercises are "for" is not so immediately obvious as with other exercises, which, say, increase bodily pleasure—especially if you are starting out and can't yet directly feel Mind in movement. In somatics, we talk about de-structuring, for instance, where attitudes that are held as bodily form are encouraged to be released fairly radically (both in "mind" and "body"), because such structures limit our aliveness, awareness, and freedom.

In this light, chöd is a very powerful de-structuring exercise directed to the attitude that consciousness, 'you,' are the body—to radically reduce identification with the body and its condition, to transform it and "give it away." This is related to what I said before about giving up the notion that 'I' am a human being—to realize that 'human being' is a structure limiting awareness and freedom. Da Free John has said, "We are a meal." Chöd is like that.

Again, in somatic terms, the practice of dissolving the six lokas is an exercise that aims at dissolving the predisposition of Mind to fix in form and identify with form. This doesn't include an intention to avoid form, however. Mind you, that's only my current understanding. I also do sound practices a good bit, because again somatically the coherent sound touches the fluids of the body in a way that no other procedure really can.

GF: By "sound practices" do you mean mantra yoga?

JH: Yes. But this isn't merely a mechanical repetition of mantras. One of the things I'm liable to get cross about is the fact that people do mantra yoga when they are completely disembodied.

GF: Ram, Ram, Ram, Ram . . .

JH: Right. The coherence of the sound can't touch them. In order to use "Ram" as a mantra, the body has to be relaxed and open enough for that sound to touch it and be felt spontaneously through the whole body. Then mantra yoga helps to restructure the tissues, helps to restructure the quality of the charge that's present. And when the opportunity arises I make love to my partner. (Laughter.)

GF: This sounds like a wonderful life.

JH: I would be in absolute agreement with you! I would say, in fact, that what has arisen in our consort practice has been the most important step forward in my own learning and practice. To be in the moment, not waiting and not yearning, has become a profound equanimity practice for me. Whatever is arising is, for me, the cauldron of joy.

GF: You are very fortunate then.

JH: Oh, yes, I should say. I celebrate.

GF: Now, for most people, this level of practice obviously is beyond reach for a very long time because you have to have a profound understanding of your own movement, your own motivations, the ability to hold up the mirror all the time, to really know what it is you're doing.

JH: Mind watching mind.

GF: Yes, but then also make that other gesture of going beyond all that.

JH: Yes, a couple of years ago I arrived at the point where I finally could sit on the beach and say, "I don't know how a person could be as dense as I am," because every time I said something like "I want to get married," I was really saying "I want an opportunity to practice surrender in this relationship." People don't get married, by and large, in order to surrender. It took me a long time to realize that they don't, because for me that's what it was all about from the beginning. I couldn't formulate my own motive with any clarity, but I know that the impulse was the same. And now, in my practice of Consort Yoga, I can at last feel free to make that gesture of surrender again and again. It's great! (Laughter.)

GF: So, should everybody get into it?

JH: Oh no.

GF: Obviously, people can be totally deluded about it. They can just fuck their brains loose and say, "That's great. I feel really ecstatic," and what not. But what they are doing is merely pleasurizing themselves, not finding the great pleasure or bliss in Being.

JH: Well, what separates the sheep from the goats in my experience is this: First of all, you have to have a mutual intention. Most people don't have a mutual intention. Most people enter a relationship because the other person's going to be what they want them to be, or do what they need them to do. Where there's a mutual intention of this quality of unfolding, or transcendence of identification with some condition, then there's a shared agreement that the other person will be present with you when the hard times come but not that they will do and be what you want. That creates, right away, conditions of enormous pressure on conditioning.

GF: Does that mean that Consort Yoga requires a commitment to a stable relationship?

JH: It requires a commitment to something before that. It requires a commitment to continuity of connection, which may or may not be physical presence with each other. It requires a commitment to surrender into what is; that is, it comes before any personal consideration. This sounds pretty extreme, but that's where the ego gets the boot, you see, because all of the stuff that comes up about "If you really loved me, you would never squeeze the toothpaste from the middle of the tube," will have to be simply dropped. It's a real fire, and the tendency to flake off is very high. So, in a certain sense, you have to be willing to surrender your preferences into, well, into Big Mind. And sometimes that's extremely hard to do.

GF: The real trick, then, is to notice when you're not loving and not joyous. Right?

JH: Yes. And that requires paying attention and also patience, as well as compassion with this body-mind.

GF: Now, your personal situation is obviously completely different from Tantrism. In Tantrism, the guru tells you the day and the minute you must show up, and then somebody else, whom you may or may not know, is brought into the circle, and that's the person with whom you're expected to practice Consort Yoga.

JH: This isn't my way. I don't say that I couldn't do it, but it certainly wouldn't be the way I would choose. I don't think it would benefit me. At least not the me I am now.

GF: Probably that would be true of most of the people who are reading up on Tantrism and perhaps get vaguely excited about it?

JH: Right. In Tantrism, as I understand it, before you are called into the circle, you might have spent twenty years or more clearing out the obstructions. (Laughter). In the West, with psychodynamic and somatic and other kinds of resources, we have the opportunity to make the relationship itself a means of cleaning the mirror. Some people prefer to do the preparation alone. Some people to do it in relationship. And I think those who prefer to do it alone have probably some hangups, adhesions, attachments, or aversive problems around connection, which they'll have to confront at some point.

Other people, like myself, find it much easier to do it in relationship, for equally neurotic reasons, or reasons that are gradually not so neurotic. So, for me, the challenge is to continue in practice and in connection when my partner is not present. That's much more difficult for me.

So what's necessary? There must be a bodhisattvic intention, that is, the willingness to embody love, joy, compassion, and peace of mind—without phonying it up, and without making it into another ritual of compliance and distortion of Being. Also required is the willingness to be present with each other, both in practicing the embodiment of these "catalytic" conditions and also, without avoidance, in confronting and resolving the inevitable bubbles of craziness that arise as we surrender and contractions dissolve. When we offer these things to each other, persistently and lovingly, together and apart, through the flux of conditions, we are offering—or so I experience—the possibility of an exacting and embodied spiritual practice in everyday life.

Erotic spirituality is not only for those who are married or in a sexual relationship. It is relevant also for single men and women. In his essay "Tantric Celibacy and Erotic Mystery," psychotherapist Stuart Sovatsky shows how voluntary celibacy can be a viable option for some people and how celibacy need not signal the end of an erotic attitude toward life. Sovatsky, who writes from personal experience, advocates celibacy as a potent means of self-transformation and self-transcendence for single men and women as well as people in relationships. Drawing particularly on Hindu esotericism, he explains how celibacy, rather than being a joyless practice of repression, can generate enormous pleasure. Dreaded by most sexually active people, celibacy does in fact entail a little-understood psychosomatic process of seminal sublimation that can not only lead to bodily rejuvenation but also to spiritual ecstasy.

TANTRIC CELIBACY AND EROTIC MYSTERY

By Stuart C. Sovatsky, Ph.D.

The terrain of conventional sexuality has been well charted over the past twenty years. Yet there are very few maps of that little-understood territory known as *brahmacarya*, or yogic celibacy. Some might think it a desert or a lonely island, others an earthly impossibility. Nevertheless, just about all of us find ourselves celibate, whether by choice or by circumstance, for at least some time during our lives. And periods of celibacy may be becoming more commonplace and prolonged these days, as our culture swings away from the freewheeling sexuality of the 1960s toward a more thoughtful and discriminating attitude toward relationship. In the following, I hope to show that yogic celibacy, like conventional sexuality, offers much to those willing to experiment with its age-old methods.

On the basis of extensive personal experience and interviews with other practitioners, I have discovered that the brahmacarya lifestyle actually has much in common with conventional sexuality. Both are erotic, at times problematic, and yet filled with life-enhancing potential. Any discussion that polarizes celibacy and sexuality distracts us from such deeper questions as "What exactly is eros?" and "What is erotic or sexual liberation?" That is, how can we act on erotic feelings in a way that secures our greatest growth, intimacy, and pleasure?

Is it possible that such feelings may in fact signal an opportune time to meditate? Or that perhaps they occur to be enjoyed in themselves, just as they are? What would happen to a person who repeatedly interpreted erotic sensations in these ways? Although we have been taught that such a person would become painfully repressed, there are other views on the matter. The great modern Indian saint Ramakrishna, for example, noted that the penultimate celibate state in yoga "was one in which it seemed that all the pores of the skin were like female organs and intercourse were taking place over the whole body."[1] In light of such an authoritative description, the sex/celibacy debate loses its potency. Rather than trying to prove which lifestyle is better or more correct, let us approach erotic feelings with what Zen masters call 'beginner's mind', that is, without preconceptions.

Curiously, 'beginner's mind' is also the central attitude behind the practice of brahmacarya. This Sanskrit word means literally 'brahmic conduct'. Here 'brahmic' refers to the brahman, the Absolute or Divine, which is conceived as transcending all qualities, including sexual distinctions. Whether explicitly or implicitly, the true practitioner of brahmacarya, who is called *brahmacarin*, is asking the question: What is the essential erotic life when I am free of accumulated concepts, habits, and social conditionings? Is it, as Wilhelm Reich and other Western theorists maintain, a system of physiological responses, emotions, and behaviors that inevitably lead to genital orgasm? Or is this just one of numerous possible ways of embodying eros in ourselves and our love relationships? In this age of sexual sophistication, it may sound strange to pretend that we do not really know all that "erotic feelings" may signify. But it is precisely through such an innocent attitude that the brahmacarin hopes to make some truly new discoveries about sexuality.

In a previous research project, I have suggested that a single eros vitalizes all of its many expressions.[2] Rather than being sheer pleasure, this eros is in fact archetypal hiddenness, or ontological mystery. Eros is "hidden" not because anyone or any moral code has hidden it, but because it is always, as itself, the most hidden and mysterious aspect of reality. Thus, the pleasure of sex comes from sensual contact with the deep mysteries of ourselves and each other—that is, from realities that we can only begin to fathom, not just from aroused nerve endings. This explains the finding of sex researchers that scantily clad persons have more erotic appeal than those who are totally naked; veiling heightens the sense of mystery. At more profound levels, the definition of eros as ontological mystery helps us understand why eros is able to overwhelm the strongest egoic controls with its seductive passions.

Spiritual authorities, both Eastern and Western, are commonly accused of hiding sexuality from us. But that is like accusing the Easter Bunny, a symbol of fertility, of hiding Easter eggs from us, when that is exactly her job, and makes for the excitement of the hunt. Scientific theory allows little room for mystery, however, and so conventional psychology has explained the mystery away: Erotic feelings are merely the urge for genital orgasm, with little or no concern for the cycles of fertility or even balanced frequency. Psychology has limited eros to a certain set of behaviors, feelings, and images; in other words, it has turned eros into sex, and has taken upon itself the task of freeing us to have as much sex as we could ever want.

When eros is understood as mystery, however, traditional spiritual teachings about sex can be understood as an attempt to protect mystery from mundane explanations and profanations, rather than as a parental prohibition against certain activities. The purposes of this protection include hygiene, a concern for maintaining bloodlines, and an understanding of the pleasures and beatitudes of mystical celibacy. These three areas of concern correlate with three great mysteries—the mystery of personal health and regeneration, the mystery of the eternal regeneration of the species, and the mystery of erotic, ecstatic union with the universe. The original intent of religion was not to repress, but rather to promote a particular approach to the mysterious workings of eros in our lives.

In the West, however, especially over the past one hundred years, people have come to believe that spirituality represses sexuality, thereby hiding it from us. In consequence, a theory of sexual liberation has emerged that is based on the desirability of increasing access to all manner of sexual stimulation. The concurrent development of effective contraceptives has facilitated this approach.

In light of this particular strategy for sexual liberation, spiritual attitudes toward sex, especially those concerning celibacy or energetic transmutation, have often come to seem asexual, or even inimical to eros. (As we shall see, this need not be the case.) The French philosopher Michel Foucault makes this point in *The History of Sexuality*, as does Julius Evola in *The Metaphysics of Sex*. I make a similar point in an earlier work,[3] and Germaine Greer also explores these issues in her *Sex and Destiny*. In short, a new history of modern sexuality has emerged that shows the limitations of the first wave of the sexual liberation movement. The next wave, which promises a further integration of spirituality and passion, has much to learn from yogic theories.

For thousands of years, yogins have been conducting research into the relationship between human liberation and sexual passion. Their hypothesis is stated most succinctly in the *Bhagavad-Gita* (VII.11), where Krishna, a representative of the highest form of bodily evolution, refers to himself as a particular kind of passion: "In beings, I am the passion that is not contrary to *dharma*." The Sanskrit term dharma stands for the cosmic order. The "dharmic" expression of passion involves interpreting and enacting erotic sensations in harmony with natural rhythms and principles of growth. These rhythms emerge at the individual, interpersonal, and cosmic levels.

INDIVIDUAL LIFE

The yogic model of the individual constitution, with its various subtle bodies, allows for a natural process of energetic transmutation from the physical to the spiritual levels of our being. Modern Western psychosexual theory does not include such a continuum, nor does it include processes of transmutation. According to Alexander Lowen and Wilhelm Reich, two of the originators of the psychosexual model, individual growth takes place within a closed system whose energetic transformations require frequent discharge in genital orgasm.

> When growth has reached its natural limits, some other use must be made of the excess energy that is being produced . . . In the higher animals, the excess energy is discharged in the sexual function, as Wilhelm Reich showed.
> Maturity means that the energy that was formerly needed for the growth process is now available for discharge.[4]

According to yogic physiology, by contrast, this excess energy is actually sublimated as part of an eight-step month-long transformation of food into bodily tissues and finally into light energy. In the seventh and eighth steps, physical sexual essence (bindu) is sublimated to subtle light-consciousness energy (ojas), thereby creating a spiritual force (virya).[5] More than one sexual release per month is considered a kind of over-harvesting, which disrupts the eighth step and depletes the individual of ojas.

We can think of this process as a bodily ecology of sexual energy, with its own cyclical rhythms. Ojas, which can be thought of as a powerful alchemical distillate of the hormones of sexual motivation, helps nourish maturation and growth processes in ways not envisioned by Lowen or Reich. Herein lies the yogic basis for the sexual lifestyle of brahmacarya; it is not a moralistic repression, but a uniquely pleasurable process of sexual transmutation in which the practices of yoga are fueled by "high-octane" ojas. As one of my research subjects noted, "It is really quite hedonistic, only of another sort. Otherwise, I wouldn't be doing it."

From the outside, brahmacarya may appear to be asexual. Yet internally, one feels permeated with eros, what mystics have called the "inward caresses of the Divine." Ordinary life activities like breathing and moving reveal a previously hidden pleasurable warmth, or glow. A pervasive, sensual, yet non-grasping intimacy with the world slowly melts egoic isolation. What was once taken to be simply and obviously sex now emerges as intricately diffuse and mysterious. As one subject reported:

> On various occasions my whole body vibrated with an erotic tingle. It was like electricity, like being totally alive. I was shaking and sweating, like an orgasm that started at the base of my spine to the top of my head.

Although this subject was compelled to use the conventional term "orgasm" to describe her experience, this was only because our language is deficient in terminology to describe adequately the full range of bodily erotic experiences, especially mystical and celibate beatitudes, ecstasies, and pleasures. But one thing is certain. The familiar truths about sex and conventional routes of sexual expression begin to appear as one largely overworked possibility among many. The erotic sense of one's own body, one's attractiveness to others, and the meaning of gender, orgasm, and psychosexual development can no longer be explained with prevailing concepts and theories.

It becomes very clear how sexual energy is both a basis for pleasurable sensation and a maturational force. In fact, one has the sense that the body is undergoing another kind of puberty, resulting in a transformation on a par with adolescence in terms of gender identity, bodily capacities, and sexual understanding. In other words, a whole new erotic universe emerges. Ken Wilber alludes to this "post-genital" sexuality when he states that the genital stage of development "beyond its normal and necessary development period represents the refusal to accept its death and discover higher states of whole-body ecstasy, ecstasy beyond the genitals."[6]

Not that the pleasures of brahmacarya are easily won. The changeover of erotic meanings and body energetics, especially in the context of our hypersexualized culture, require a steadfast discipline and a sensitive appreciation for subtle, incremental changes. Sexual desire, in fact, often increases during brahmacarya—a sign, paradoxically, that transmutation is taking place. Obviously, this may also create inner struggles for the advanced brahmacarin as well as for the beginner. But even a conventional sexual lifestyle confronts one with problems, and brahmacarins must learn to accept and work with any issues that arise. They must discover ways of expressing these heightened feelings of love and attraction that are consistent with their brahmacarya sexuality. They must watch for the ego's attempts at "spiritual materialism"—that is, the tendency to use spiritual practice to feel superior to others. At the same time, they must maintain the regime of yoga practices and pure diet needed to assist in rechanneling the energy "up and in," rather than "down and out." Above all, brahmacarins must keep a positive and accepting attitude toward sexual feelings. Otherwise, repression may very possibly occur.

In his celibate exploration of the mystery of eros, the yoga teacher Kripalu noted two forms of passion: mental-sensual and physical-spiritual.[7] His distinction is a useful one because it shows that a single intelligent energy, which the Hindus call *prana*, vitalizes the activities, pleasures, and personal development experienced in both conventional and brahmacarya sexualities. The difference lies in their ways of provoking and sustaining passionate feelings.

In mental-sensual passion, the various sexual images we imbibe from the culture and from past experiences combine with what Freud called "genital strivings," the drive toward orgasmic release and exchange. In the process, erotic mystery and erotic feelings are shaped into more and more well-defined sexual desires, behaviors, and relationships.

In physical-spiritual passion, by contrast, conventional sexual images dissolve, and the mental, emotional, and spiritual bodies absorb and transmute the erotic energy that was held in the image. The mind becomes more meditatively empty, and feelings of joy, love, warmth, and vibrancy begin to pervade the whole body. As one subject noted:

> In the beginning of a meditation there would be a lot of sexual imagery. When my mind calms down, the imagery would be gone, the energy would raise to the heart cakra . . . all the cells would open and you feel just beautified, no matter how strong the sexual feeling [is at first].

This phenomenon is what is meant by "rechanneling" erotic energy inward and upward. The flow of energy and awareness moves less toward the temporary gratification of transitory desires and more toward the contentment found in the timeless dimensions of one's being.

Instead of leading toward genital sexual activity, physical-spiritual passion fosters a general intensification of *prana*, a process known in yoga as *prana-utthana*, or release of prana. In prana-utthana the passionate, uninhibited body movements, breathing patterns, and emotional releases of conventional sexual activity shift their genital focus to the whole body, animating all the practices of hatha-yoga with physical-spiritual passion. As a result, yoga practice is no longer just a system of disciplined exercises, but a spontaneous "love-making" relationship between the physical and subtle bodies and the spiritual passion hidden within prana. Postures flow from one to the next, coupled with breathing patterns and emotional expression, in a manner perfectly and spontaneously tailored to the individual's needs. The American adept Da Free John describes a similar state of erotic freedom as "whole bodily Communion with Life."[8] And Bhagwan Rajneesh characterizes the transformation as follows:

> I wish to tell you that sex is coal, whereas brahmacharya . . . is diamond. Celibacy is a form of sex; celibacy is the transformation of sex.[9]

These descriptions are certainly compelling. But to live brahmacarya in our culture is no easy task. The internal gains one achieves may seem overshadowed at times by how far one has diverged from the sexual values of one's peers. During my own ten-year practice of brahmacarya, I found that one of my greatest interpersonal needs was the need to be understood. I now see that the intimacy I was seeking through being understood (and that others perhaps seek through sex) actually comes from a deeper level, from the very heart of this erotic mystery itself. I hope this essay assists in bridging the gap between these two forms of sexuality and helps us see that the great, mysterious eros knows of no such distinctions, but is always leading us to deeper and deeper experiences of intimacy with each other, our planetary home, and our spiritual source.

Ultimately, brahmacarya supports perhaps the most mysterious process in kundalini-yoga, known as *urdhva-retas*, the complete sublimation of bodily energies. This process culminates in the "divine body" (*divya-sharira*) of hatha-yogins, which marks the highest possible evolution of individual incarnation. However, it should be noted that, according to some yogic sources, no one has achieved this state in over five hundred years. If you are interested in experimenting with brahmacarya, you would do well to set a more moderate goal for yourself.

Brahmacarya takes on an even more interesting dimension at the relational level. The same basic principles of sublimation apply, but we are now also dealing with the phasing together of the energetic rhythms and belief systems of two individuals. One goal is a form of intimacy in which each person's consciousness is saturated with sublimated passion, such that "in the absence of forceful physical excitement between them, their love has a sweet serenity. Indeed, their love-drenched minds embrace each other."[10]

Conventional sexual relationships are centered on genital puberty and genital strivings. In contrast, a relationship founded on the practice of brahmacarya surrenders its genital basis through continuously unfolding "post-genital puberties." This leaves the couple without the ordinary frame of reference for their feelings of attraction and love for one another. As I noted in describing the celibate lovemaking practice, the "Great Gesture":

> We become partners in this most uncommon and uncharted exploration of brahmacarya relationship; perhaps also sharing how little we actually know about erotic mystery, rather than how much sexual skill and prowess we have. That is, a literal sharing of innocence, wonder, and awe. Sexual thoughts, should they emerge, can seem like a refuge from this nakedly intimate contact in which we are seeing into one another's ever-shifting mystery. Longings intensify and subside, over and over again, as various emotional peaks are released into an utterly desireless rapport. An hermetic alchemical passion energizes lachrymose, salivary, genital, pineal, hypothalamus, and pituitary functions as well as the cakras and subtle energies.[11]

Here, I would say, eros is experienced as an unfolding mystery where the experience of erotic union keeps emerging in new and changing forms. Sex becomes a state of mind and an ongoing condition of the relationship, rather than a set of circumscribed behaviors. In his examination of sexuality, Sartre calls this state "double reciprocal incarnation," where lovers passionately behold one another in a unity of consciousness and body—a unity that, Sartre feels, is always "ruptured" when it is translated into the activities of sex.

In simple terms, double reciprocal incarnation is an ever-spiraling turn-on; each partner sees the effect of his or her passion on the other, which increases the passion, which then increases the other's passion, and so forth. Instead of the linear model's sharp peaks of foreplay and orgasm, this model of erotic exchange is more circular, and very possibly endless. I remember at times experiencing my partner's femininity as a slowly rotating cornucopia of love and desire capable of creating infinite worlds and pleasures. In such moments, the great mystery of procreation, as the seeds of all future humanity slumbering in our loins, became awesomely real. A kind of peaceful at-one-ment seems to follow such experiences.

Rajneesh and Da Free John have outlined how couples can move from conventional sexuality toward this unbounded relational communion. They tend to agree on a three-phase progression from (1) genitally focused, orgasmic sexuality to (2) orgasmless sex (*maithuna*), and then to (3) spontaneous bliss-communion with the immanent spirit-energy. Also, two recent books on Taoist sexual yoga, Mantak Chia's *Taoist Secrets of Love* and Stephen Chang's *Taoist Sexology*, give many practical techniques for moving from conventional, orgasmic sexuality toward more circular and subtle erotic unions. All this new information is extremely important in furthering our erotic liberation and the integration of spirituality and sexuality. However, it is essential to remember that techniques—whether orgasmic, tantric, or brahmacarya—are not "the way." Techniques are merely doors that lead us just alittle further into the great mystery of eros.

The three phases of a gazing meditation from tantric yoga provide an interesting example of how sexual bonding can express itself at a post-genital level. Whereas the American sexologists Masters and Johnson speak of the four phases of genital sexual response, these three Tantric phases refer to stages of the heart's opening. The first phase is signified by the flowing of tears as the partners gaze into each other's eyes. The second is denoted by an increased flow of saliva, and the third by secretion through the nose. These three common signs of tearful compassion represent, in this meditative context, a kind of post-genital "heart orgasm." Other blissful, quasi-orgasmic responses may occur—for example, as a result of chanting or breathing practices. Finally, the love relationship itself is a mysteriously continuous flow of erotic feeling.

Needless to say, brahmacarya sexuality can also have an obvious and profound impact upon procreation. In the ideal form, problematic contraceptives, unintended pregnancy, and sexually transmitted disease recede from one's concerns, without a loss in relational intimacy.

COSMIC LEVEL

The contemporary notion of sexual liberation interprets erotic sensations in terms of the primacy of the genital orgasm. Thus, sexual liberation has come to mean freeing oneself from externally imposed restrictions on having sex. As Foucault notes, we have become the unwitting victims of a kind of inverse restriction, which mandates that the sensations of eros should lead to a desire for sex. Through brahmacarya one can step back from this hundred-year-long experiment in sexual liberation and approach the matter with the innocence of "not knowing." The erotic world that emerges may reveal that, after all is said and done, the experienced mystery of eros, of love-attraction, of procreation, birth, and rebirth, and of individual psychosexual unfoldment is deeper and more subtle than the words of any theory can describe. And, as we in the West learn more about yogic understandings of psychosexual development, we might humbly admit that we are just beginning to fathom the full expanse of the erotic universe. If we are to go more deeply into the mystery of eros, we must certainly be prepared to let go of habitual behaviors, preconceptions, and predispositions. As Lao-tzu says:

> Always without desire we must be found,
> If its deep mystery we would sound;
> But if desire always within us be,
> Its outer fringe is all that we shall see . . .
> Where the mystery is the deepest is the gate
> to all that is subtle and wonderful.[12]

NOTES

1. E. Dimock, *The Place of the Hidden Moon* (Chicago: University of Chicago Press, 1966), 4.

2. See S. Sovatsky, *A Phenomenological Exploration of Orgasmic, Tantric, and Brahmacharya Sexualities.* Doctoral dissertation. San Francisco: California Institute of Integral Studies, 1984; and "Eros as Mystery: Toward a Transpersonal Sexology and Procreativity," *Journal of Transpersonal Psychology* (Summer 1985).

3. See S. Sovatsky, *A Phenomenological Exploration.*

4. A. Lowen, *Love and Orgasm* (New York: New American Library, 1967), 57.

5. See R. Dass and Aparna, *The Marriage and Family Book* (New York: Schocken Books, 1978), 66; and Sri Aurobindo and the Mother, *On Love* (Pondicherry, India: Sri Aurobindo Ashram, 1973).

6. See K. Wilber, *Up From Eden* (Garden City, N.Y.: Anchor/Doubleday, 1981), 213.

7. See S. Kripalu, "Success or Freedom?" *Vishvamitra*, vol. 4, no. 1 (January 1977), 1-3.

8. See Da Free John, *Love of the Two-Armed Form* (Middletown, Calif.: Dawn Horse Press, 1978).

9. B. S. Rajneesh, *From Sex to Superconsciousness* (Pune, India: Ma Yogi Laxmi, 1979), 92.

10. S. Kripalu, *Premyatra* (Summit Station, Pa.: Kripalu Yoga Fellowship, 1981), 10.

11. S. Sovatsky, *Tantric Celibacy: Beyond the Last Taboo and Other Erotic Mysteries* (New York: Dutton, 1989).

12. J. Legge, transl. *Lao-tzu, The Tao Teh Ching* (New York: Dover, 1962).

This autobiographic account was written especially for the present volume. David Ramsdale, who teaches a form of neo-Tantrism, is the author of the popular book Sexual Energy Ecstasy. *This work shows in detail how those wishing to practice sexual communion can become more sensitive to their own psychic energies and those of their sexual partners. Ramsdale, however, also makes it clear that beyond the experience of the energy dimension of sexuality, we must remain cognizant of the spiritual Reality, what he calls the "Crystal Rainbow Heart."*

REMEMBER THE CRYSTAL RAINBOW HEART

By David Alan Ramsdale

Thirteen. I was at a social gathering with my parents where there were a lot of adults I didn't know. Spontaneously, I felt a magnificent wave of warm good feeling towards these strangers rise up within me. I felt love for everybody. I walked over to a group in the corner, my arms outstretched. Standing in front of them, I proclaimed "I love you!" Naturally, they looked at me as if I was crazy. I was completely devastated. The wave of love crashed as a torrent of fear ripped through my frail thin frame.

I felt a sharp searing pain in the middle of my chest. The pain spread to an area the size of a pancake. It went deep into my chest, almost to my spine. "This is so painful," I said to myself, "that I never want to feel this again. Never!" I was so stuck on myself, so self-involved, that this grossly defensive posture made perfect sense.

In psychic language, my heart cakra had cracked. The human psychic heart (the personal core of deep inner feeling) can definitely become damaged. A bitter romantic loss is just one way (the proverbial "broken heart"). A shocking rejection while in a hypersensitive state, such as I had experienced, is another.

True to my word, I managed to suppress my ability to feel for years. I developed intellectually and used my analytical abilities to deny and destroy feelings, to literally cut them off. It was a big mistake, but I learned a tremendous lesson. Do not block anyone, yourself included, out of your heart. "Do not, at any cost, close your heart!" is now my guiding thought, much as the thought "Avoid this pain at all costs!" guided me as a naive teenager.

I had other unusual experiences as a teenager. I left my body and went on a tour of the planets. I foretold the future, heard voices, saw colored lights, smelled ghosts, received mystic teachings in my dreams, read a deck of playing cards face down, performed sophisticated classical music on the piano without taking lessons. Yet, in the midst of all this psychic flimflam, the anger in my heart raged on.

Indeed, while I was out of my body, a commanding male voice asked me quite clearly, "Are you ready?" I knew what he meant. Was I ready to take responsibility for all these psychic abilities? "No," I replied, for in my heart I knew I was too confused, too immature. Soon afterwards, most of the psychic experiences stopped. It would be years before my psychic abilities would again blossom, and then in a gentler, much more uplifting way for the service of others.

I also met several talented psychics at this time. A very loving psychic woman predicted that I would meet my wife, who would help me fulfill my life's mission, "soon after I became thirty." In fact, I did meet her—at thirty one.

I was about fourteen when my father spanked me with the "business end" of his belt. He had found some *Playboy* magazines under my bed. The spanking made no sense to me then. It still doesn't. Sex is real. It cannot be denied. If he wanted to block that particular outlet, that's all right. But he should have supplied alternatives: taken me to a whorehouse or a dirty movie; openly talked about sex; told "dirty" jokes. Like a mighty river, sex energy will find another outlet. If creative, life-affirming outlets are not provided, then it will give power to life-denying destructive outlets that may include violence towards self as well as others.

I remember starting to make out with my high school sweetheart Jennifer in the back of a pickup truck and suddenly stopping. "I can't go on," I said, "it's too dirty." True, we were lying on some dirt and hay, but that wasn't it. I felt dirty because I was engaging in sexual activity.

Tantra exploded into my life between the ages of fifteen and sixteen in the form of several awe-inspiring romantic psychic events with Jennifer. While the relationship lasted for only a year and a half, it took me more than five years to get over her. Jennifer is an extraordinary woman, a truly intelligent, elegant, compassionate being. Falling in love with her was a great blessing.

The most dramatic experience took place at a MENSA party in Hollywood. I was waiting for her to come down the stairs. As I watched her descend from the second floor, time literally stopped. Her foot seemed to freeze in midair. Everything around us disappeared. All I saw was her face with a glowing egg-shaped aura around it. My body was filled with bliss. The experience seemed to last for a full half hour at least. Then her foot continued to the next step and the noise and music returned. Remarkably, I later saw my vision duplicated as a special effect in movies to show what two people madly in love see when they look at each other.

I would dream splendid dreams of her. In one dream, still vivid to me now, I reclined next to a pool of gold. The air was filled with a shimmering radiance. Dressed all in white, she sat regally in a huge silver abalone shell nearby. As a token of my devotion, I offered her a golden leaf.

Having parents who are paragons of virtue has its disadvantages. For one thing, it's rather hard to find really good reasons to hate them, to justify your separating from them as you get older and go to college and so on. Sure, Mom and Dad were sexually uptight, but they rarely raised their voices, they didn't smoke or drink, they were affectionate in public, they had a great marriage, they were pillars of the local church. I wanted to scream "Will you please do something horrible to me so that I can justify hating you?"

College. Like many students then, my curriculum consisted of three units of booze, two units of psychedelic drugs, one unit of studying and eight units of chasing the opposite sex. I was determined to blow away, by force if necessary, every remnant of inhibition and prudishness my parents had vested in me.

To further my spiritual seeking, which I began as a teenager, I started a Bhakti Yoga Society at UCLA. This actually gave me the power to bring spiritual groups to me since to put an event on at campus they needed a student sponsor, namely me. I got more than I bargained for.

I don't remember her name but she was hooked up with some group that did Enlightenment Intensives in the desert. They would sit and face each other and ask the question "Who are you?" for hours on end. I still remember her back. Incredible. The sexiest, most lithe, most wicked back in the world. She was flexible to an amazing degree, which she demonstrated to me with great enthusiasm. There I was in my freshman dormitory room, President of the Bhakti Yoga Society, with this astonishing Tantric yogini in my arms. Looking straight in my eye, she whispered in a tone that made my skin groan for her caress, "Do anything you want with me. Anything. I'm yours." Totally intimidated—I was still a virgin—I mumbled something and backed away. The conversation shifted into an intellectual frequency and she soon left.

In retrospect, though, the experience was far from a total

loss. Transmission still took place. By transmission I mean she affected me, even overwhelmed me. She got "under my skin." She demonstrated to me the commanding sensuality of a power woman. She proved to me that such women do exist. She inspired me to explore Tantric sex more deeply. Though I did not penetrate her physically, her potent aura nonetheless penetrated me, lancing my fragile intellectual myopia as if it were an ugly scab over my life, allowing fresh blood into the starving heart beneath. I had been initiated.

In spite of all my psychic experiences (or perhaps because of them), by the time I was in college, I had actually gone in the other direction. I was no longer fascinated by psychic phenomena, energies, ghosts, magic. I embraced a laissez-faire lifestyle with underpinnings of existentialism. I courted the ordinary ecstasies of life that I, as a high school egghead with but one close friend, had denied myself. This included drinking screwdrivers at parties for entire weekends and waking up Monday morning temporarily deaf because the alcohol had deadened my auditory nerves. Or staying up all night guzzling coffee and writing poetry with an artist friend, then driving to the ocean to see the sunrise. And, of course, there were the obligatory psychedelic journeys. More and more, I viewed my life as an experiment. I felt free to try anything once or twice.

My one brave effort at unconditional love long forgotten, I embarked on a series of sexual escapades that spanned the next decade of my life. Emotionally immature, my ability to feel castrated by my own hand, I found myself embroiled in Don Juan scenarios where I would seduce the woman by telling her I loved her just to get her into bed. I really did this! I did, that is, until one woman took the game to another level. While the relationship was just a fling for me—a way to get laid on a regular basis during summer vacation—for her it was much more serious. I knew this and used it to my advantage.

One hot August night—just after we had sex, I think—I announced that I was leaving town the next day. I had been planning this all along, of course. A few tears came to her eyes and without a word she ran to the bathroom and slammed the door. After about ten minutes I became concerned and investigated, only to find her unconscious on the floor, a half-empty bottle of pills in her hand. I called the paramedics. They pumped her stomach. The drug she had taken was not particularly lethal, so the overdose would not have killed her. But I stayed up all night holding her, comforting her, and attending to her needs. I left on schedule the next day but not without proving, to her satisfaction at least, that deep down I really did care for her as a human being. That was the beginning of the end of my Don Juan days.

In spite of my game-playing, I continued to meet women with whom I would get deeply involved and, on occasion, have erotic experiences with mystical overtones. I loved women. I loved sex, and I simply had to be in a relationship. Even lousy sex and a lousy relationship seemed better to me than being alone.

My most common psychic sexual experiences were ecstatic visions during sex. But I didn't have the slightest idea what caused them or how to repeat them. I didn't know about sex yoga skills like preparing the environment, harmonizing with your partner, or joint sex energy meditation. What I did know was that ordinary good sex didn't satisfy me like it used to. It also bothered me that my partner could not share these experiences with me. I knew from books that the ultimate erotic high was supposed to be a blissful fusion of identities. How could what was happening to me be the ultimate sexual experience when only one of us was enjoying it?

Still, these peak experiences inspired me to continue experimenting with sex energy and to keep working on myself. They pointed to a distant horizon of happy transcendence where the sex act might actually become an act of holy worship and spiritual illumination. If this awesome energy could only be harnessed!

Sometimes I felt very close to a breakthrough. I was much more ignorant than I realized, though. I had the karmic tendency to have these psychic sexual experiences, but that in itself guaranteed nothing. I needed guidance. And I needed to do a lot of growing as a human being.

Occasionally I fell into deep depressions that lasted for days. Sometimes I contemplated suicide, which, fortunately, my intuition of a life after death circumvented. A fortress cold and mighty still guarded my angry broken heart. Nonetheless, my heart was mending. The fortress was coming down.

My first Tantric teaching transmission where I had some sense of what was going on occurred several years later. I had worked through a lot of the psychological flotsam with the unreasonable persistence that sometimes comes to the deeply desperate. At least now I could admit my error. I knew I needed help. I dropped out of college to join an educational commune experiment near Mendocino, California. It was a great place to consider the direction of my life and meet interesting, even wise, people while enjoying nature.

I arrived in the winter. That spring I met the Bird Lady of Mendocino. I don't remember her name. We saved ten sea gulls from an oil spill that day. To show her appreciation for my help, I suppose, she made lunch for me. I watched in amazement as she skipped around the backyard of her friend's house where she was staying—she was a wanderer, essentially—picking flowers, weeds, leaves and herbs. The lunch was excellent.

She was also a gifted yogini, for she slid easily into poses which I knew from reading (but not doing) were very advanced. She must have seen something in me because it was that night or the next that we ended up in bed. I had a cabin, a shack really, that overlooked the juncture of three rivers. It had no windows and the wood was rough. But the bed was quite good.

The sun was going down, filling the cabin with a brilliant orange-bronze radiance. I remember sliding inside her and feeling the taut muscularity of her slick vagina. She raised her legs somewhere over her head for maximum penetration. And then, I can't explain exactly how, the breathing started. It was not like any ordinary breathing.

Really, the whole relationship had not been ordinary. I had had the sense pretty much from the beginning that she was superior to me, wiser than I. I felt fortunate to be with her. She was going to teach me something, something about love or truth or happiness—that much I knew. Following some unspoken protocol, I had meekly followed her lead from the moment we met.

Somehow, then, the breathing began. It was like a slow steady pulse that filled our bodies and the space around us. It expanded and contracted with its own rhythm and we moved to it. I moved in and out with it. We breathed together with it. The pulse became slower and slower, the breathing deeper, the pauses between breaths longer. Soon it felt as if we were literally breathing each other. A moment arrived when I could not tell who was who. There was no movement, no sound, no separation, just a primal dreamlike fusion that melted my mind into an endless glowing void.

At this time, too, came the open-eyed vision of a colossal red pyramid pulsating with elemental power. I don't remember having a conventional orgasm. The notion of coming or not had been totally eclipsed. This was our only sexual encounter. A few days later we were drinking coffee in one of the tents at the commune. As she poured me another cup, she calmly remarked, "You really are very immature, you know." She put the pot back on the stove and walked out of the tent. I never saw her again.

Nevertheless, I have remained in her loving embrace ever since. A powerholder, she transmitted the Tantric nectar to me. Then, like a bee pollenating first one flower and then another, she moved on, following the dictates of the Spirit. Like a true teacher, she did not initiate me without also forcefully reminding me that the foundation of Tantra is purity of heart. Unlike my other experiences, which had always seemed so random, this one had been largely under my mistress' control. So there is a sexual yoga after all! The pervasive notion that if you were serious about God you would choose to be celibate had troubled me deeply. If you were still hung up on having sex, the theory said, we'll see you back here again soon and better luck next time!

Paradoxically, this experience of Tantric Orgasm with the Bird Lady ushered in a phase where I was much less interested in sex than before. The conflict that had raged within me about the separation of sex and love and God was largely quenched. Now I knew, through direct experience, that sexual intercourse can be a sacrament. Through awareness, compassion, and yogic skill the primal forces that are evoked can lift the Tantric practitioner into a state of cosmic blessedness.

A few years later, I returned to school and completed my degree. I became interested in a guru, to whom I gave three years of my life. When I chose to leave the organization, it was with another ex convert. Estranged from our parents, our old friends gone, we struggled for direction in a world that we had vowed to discard. Frightened and lonely, we ended up marrying. It was a bad idea. The separation and divorce which came four years later in 1980 was so painful that I literally could not talk to her at first. If I tried to hold a conversation with her on the telephone, my body would begin to shake and I would start to scream at her. Nothing she or anyone else could say would shut me up. I would smash the receiver down and disconnect her or someone else would have to grab the phone from my hand. I was a mess!

I had the very good fortune of finding a yoga center to live in. The room and board was minimal and my savings could easily handle it for a few months. I was finally free to face myself. For the first time in my adult life, the choice of love versus hate was so starkly defined that I simply could not deny it. I was at a crossroads. I could choose love. I could choose hate. I could step into the light. Or I could crawl back into the darkness. The choice was completely and obviously mine.

Several years later, while listening to Zen-inspired jazz at the Bodhi Tree bookstore in Los Angeles, I was inundated with memories of a past life in Japan as an alcoholic samurai. Though reasonably successful, I wanted to be known as the greatest Samurai in my region. I really did not have the talent to match my ambition and, in my heart, I knew it. I saw myself, much bigger and stronger than I am now, coming home late at night, drunk and bitter. Horrified, I watched as my Samurai self took those frustrations out on my pretty young wife.

I yelled and cursed at her as she cowered on her knees before me. I hit her again and again, hard with the back of my hand. Finally, she crawled to the corner and collapsed, sobbing uncontrollably. The scene was repeated several times.

My delicate Japanese wife of five hundred years ago is now the beautiful ex-wife who so skillfully skewered my selfish heart. Yet she did this to liberate me, not to hurt me. At the time of my separation, though, I had no such logical explanation to fall back on. Verily, the wheel had turned full circle.

This time I chose to listen to the still small voice of wisdom in my heart and I opened my heart wide. I consciously chose to love and forgive both of us unconditionally. I began to meditate in earnest. My life made sense at last. Soon I met Ellen, now my wife, whose role in my life had been predicted twenty years before. A few years later I met my meditation teacher. Under his guidance I practiced Buddhist meditation and went through a series of purifying spiritual experiences that have greatly enriched my life. Above all, I was guided to understand that the heart is the very core of spiritual life.

With my wife Ellen, a true *karmamudra*—natural, uninhibited, enthusiastic—I was able to do serious research into the various techniques that lead to Tantric awakening. This research became the book *Sexual Energy Ecstasy*. As a couple, we also gave numerous Tantric Sex workshops around the country.

With her help, I developed a simplified approach to the Tantric style of lovemaking.

First, begin at the beginning: the map is not the territory. Approach the entire subject of sex with a new mind, with a mind that does not know what sex is. Experience sex directly, without preconceived notions or priorities. Allow whole-body ecstasy the way an infant does without isolating it in a few nerve-rich pockets of the body.

Just as there is yang and yin, so there is good hard sex and good soft sex. When good sex is very hard, it verges on violence, yet between consenting adults it may bring great pleasure. When good sex is very soft, it may take the form where the couple unites bodies in a motionless meditation posture that awakens the power of Mother Kundalini.

The middle path is the conscious, compassionate, creative, inspired use of the elements of the sexual act: breath, touch, rhythm, heartfelt feeling, eye contact, holy sound, slow motion and no motion, sex muscle yoga, the exchange of life force, surrender to the feminine principle, the inner mounting flame, romancing the Divine, the timeless paradisiacal dalliance. Most couples take from the yang and the yin, the hard and the soft, to develop their own individual styles.

In the workshops, which I now give by myself except for the all-couple workshop retreat Ellen and I offer once a year, I begin with a simple five-step formula: (1) relax deeply, (2) breathe completely, (3) be totally in the moment together, (4) let go of the goal of orgasm and (5) open yourselves to new experiences of bliss and insight.

I believe that working with these basics is the key for most people. Keep it simple and practice, practice, practice. It is important to understand, too, that Tantric sexual practice is a supplement. While it is a valuable part of your Tantric tool kit, the chief ingredient is the regular practice of some style of meditation or the equivalent. Meditation develops the master skill of being fully aware in the moment. There, in the Cosmic Now, resides the eternal perfect Divine realm of never-ending happiness and harmony.

In Tantra, we work hard to soften, open, and heal our own hearts. We strive to open our hearts wider and wider. So, there is effort. We understand that we must start where we are. We acknowledge that we are in denial of our subconscious pain with its many changing faces.

We work with and through the negative appearances, for

they are the ground upon which we stand as we reach up for the fruits of the Spirit. They are seen as hidden opportunities, as open doorways, as powerholding mudras—graceful liberating lovers—eager for transformational embrace. Through the light of conscious awareness, these dull dark dense habits are able to evolve into their luminous benign essence equivalents. Just as caterpillar becomes butterfly, anger can become the ability to accomplish.

At the same time, we are reminded that it is all grace as well, for everything is already perfect. It is also understood in Tantra that grace and understanding can be transmitted through the sexual act, in erotic mystical symbology, via any kind of erotic interplay, even a brief eye contact. This transmission can even taken place purely on a subtle plane without physical intervention.

The creative power that generated our bodies can regenerate the spirit of the sincere Tantric practitioner. Such a practitioner, who is called a hero or heroine in the old scriptures, is earnest, patient, mindful, and full of good will. He or she is able to consciously generate positive warm regard for the self and other beings. Such a hero or heroine reaches total fulfillment and finds Truth.

You will know the real Tantra when you see it. Real Tantra teaches the personal experience of Cosmic Love and the transcendence of duality in unconditional peace-wisdom-bliss. It teaches love and surrender and meditation, not just pleasure and power and getting high under a fancy name. Real Tantra teaches the enduring ecstasy of love and not, as one of my teachers described it, "souped-up nookie."

The key to it all is quite simple. This key, whether you choose to tread the path of Tantra or not, is to make a noble effort to purify your own heart through prayer and meditation. Work hard to soften, heal, open, and strengthen your heart, for it is your own spiritual home.

Your heart is the Holy Grail, the Philosopher's Stone, the alchemical crucible where the lead of human ignorance is transformed into the gold of enlightenment. This pure heart of pure gold, clear as crystal, radiant as rainbows, is the lighthearted secret of the Buddhas and of the Christs and of the great Tantric Masters and Powerholders.

This pure heart of pure gold is already truly happy, utterly content, indelibly serene, completely at peace. Yet it sings with sweetness, jumps for joy, shakes with laughter, swoons with love, soars in celebration always and everywhere.

This heart, this crystal rainbow heart, is where You are. That, more than any technique or phenomenon of the Tantric way, is the secret. Remember the crystal rainbow heart.

Robert Edwin Svoboda recorded for us the teachings of his guru, the late Vimalananda. His essay emphasizes the fact that Tantric sexual practices call for immense self-understanding and discipline. This is often overlooked by Westerners trying to adapt ancient Tantric ideas and practices to their modern needs. Yet true Tantra is, like any spiritual path, a sacred ordeal involving our own transmutation, which is never easy or free from pain. Svoboda's essay introduces a radical spiritual orientation that takes us to the borders of what most people will find intelligible and acceptable. The Aghora tradition of Hinduism is Tantra at its most extreme. It confronts us with our own preconceptions about life. Above all, it cures us of any illusion about sexual spirituality being a quick-and-easy route to spiritual enlightenment. It demands a level of self-surrender, or ego-transcendence, that most of us find utterly intimidating, which reveals more about us than about the Aghora tradition.

SEX, SELF-IDENTIFICATION, AND THE AGHORA TRADITION

By Robert Edwin Svoboda, Ph.D.

Many people sincerely believe that true spirituality is possible only in the complete absence of sexuality. I was fortunate to discover otherwise early in life when I first visited India and was introduced to Tantra at a Tibetan Buddhist Kalacakra initiation in Bodh Gaya. I was spiritually illiterate then, and felt an immediate sensual rapport with what seemed to be a system of carnal Yoga. I longed to learn how to make love in a sublimely meditative state, achieving thereby pleasure many times more intense than that available through normal sex. The powerful image of the Deity in continuous copulation with His Consort entranced me, and mentally I transposed myself into that Deity, holding scepter (*dorje*) and bell and enjoying great bliss!

When I learned, however, that to gain this bliss I would have to vow that I would never again in this lifetime discharge semen from my body, I realized that I personally, at age twenty, would be unable to swear such an oath and keep it. I left Bodh Gaya, but retained my interest in Tantric sexuality. Only in 1975, when I met my teacher, the Aghori Vimalananda, did I realize that there was more to spiritual sex than merely asserting deityhood and plowing ahead with intercourse.

An Aghori is a practitioner of Aghora, the ancient, secret spiritual tradition that goes beyond what is commonly understood as Tantra; it takes up where Tantra leaves off. Aghora has no set dogma or doctrine. Although some groups of Aghoris are recognizable by their special earrings or their firetongs or by the way they swathe their naked bodies with ashes, there was nothing about Vimalananda's deportment to suggest that he was in any way different from his fellow race horse owners. Only his attitude, a "succeed or die" approach to everything in his life, set him apart from the flock.

The decades Vimalananda spent worshipping the Mother Goddess transformed him into the ultimate mother, a being who supported each of his "spiritual children" fully and unconditionally with a pure and abundant love which eased even the harshest of lessons. He refused to allow me to accept any of his ideas uncritically, and insisted that I experience personally the validity or falsity of what he taught so that I would be fully convinced of its accuracy. "If you have good blueprints and a good foundation, your building is bound to hold up," he used to say. "But if you have built on shifting sands, or your blueprints are faulty, no structure you erect will ever be able to stand for long."

Vimalananda's foundation and blueprints have always served me well, especially in the realm of sex, and this essay reflects the debt I owe to his teachings and to the hoary Aghori tradition of iconoclastic spirituality.

The sexual ritual of Tantra and Aghora is an extremely exalted form of spiritual discipline, elegant and powerful. Modern popularizations of Tantric techniques have usually presented the external ritual without its requisite internal mental discipline. Vimalananda strongly resented this perversion of wisdom, and vigorously asserted that the external trappings of Tantra were incomprehensible unless one knew their inner intent. His was a living tradition of spirituality, a system of "internal sacrificial rites." Sex plays an important role in this path.

Because the universe's fundamental duality is the male-female polarization, every approach to spirituality must come to terms with sexuality. As long as we retain our sense of gender identity our human nature makes us crave closeness with the opposite sex. Because male is half and female is half, we all tend to search outside ourselves for that other half which will complete us and make us whole again.

We cuddle and fondle one another, attempting to find completion and unity in another being. Cuddling and fondling produce some closeness, and enhances the desire for more. A man and a woman engaging in sexual intercourse are closer than when they merely cuddle and fondle; and temporarily, in the explosion of sexual energy occurring during the brief moment of orgasm, they sense the primordial Unity that was lost when the cosmos manifested.

Some Tantric yogins of the Uttara Kaula sect even masturbate occasionally, to remind themselves with an orgasm of the bliss of Unity consciousness.

Orgasmic sex can never satisfy for long, though, because Unity consciousness is achieved for too short a time. After a few instants of union, the couple is returned forcibly to separateness. Because they yearn to recapture this experience, most people return to sex again and again, though the result is the same each time: a few moments of pleasure followed by a hard landing on the surface of manifested reality.

Engaging in sex usually involves projecting an image of one's ideal mate onto the partner of the moment in the hope of finding a good fit. A perfect fit is impossible in our world, though some couples come very close to it. Because of the high expectations each partner has for the other, however, ordinary sexual activity often becomes frustrating and destabilizing because it continuously demonstrates that no partner is quite that perfect fit needed for completion.

Ordinary sex, no matter how enjoyable, is a poor way to return to a state of union, but for most people the transcendence obtained during sex is the only transcendence they ever experience. Good, satisfying sex is therefore essential to their spiritual health. While both men and women love to have sex, good sex is much more important for a woman than for a man. The pheromones which she inhales during intimate contact with a male and the total relaxation and satisfaction that flood her during and after a string of orgasms fill a woman with joy. Parvati Herself, the Queen of the Universe, the Grand Consort of the God of Death, Lord Shiva, states unequivocally in the *Brahma-Vaivarta-Purana*: "Among all the pleasures of women the greatest pleasure is to unite with a good man in private, and the misery that arises from its interruption is not equalled by any other."

The female polarity in the cosmos is in charge of creation. Unsatisfactory sex makes a woman frustrated, causing hormonal changes that imbalance and upset her system. As an Ayurvedic doctor I have occasion to consult with all sorts of people on all sorts of conditions, and I have found that Vimalananda was correct when he taught me that an unsatisfactory sex life is the root of many or most of the diseases that afflict women. When a woman's internal environment is disturbed by sexual misery, it impairs her creativity, and produces disharmony in the home and family, and in the nation and the world.

The male polarity is the cosmic principle of control and direction. A man's responsibility is to satisfy his woman, to direct her energy so that she can create or procreate. Sex forms an important part of this direction. He must make sure that she is satisfied, and no man who values his own happiness can afford to accept this responsibility lightly. A woman's enjoyment of sex occurs through intimacy and orgasm, but a man's enjoyment is the enjoyment of control and direction. His enjoyment begins the moment the woman yields to his advances and ends when she is so full of satisfaction that she can take no more.

According to Vimalananda, a good man knows how to play his woman like an instrument, producing the music of orgasmic delight. Most men are unaware of this and fail to fully satisfy their women. Many men are so concerned with their own gratification that they indulge in their own orgasms and deliberately neglect their partner's enjoyment. Whenever a man fails in his duty to his woman, her ability to create a happy home suffers, and life becomes hellish for them both.

Millions today suffer from sexual dysfunctions caused by fear of intimacy, by anxiety over performance, and by other misunderstandings created by miscommunication. For such people who suffer from inhibited sexual desire, spiritual advancement begins with the awakening of sensuality. A healthy attitude toward sex is an essential prerequisite for spirituality, because people who cannot be intimate with one another will have difficulty being intimate with God. Satisfying sensuality can improve relations between man and woman, and between the couple and the cosmos, as long as the relationship does not end in sensuality.

Homes can also be ruined, though, when a couple uses "spirituality" as an excuse to avoid intimacy with one another. "Yoga is not a system of physical jerks," Vimalananda would say; "Yoga is meant to make every home a happy home. What is the use of that so-called spirituality which promises you advancement in other realms while destroying your mundane life? If you cannot meditate in the privacy of your own home, and create harmony and stability there, how will you ever be able to go out into the jungle and perform penances?

"When two people love one another deeply it is natural for them to express that love sexually. I will never say, like so many so-called holy men do, that sex is evil. Addiction to sex is unwise, yes, but only someone who is afraid of being tempted could ever say that sex and women are bad. How can sex be bad, when all of us have been born through it? How can women be bad, when it is the female who creates the entire universe? It is easy for a man to say he wants to be celibate if he does not want to satisfy his woman, or does not know how to do so. But that is simple cowardice. The sort of Yoga which is best for most householders is the Yoga in which the woman is fully satiated by her man. This sort of Yoga stabilizes society and nurtures the children who grow up within it. It helps heal and harmonize the home, making it a heaven, and a haven."

While this state of satisfying sensuality is the foundation of a happy life, it is not the ultimate in spiritual advancement. Vimalananda was certain that true real spiritual growth can occur only when people lose their fancy for flesh. Flesh is ephemeral: breasts sag, faces wrinkle, erections droop. To limit a relationship to sexual pleasure is to ensure eventual frustration. Ordinary human relationships, characterized as they are by a lack of clarity, tend toward turmoil, while relationships in which spirituality plays a part can develop a clarity of great precision. Most people follow paths that take them further and further out into the world of the senses. Spirituality requires a change of direction, a loss of one's fascination with sense objects.

Worldly people are satisfied with bodily pleasures; spiritual people redirect this energy to obtain spiritual bliss. Though good sex is satisfying and healthy, it cannot in any way be compared with the personality transformations that occur in the sexuality of Tantra and Aghora.

To an Aghori, the difference between misery and bliss in life is *sadhana*. A sadhana is any repetitive action that introduces a new, divine pattern into the consciousness. Any action can be made into a sadhana; singing devotional songs, repeating mantras, serving the poor, avoiding injury to any being, and concentrating on the "third eye" are examples of sadhanas that have been successfully used to extricate the mind from the web of delusion it creates for us.

Aghoris worship in cremation grounds because death is the ultimate reality in our world of name and form. To an Aghori, remembrance of one's own impending death is the fundamental sadhana. All of us who are born are doomed to die, and an Aghori has no interest in waiting until death to find out how to live without a body. Every human body is basically a corpse, because even though it temporarily lives and breathes its ultimate fate is the boneyard. A body is necessary if you want to perform sadhana, so having a body can be very helpful as long as you use it for sadhana and not for indulgence.

While performing a sadhana, many common, comforting actions that tend to reinforce the old, tired patterns that the sadhana is trying to erase must be limited or eliminated. The sexual urge is the most powerful of all urges, and sex is the hardest habit of all to drop. One of the reasons that some yogins disparage all sexual contact is that every sexual experience further inflames outward-looking sexual desire when an inward-looking attitude, which Vimalananda called "interior-ity," is essential for sadhana. "Where there is lust there is no God, and where there is God there is no lust." Because lust is so difficult to overcome without abstinence, most spiritual tradi-tions support chastity, at least in the initial stages.

The influence of external reality intrudes into the deepest recesses of the human being, and must be overcome before the new reality can gain sufficient solidity to project itself. All of us continually refresh our remembrances of external reality through the conjunction of our sense organs and their objects. Thus Tantra and Aghora, like Hatha Yoga, insist upon restraint of the senses until they are completely brought under the control of the will. Adequate energy is also essential to make a success of a sadhana. Every activity that expends the body's energy must be limited before serious sadhana is attempted so that enough energy can accumulate to effect changes in the consciousness. These activites especially include eating, sleeping, and sex. Of the ten sense organs (the five we know plus the tongue, hands, feet, anus, and genitals), the tongue and the genitals cause in most people the loss of the greatest amount of energy. When the use of these two organs is restricted, by keeping silence and observing chastity, energy loss to the outside world is signifi-cantly reduced.

The sex energy, the strongest energy in the body, requires the most stringent control. Ejaculation especially weakens a male's nerves and prostate, and lowers his digestive power and immune strength. A female's orgasm wastes less energy than the male's, but in both sexes ordinary sexual activity destabil-izes the mind and promotes a desire to indulge in more sex along with a willingness to be sweet-talked into such indulgence. Control of sexual excitement is critical in Aghora, where a single mistake in certain powerful sadhanas can mean disaster.

Tantra and Aghora believe in renunciation through satia-tion with life, including sex. If flesh is used to go beyond flesh, the union the partners experience is far more intense than if the mind and body are allowed to interfere. Sexual sublimation is, however, an essential prerequisite to the use of sex in sadhana. You don't become a Tantric merely by asserting it, nor can you use sex as a sadhana without first bringing your sexual re-sponse under the absolute control of your will.

Vimalananda suggested this possible scenario: Before sublimation you should live together with your partner and enjoy full sexual enjoyment for a time. Then you must restrict yourselves to sexual continence while you perform spiritual disciplines. When your interiority is strong, and you have developed control over your sexual response, you finally return to sexual activity, ready to use it for true spiritual advancement. Before you can really enjoy sex, you have to learn how to forget both your body and your sexual desire; only then can the spirit manifest through you sufficiently to make your sex spiritual.

When Tantra surfaced in the wild waters of the Western world, many seekers latched onto it like remoras to a shark and convinced themselves that it gave them licence to enjoy limitless sex in the guise of spiritual advancement. Ignorant of the Tantric tradition, many people jumped to the erroneous conclusion that Tantra is somehow "pro-indulgence" because some Tantric rituals enjoin the use of intoxicants and sex. This sort of misunderstanding, which was perhaps inevitable given the surpassing self-indulgence of modern life, characteristically occurs in a mind which is still wedded to the desire for indulgence in pleasure and the avoidance of pain. The same people who so enthusiastically jump into sexual "yoga" usually leap equally enthusiastically out of the path of other, less pleasant rituals like meditating with skulls or repeating mantras while sitting on top of a corpse.

Tantra is neither pro-flesh or anti-flesh; it neither celebrates nor decries life. Tantra and Aghora believe in truth and reality, and in the facing of facts. The first fact to be faced is that all of us are part of the manifested universe until we cease to define ourselves in those terms. Tantra means "process," "method," or "technique"; it is a system of procedures that can be used to disengage the ego from limiting itself to the body, making it *svatantra*, self-functioning or free. The ego can then redissolve into the Absolute Undifferentiated, or it can redefine itself in this world in the context of a new reality.

An ordinary person like me possesses a personality that is created by the likes and dislikes I experience, and is influenced by how these likes and dislikes affect my family, my neighbors, and the other people who live around me and interact with me. These other people are part of my environment, and I am part of their environment. All of us get caught in one another's projections of how we imagine ourselves and each other to be. These projections of reality bind us together like nets or webs, and by limiting us define us. All of us who are not enlightened are defined by our environments.

Aghora is the path that goes beyond all limitations, and no

Aghori would ever permit himself to be defined by his environment. Rather he defines himself, according to his own personal rules of sadhana, and then that definition defines his environment. An Aghori is someone who believes in using fast, intense methods to transform his limited consciousness into the unlimited consciousness of a deity. His reality is entirely subjective, created by his own thoughts, opinions and attitudes. An Aghori is equally comfortable in a cremation ground and a five-star hotel because he has minimized the influence of his environment on himself. He defines himself as unlimited, and by determined hard work eventually *becomes* unlimited. Vimalananda lived for his sadhanas; everything he did, including sex, was a sadhana for him.

Instead of allowing wants and desires to fragment the concentration, an Aghori selects a single thought form and a single process for manifesting it, and continuously energizes that thought form with his collected energy until eventually a new, coherent personal reality crystallizes. This is the traditional Law of Caterpillar and Butterfly. Just as a caterpillar in the cocoon takes on the form of the butterfly it contemplates, the consciousness takes on the form one visualizes. The form provides a focus for one's concentration and a pattern for one's self-definition. If this form is that of a deity, the consciousness will take on the deity's form. This is the aim of most Aghora sadhanas. Aghoris believe in the superiority of the personal God, the God with form.

There are different approaches to sex even within the Tantric tradition, but fundamentally, all sex involves personalities. In Tantra, the science of personality, sexual compatibility occurs when two aspirants develop new personalities that mesh perfectly and harmonize one another when they are united in the sex act.

Because the ego, and hence the personality, is so important to sex, Tantra and Aghora believe that the personal God is essential for sexual sadhana. Since identification of the ordinary ego with the body directs the consciousness externally, Tantra insists that the forms of the Deities worshipped must first be created within the bodies of the celebrants before sexual sadhana is even contemplated.

As long as you remain alive it is impossible to completely divorce your ego from your body and mind; the ego completely stops self-identifying with your humanness only at the moment of death. The closer you get to death, the weaker is the ego's bond to the body; death is the only absolute that exists in our world of relativity. An Aghori worships in charnel grounds and meditates on burning bodies because he wants to convince himself of his own mortality and learn how to disentangle his ego as far as he can from his inborn personality so that his Deity will have room to enter his being and manifests in the world through him.

Vimalananda used the word ego to refer to the force that accretes and preserves the personality by means of self-identification. The Sanskrit term for this force is *ahamkara*, which literally means "I-creator." I am able to go to bed tonight as "me" and wake up again tomorrow morning as "myself" because the ahamkara ceaselessly reminds me who I am.

My identity is composed of my memories, imagined and real. My body is a great help in this process, since it provides ahamkara with a relatively stable form with which to identify. Ahamkara continuously reminds each body cell that it is part of the organic whole known as "me." When any of my cells die, the ahamkara forgets them. This allows my immune system to identify them as alien and destroy them. A weak ahamkara means a weakly integrated personality, and thus weak immunity, which allows alien cells or traits to enter the organism and thrive. Whenever the ahamkara totally relinquishes remembrance of the body, all cells forget to whom they belonged and the body disintegrates.

It is essential for life that the ahamkara self-identifies with the body, but this self-identification is inherently non-spiritual because it continuously redefines the individual in terms of his or her body, and of the limited sheltered therein.

Because good health occurs when ego, personality and flesh are well-integrated together, some renunciates believe that they can make spiritual progress by torturing their bodies to disturb this integration. But poor health cannot provide the mental and physical stability necessary for stabilizing spiritual advancement in one's consciousness, which is why Tantra has never valued body-mortifying penances for their own sake.

The ego is the Kundalini-Shakti, the source of all energy in the body. The ego/Kundalini-Shakti is referred to as "she" because all Shaktis, or energies, are female. In ordinary people the Kundalini remains dormant, sleeping peacefully at the base of the spine; the ego is fully self-identified with the body and the limited personality, and all actions are self-centered. Tantrics and Aghoris believe this is a terrible waste of potential, and use this powerful innate energy to create their new realities by awakening the Kundalini from her slumber and making her ascend in a controlled way up the spinal axis to Shiva, the cosmic male principle, which lies awaiting her in the brain. When she reaches Him, her power fleshes out the form of the reality He has created, and a new being is born.

The Kundalini's upward progress continues only so long as there is no obstruction to her course caused by attachment to indulgence in external sense objects. *Asanas* (Yoga postures), *pranayama* (breath control), recitation of mantras, devotional singing, the intake of alchemical preparations, the use of various intoxicants, and the worship of *yantras* (mystical diagrams representing the body of the Deity) are some of the methods Tantra and Aghora use to help free the Kundalini from her misguided moorings.

Liberation can be achieved by the very things that cause bondage, including sex. For example, a Tantric may choose to perform *homa*, or fire worship, to purify the Fire Element in his body and mind, by offering the fuel of his penis into the fire of a woman's vulva instead of using external fuel and flames. Sexual practices find a place in Tantra because both the sexual energy and the ability to advance spiritually are dependent on ahamkara. For spiritual advancement the ahamkara, or ego, must be detached from the body and mind; in sex, though, the ahamkara must self-identify strongly with body and mind. A penis becomes erect only when an ego makes it erect. Who the ego belongs to or belonged to is unimportant; what is important is that some ego or another must identify with the body to inflate the organ.

In the human body, Vimalananda would say, there are two organs which though boneless can move: the tongue and the penis, or clitoris. These organs can move only when they are invested with the power of the ego. Until the ego identifies itself with them, they remain limp and inert; filled with ego, they become firm and active. When properly controlled they can lead you to the heights of spiritual achievement, and when left uncontrolled they drag you down into the depths of misery.

Most of the methods of awakening Kundalini involve some use of the tongue, whose control is far easier than is control of the genitals. Breaking off a kiss, no matter how intimately entwined the tongues, is much simpler than disengaging from sex once the penis has entered the vagina. Less energy can be transmitted between the partners by a kiss, but that energy is more easily assimilated into the organism than is the energy aroused and released in sex.

As the penis and vagina/clitoris stimulate one another during their union, the nerves of both partners' bodies are strongly stimulated. Ordinarily this stimulation proceeds uncontrolledly, until the entire nervous system overloads and the energy is released explosively outward in an orgasm. If instead of this outer release the energy is forced inward into the spine it can awaken Kundalini very quickly.

Speed is often scary, though, especially when it involves the awakening of the Kundalini. When the Kundalini wakes too quickly, before adequate control over her movement has been obtained, she may force her way through closed or blocked passages, causing the sort of physical and nervous breakdown that is often referred to as a "Kundalini crisis" and which may be quite severe. Physical and mental purification before attempting to raise the Kundalini is essential to avert such a crisis.

This is true dozens of times over if sex is used as a sadhana. Tantra believes that seminal fluid (bindu, retas) is exceptionally valuable to the organism's immune system, and that blithe release of semen also weakens the ability of the nervous system to withstand the tremendous power of Kundalini. Hence, the promise I would have had to make in Bodh Gaya. Frequent orgasms disturb the movement of prana, the life-force, in the body, which can cause disease. As the Kundalini moves upward, the "semen" should also move upward. Sticky white semen does not move upward through the spine, of course; what moves is the prana. Much life-force is expelled from the body in orgasm, which would otherwise have been available to speed the Kundalini on her way to her tryst with Shiva.

With adequate control it may be possible for an aspirant to raise Kundalini safely by means of sexual sadhana without becoming a rapacious lecher. But the intense stimulation that an aroused Kundalini produces inflames the sex centers to such a degree that it is impossible for most people to withstand the deviation of this energy into passion.

And what passion! Kundalini is the source of all human power, and if her current is diverted full force into the genitals, you will begin to live, eat, and breathe sex. This is common among those people who come to Tantra believing that it espouses indiscipline. Intensity may delude them into believing that their colossal lusts are really spiritual experiences. Sex, when the Kundalini is being aroused, usually becomes obsessive as long as the mind is still turned out toward the world.

During ordinary sex the ego identifies with the body and with the limited personality which craves physical satiation. This has nothing to do with sadhana. If you hope to practice spirituality in the true Tantric sense, you must utterly forget how to take, and learn only how to give. You must renounce the desire for all enjoyment of sex if you ever hope to succeed at sexual sadhana, where there is no place for indulgence at all.

Unfortunately, humans adore indulgence. The craving for sexual satiation is so powerful that, especially here in the West where we regard instant gratification as some sort of birthright, it is very difficult for anyone to get far enough away from themselves to do real Tantric sexual sadhana. How spiritual one's sexual activity becomes depends on the nature of the relationship that exists between the two partners. Most couples get trapped in the webs of each other's projections of reality. Two confused people will breed confusion in one another; two harmonious people will exchange and augment harmony.

If the Kundalini is first awakened and stabilized, and her path is cleared of all obstacles in the cakras (the subtle plexuses through which the Kundalini moves), sexual sadhana may be useful to arouse sufficient energy to create and manifest the desired Deity. This assumes that the Deity in question finds sexual sadhanas agreeable (not all do), and that a subtle form of the Deity has already been created and is residing in the aspirant's astral body. The Kundalini is a Shakti, a power. She will do whatever she is told to do—she can self-identify with anything—but she must be given something with which to self-identify.

Sex has nothing to do with the body. It is true that the body should be complete for the sex act to succeed, and that sex is best enjoyed when the body is healthy, but sexual response is all in the mind. The body without the mind and the ego is a corpse. When Tantrics or Aghoris perform the *panca-makara-sadhana*, the ritual of the "five m's," in which they use *mamsa* (meat), *matsya* (fish), *mudra* (parched grain), *madira* (wine), and *maithuna* (sex), they do not consume these things with their own egos; they offer the articles of worship to the Deities which they have invoked into their bodies. Externally it appears that the practitioners are having a fine old time; internally the deities enjoy the bliss.

Only the lowest category of aspirant offers the "five m's" in worship without also using their internal correlates: silence for meat, breath control for fish, Yoga posture for grain, devotion for wine, and union of the individual's consciousness with the deity for sex. Some innately spiritual people use only the internal forms of the "five m's," and a small number of "heroic" types are fit to worship both externally and internally simultaneously.

Use of the external forms of the "five m's" increases the likelihood of semen loss from the body. Ideally, the sexual intercourse that occurs during the panca-makara ritual employs a practice called *vajroli-mudra,* in which a man both restrains the outward flow of his juices and also sucks up the vaginal secretions of his partner, who, if she knows vajroli, uses her vagina in turn to suck up any secretions he may choose to release.

Practices like vajroli obviously require the sort of tremendous physical and mental control that is obtainable only after years of practice. Before vajroli can even be considered, the *shiva-lata-mudra* must be perfected. The Sanskrit word *lata* means "creeper," the sort of creeper that twines around a tree. In the first phase of lata-mudra, the female sits on the male's lap and twines herself around him, as they recite mantras together. While they sit together they must both forget to identify themselves with their ordinary day-to-day personalities. He visualizes himself as Shiva, the ultimate expression of consciousness in the universe. She visualizes herself as Shiva's Grand Consort Parvati, the embodiment of universal energy

As they concentrate, they exchange energy. He directs his energy to her with profound affection, and she returns it to him, adding some of her own. The energy begins to resonate, much as sound resonates in a musical instrument when it is played, and it builds in power and sweetness. If the couple is sincere and hard-working, they soon lose themselves in this play. When they can relinquish the last vestiges of their self-awareness as human beings, they unite completely with their Deities and their new realities are complete.

Frequently, the couple is unable to perfectly forget themselves, and some elements of their own individualities remain. If they can continue to practice lata-mudra without falling into pure passion, their personalities will eventually fuse. They will still have two hearts between them, but there will be only one beat. This is a spiritual achievement, in a sense.

Usually, though, two people who try to practice lata mudra can maintain the energy flow only temporarily, because their ability to disassociate themselves from their egoic personalities and to identify themselves with their Deities is weak and limited. As soon as they begin to remember who they are, human possessiveness and selfishness return, and soon each is attempting to collect and hold onto the energy. This inflames their sex centers, and both of them become ravenously lusty. They then turn on one another and devour each other sexually. This is a great feeling, and can do wonders for the relationship, but it is not the ultimate.

An essential preliminary before attempting even lata-mudra involves learning to sleep together with your partner in a tight embrace, like two spoons in a silver chest, without the least amount of sexual excitement. Until a couple can succeed at this exercise, they will be unable to succeed at lata-mudra, much less vajroli.

Most people though have their egos so firmly enmeshed in their flesh that no matter how hard they try they cannot draw back far enough to relinquish their lust, and often do not even recognize the need to do so. This used to annoy Vimalananda. "If I could," he would say, "I would decorate a big room with skeletons. I would pose them as if they were performing their daily activities. I would lay one pair of skeletons on top of one another as if they were copulating. Whenever anyone would come to visit me to ask questions about sex and spirituality, I would take him to this room, show him this couple, and tell him, 'Do you see? Can you understand? This is what you look like when you have sex with someone. There is no male and no female; there is no such thing as gender. There are only skeletons, because you and your partner are only corpses.'"

When people would ask him about Tantric sexual rituals, Vimalananda would tell them about lata-mudra and then say, "No matter how much you try, you will never be able to succeed at lata-mudra without a teacher. Until you can disengage yourself from your limited human personality, you can try lata-mudra all you like, but your control will invariably fail you and you will fall into ordinary passion." Success at Tantra and Aghora sadhanas can be achieved only when they are directed by a guru, because only a guru can force a human to relinquish all attachments to the comforting limitations of the human personality. You or I cannot hope to perform lata-mudra properly; only Shiva can.

Vimalananda encouraged my own initial experiments at lata-mudra, which, as he predicted, served principally to inflame my own lusts. Over the years his teachings have proved their truth to me over and over again, and I have found that all sexual activity, no matter how subtle, remains ego-based, and therefore self-indulgent, until the personality of a Deity can manifest itself in one's consciousness. And because self-indulgent sex is not truly satisfying to either partner, it can never be particularly spiritual. It can lead in that direction, and can provide rest and refreshment along the way, but only that sexual experience in which the experiencer is no longer present can ever satisfy in the way God means for sex to satisfy.

Actually, until you realize God, everything you do will be ego-based, and thus imperfect. An Aghori's answer to this problem is simple: God has created all of us, and all of us are part of Reality. If every act we perform is first offered as worship to God, the karmas involved in self-identification with our actions are minimized; not elminated, but rendered less harmful. Sex, the expression on the human level of the union of the universal male and female principles, is a fit offering to the Divine.

Therefore, if you wish to be sexually active and do not yet have a guru to teach you Tantra, the best path to follow is the path of the happy home. Select a partner and commit yourself to a relationship, and when you have experienced full enjoyment, begin to experiment with periods of sexual continence to deepen the relationship and enhance your spiritual development. At all times, in all interactions with your partner, offer all your pleasure to the Divine and let It guide and direct you. It may not be the highest possible expression of sex, but spiritualized sexuality can become the beginning of sexual sadhana.

This piece, reprinted from the book Healing Love Through the Tao: Cultivating Female Sexual Energy, *balances the other more male-oriented essays in this anthology.*

This interview with a female Taoist practitioner was conducted by Michael Winn, a student of the Taoist teacher Mantak Chia. The interview, entitled "Taoist Sexual Practice: Ovarian Kung Fu," focuses on the art of using the breath to conduct sexual energy from the genitals to the whole body.

The Taoist masters believe that the principal energy (called jing) of a woman is largely accumulated in the ovaries and that conscious breathing releases that energy and makes it available for the spiritual process as well as the rejuvenation of the body. Similarly, the principal energy of a man is found in the testes and is utilized by an analogous discipline of controlled breath and concentration. Both Taoism and Tantrism emphasize the importance of taking charge of one's psychosomatic energies. Ordinary sexual activity is thought to squander those energies, primarily through orgasm. Through sexual practices this waste can be prevented, and the life-force can be used to intensify our awareness and, ultimately, to reach the state of spiritual enlightenment.

TAOIST SEXUAL PRACTICE: OVARIAN KUNG FU

Interview by Michael Winn

Question: How long have you been practicing Ovarian Kung Fu?[1]

Answer: For three years.

Question: Did you find the techniques difficult to learn?

Answer: I found them easy to learn, especially since from the very beginning the benefits were so immediately obvious. I was motivated to practice, but it did require a certain amount of time to completely embody them and make them a part of my life.

Question: Did you learn them alone or with a partner?

Answer: Initially I practiced alone having just ended a relationship. I immediately found they empowered me with control of my own sexual energy, and rediscovered sexuality as a resource for cultivating myself.

Question: What do you mean by resource?

Answer: In the sense that the Taoists speak of cultivating one's nature, refining energy for personal and spiritual development, with sexual energy being one raw material from which that refinement is accomplished. I actually had the experience of being able to direct my sexual energy within my body, and watch it transform my body and my emotions.

Question: Did you have a sense of sexual energy as a resource before you began Taoist practices?

Answer: No, not specifically as a resource. I felt confused after growing up in this Western culture which perpetuates a sense of separation of body and spirit. I am naturally a very sensuous person and totally enjoy the physical aspects of sex. I always had a sense of the mystical quality or spiritual communion possible in a sexually and emotionally intimate relationship. I longed for inner union and knew I would need to experience that union within myself before I would be able to experience it with a partner. This longing fueled my spiritual quest, leading me to meditation and eventually to the Taoist sexual practices.

Learning the Taoist sexual practices helped ground my meditation in my body and in my daily relationships. I was attracted to them because of the value placed on harmonizing heaven and earth, spirit and body. Sexual energy became for me a valuable resource, a fuel for my spiritual journey. I discovered I could enjoy sex and transform it into spiritual energy at he same time. The pleasure of sex actually became more intense and exquisite. Pleasure became ecstasy and ecstasy grew into bliss.

Question: Does this mean that sex is now something that you can have with yourself?

Answer: Yes. Almost like a twenty-four-hour-a-day experience of my being alive as a sexual being. That energy is now there and available to me constantly. Before, I was stuck in a bit of a polarity: I was either blocking the sexual energy if I wasn't in a relationship in which I could express it, or feeling impelled to get involved in a relationship in order to experience it. Now, I feel more sexually aroused and alive. I feel my energy is at its fullest potential, and am more "turned on" by life all the time. Now, I don't feel that I always have to interact with a man in order to express it. Because my sexual energy flows in clearer channels, I can tolerate a higher level of energy without feeling an urgency to discharge it.

Question: What happens with the sexual energy when you are not interacting and making love?

Answer: When I first began doing Ovarian Breathing,[2] I discovered immediately that I could move the sexual energy easily from my genitals throughout my whole body. It's very simple, but very powerful. I can increase my ability to be connected and present in life. Over time I have been able to refine it so that I can share more energy with other people in my work and daily relationships. It doesn't come across necessarily as purely sexual, but I know it is my sexual energy that I have transformed into healing and loving energy.

Question: Do you think that men are more attracted to you now that you do the Ovarian practice?

Answer: They seem to be.

Question: Has it changed the kind of men that you attract?

Answer: I would say that I seem to be more attractive to people in general. Although I seem to be more attractive to men, judging by the feedback that I get, I am attracting in a way that feels comfortable. I do not feel that men are leering at me. I used to feel that whenever I was strongly in touch with the full power of my sexual energy that I was somehow putting out a strong sexual message, inviting a kind of response that I really didn't want. Now I feel that people are interested in me as a whole person.

Question: Would you call this a personal magnetism?

Answer: Yes. A personal magnetism.

Question: Have you ever practiced Ovarian Kung Fu with a man?

Answer: Yes. I practiced by myself for about three months, and then I was very fortunate in attracting a man who had been doing the Taoist sexual practice for a period of time.

Question: During those first three months, did you see any changes in your menstrual period, or did you experience any other physical changes?

Answer: My periods had been healthy and trouble-free so I really didn't notice any change. But friends who have begun the practice who have had any kind of difficulty before have experienced dramatic improvement in terms of a relief of menstrual cramps, a shorter flow and fewer pre-menstrual symptoms.

Question: What about emotions? Sexuality is supposed to be linked with emotions in many different ways. Once you began this practice, did it change your connection to your emotions?

Answer: Yes. Since at the time I began Ovarian Kung Fu I was already involved with other Taoist practices, it's difficult to differentiate which was having the effect on my emotions. I know that the Fusion of the Five Elements,[3] Part I, had a profound effect on my emotional state since it involved recycling negative emotions into a pure form of energy. Combining that with the Taoist sexual practice, I gained a tremendous sense of personal responsibility, of being in charge of and able to direct both my sexual and emotional energy.

Question: Do you feel the Fusion and Ovarian Kung Fu

practices go together?

Answer: Yes. It is wonderful to do the Taoist sexual practice with a partner, but it is extremely helpful to do the Fusion practice because it keeps the emotional energy so clear. It puts a relationship on a wholly different level without the normal kind of emotional confusion that often comes into a male-female relationship.

Question: Do you feel it is dangerous for someone to do just the sexual practice if it is not balanced by clearing out all the negative emotions?

Answer: I would say that really depends upon the person. If two people are very responsible about their emotions, acknowledging them so that they are able to let them go, then they will probably do well with just the sexual practices. But they would still benefit from doing the rest of the meditation practices as well. For couples who have any confusion, I would say it is essential to do Fusion at the same time as the regular sexual practices.

Question: Do you know of anyone who is doing these practices who has had problems with them?

Answer: No, I don't. Everyone I know who has practiced them has been quite enthusiastic about the benefits.

Question: And there are no side effects?

Answer: I have never known anyone, male or female, who has any side effects. This practice allows sexual energy to be transmuted and not just conserved. It also refines and spreads it throughout the body, revitalizing the whole body in mind and spirit. So the practice itself removes the negative side effects of sexual desire, which for most people appears as sexual frustration. Sexual frustration is simply blocked sexual energy.

Question: Once you became involved with your lover, did you find a big difference between the other lovers you've had who were not doing these practices?

Answer: Yes. It was quite dramatically and wonderfully different. This relationship, which continues happily, has all the elements that had been wonderful in my other relationships in terms of closeness and pleasure, but goes far beyond anything that I have ever experienced before. The whole quality of the relationship is very clear.

We experience very clear communication, a flow, and a true bonding on many, many levels that I hadn't experienced before. We are connected emotionally, mentally, and psychically, and are often able to know what the other is thinking. We feel that even at long distances we are able to make love. We have a feeling of the spiritual connection that is very, very satisfying.

Question: What about women who learned the practices but who have been unable to find a man who would do these practices? Do you have any friends like that?

Answer: I think everyone I have known who has learned the practices has wanted to find a partner. It is interesting to me that people I speak with about the benefits of the practice are all initially cynical and suspicious. Most of us experience a lot of our greatest pleasure in life sexually, so we do not really want to give up the known for the unknown. Since this practice has spiritual benefits, most people think that it won't feel quite as good on the physical level. People are often a little reluctant initially to try. But everyone I know, once they learn the practices, wants to find a partner with whom to practice because they find the quality of their sexual experience far more pleasurable and satisfying, and they want to find someone with whom to share.

Question: What problems exist for the woman who does the practice while her partner does not?

Answer: The quality of these relationships is probably better than previous relationships. Some of the refined sexual energy spills over, and the partner probably picks up on it on subconscious levels.

Question: Do you think there is danger of abuse, of someone drawing the energy out from the other person, something like "sexual vampirism"?

Answer: A method can always be abused. It is very important for anyone planning to do these practices with a partner to have a clear commitment to sharing fully to attain mutual spiritual growth.

Question: Can you describe your experience of orgasm with your partner?

Answer: The orgasm is a Valley Orgasm,[4] rather than a Peak Orgasm. I experience a slow wave of energy rising within me. This actively stimulating phase rises to a prolonged peak of excitement, then I deeply relax in the "valley" for a period. I repeat this cycle two, three or more times. Each succeeding peak of excitement is higher and each valley is more deeply relaxing so that more and more of my whole body-mind-spirit is at the same time aroused and deeply surrendering.

The Valley Orgasm occurs spontaneously in the state of deep relaxation, and it is a very powerful experience which I feel in every cell, every particle of my being as an exquisite, ecstatic melting. The feeling of connection with my partner is profound. My whole being is shared with his, and his with mine, as one flow that knows no boundaries.

Sometimes our awareness expands to include the whole cosmos, and there is a powerful sense of being omnipresent and a part of all things. Sometimes the orgasm has felt like nuclear fission and fusion occurring simultaneously, as thought I am both expanding infinitely and fusing into a point of nothingness. I have experienced a tremendous spectrum of sensations each time. In the beginning sometimes we spent the whole day making love and meditating with the energy we generated. I am always in awe of the tremendous power residing in male and female. We are all closer to being gods and goddesses than we think.

Question: Are you able to distinguish your energy from his during the cycling and sharing?

Answer: I definitely can distinguish his energy and can also feel the quality of the merging. I had been practicing the Microcosmic Orbit Meditation[5] for about a year before I began doing the sexual practice, and had practiced the Single Cultivation of Ovarian Kung Fu for several months before actually being with my partner. Because my partner was also experienced in the practice, our merging was really spontaneous without any need to control it. I could feel from our first sharing the energy moving naturally into the Microcosmic, Belt, and Thrusting Channels[6] If you meditate in these channels daily, your lovemaking energy will flow effortlessly into them.

Question: How long do you make love during this practice?

Answer: Several hours. Sometimes two hours, sometimes three or four. Quite frequently we experience the peaks and valleys all night, but with naps during some of the valleys. There is a saying that in love there is no sense of time. This really describes Taoist lovemaking. There is a sense of all the time in the world, of being in eternity, and of having more and more energy available. Now that we have created so many connections, we don't really need to spend as much time. Once we made love for only 30 seconds before experiencing a Valley Orgasm, but the polarity between us was so powerful that the Valley Orgasm lasted for hours. Now we are much more tuned to each other and feel that we are making love all the time.

Question: Are these cycles of the peaks and valleys determined by the male's erection?

Answer: I would say that the cycles of peaks and valleys is determined by both people. Both partners move to greater and greater excitement, and when a partner feels he or she is coming to the point of no return, then both partners pull the energy up to mingle it and share it in the quiet valley stage. It has always seemed spontaneous when another crest and wave begins, drawing both of us into it.

Question: During the resting period when you have reached the high peak of stimulation and have allowed the CHI[7] energy to move up the body until the whole body feels tingling, warm, and vibrant, is there a danger of feeling unconscious with this energy?

Answer: If I'm extremely fatigued there is a tendency to be more unconscious with it. My experience in general is of going into a totally altered state, finding a melting point with my partner in which I am very aware and yet very at ease. Then I can meditate and further refine our lovemaking.

Question: The technique of the Valley Orgasm as it is described requires you to meditate at different levels, or Tan Tiens. Did you find yourself able to meditate at specific centers with this energy?

Answer: It's very hard to generalize because every experience is unique. I found initially that the energy first moved in the Microcosmic Orbit, but I also started noticing that it would move through the whole body. It would tend with each valley to move up through another center. There would be times in the valleys when it would seem like a showering-up, sometimes more in the center or in the back, while at other times it would be like the rush of a rocket taking off, straight up.

Question: Does this feeling linger after lovemaking?

Answer: There is the sense of being a unique male and female each in our respective bodies, and yet being all man and all woman, god and goddess. I have clearly experienced this before in other sexual relationships, but in this relationship it exists all the time.

Question: After practicing in this relationship for almost three years, what has been the evolution of this practice?

Answer: I would say that one of the aspects of all the Taoist practices is the sense of active awareness of drawing energy in directly from the stars, the sun, the earth, and from one's sexual partner. What I feel is that I have been able to absorb, be nourished by, and bring into my own life some of the real masculine, Yang, qualities of my partner. With my partner's Yang energy as a resource available to me, I have been able to be more assertive, more creative, and more outspoken. The exchange with my partner of the whole essence of his being has enabled me to amplify my own personality and to include his qualities.

Question: How has the male energy you absorbed affected your daily meditations.

Answer: I want to be more integrated, including integrating the male and female energies within myself. Becoming more integrated and more balanced is one of the benefits of this practice. Being able to exchange with my partner has really enhanced my spiritual growth.

The same energy that could have been lost at times in emotional confusion or through miscommunication has become an energy resource that is available for my own growth. There is clarity that is illuminating in terms of my emotional and spiritual life. It is also more refined energy. My partner's energy is now available for my spiritual growth, and my energy is available for him.

Question: What do you feel is the highest level of this practice?

Answer: Refinement of one's own sexual, emotional, and mental energies into subtle spiritual energy and into a spiritual body that lives within the physical body, yet is free to move anywhere in time and space is the highest level. The sexual practice conserves and refines the fuel, but it is within the Kan and Li meditations that the real alchemy occurs. The essence of the Kan and Li practice is fire and water, male and female energies uniting creatively within each Tan Tien or center in the body.

Through the self-intercourse of Kan and Li, one impregnates oneself, nourishes the fetus, and finally gives birth to a spiritual child that dwells within. Then the challenge is to nourish the spiritual child with strong, refined energy and virtue through the ups and downs of daily living. And how does my partner fit into this? I enhance his self-generation as he helps me with mine.

Question: You can be both the mother and father of this spiritual child by having the additional help of outside masculine energy?

Answer: Yes. What I like so much about the Taoist practices is that in cultivating our own nature, we attain our fullest flowering and give birth to ourselves. With a partner in Dual Cultivation, there is obviously an added energy and mutual support in addition to joy and pleasure. I also know that I can cultivate my own sexual energy myself, and be creative with it.

Question: Do you feel the sexual cultivation practice is essential to your spiritual growth?

Answer: Yes, but it is not essential to have a partner. These practices can be done by a woman who has commitment to celibacy as a way of utilizing her sexual energy for her own spiritual growth and directing the transformed energy toward service to others. For a woman who does want a partner eventually, Single Cultivation allows her to take her time to choose her partner well without rushing into a relationship purely to satisfy sexual needs. So I would say Single Cultivation is essential. Dual Cultivation is valuable, but optional.

There is something else that I feel is very important since we are talking about the benefits. From the beginning these practices were very transformative, enhancing my sense of being in control of my own energy and my own destiny. I have grown more responsible and able to use my energies creatively.

Question: Is the Tao all about controlling your emotions and energies? How does this figure in being effortless and flowing free?

Answer: I think about life as a river. Before I practiced Fusion and Ovarian Kung Fu, I felt in my emotional and sexual life as if I were a leaf on a current, and it was the current of circumstance that would sometimes direct me. Now, knowing these Taoist practices, I feel that I am more like a raft, and I can use the current for the purpose of following the river. When I look at my past and all the suffering that I went through in some of my emotional and sexual relationships, and I look at friends now, I see that the Taoist practices allow us to be in the river in a way that's harmonious and flowing without being knocked against the rocks. We are the navigators.

Question: Let's talk a little about the psychology of relationships. How do you feel this practice changes the psychology of the battle of the sexes?

Answer: I think it is essential for both partners to enter into a relationship with the intention of moving the energy up and fully sharing, because it is an exchange of energy designed to be redirected toward growth. This growth will naturally take its own direction, emotionally and spiritually. As the energy moves up during the practice, it takes care of itself. Everything else will flow naturally from that. The power struggle tends to dissolve. When things occur that must be clarified, the tools are available. It seems there is a harmony and a flow that is present that really extends far beyond the sexual act. There is also the other tremendous benefit of feeling attuned to the other person, wherever he might be.

Question: Why do you think this happens?

Answer: My experience is that as the energy moves up there are bondings, at the heart level, and at the mental and spiritual level, and those bondings are very profound.

Question: I have some specific questions about the actual technique. Do you really feel the energy flow up the spine in very direct pathways? It seems when you are making love these energies all get mixed together. This is a little confusing.

Answer: I think there is an interesting distinction between practicing on my own, if I am stimulating myself, than when my whole being is totally involved with another person. More of my whole body gets aroused when I am with my partner. So when the energies move up, they are more likely to expand and to fill my whole body. When I am alone, I have a clearer sense of the energy going up my spine. If I'm with my partner, I have a sense of the energy moving up through my whole body. Sometimes I have the sense of not only my own energy, but also of his, as one column or wave moving upward.

Question: Have you discovered any additional techniques to aid this sexual practice?

Answer: My lover and I have discovered certain things spontaneously. It requires a great deal more discipline for men to cultivate this practice than it does for women. For women, it is really control of the pelvic-floor muscles. All I really need to do is contract my pelvic-floor muscles in the direction of my coccyx and tilt my pelvis slightly, and the energy will just begin to move up. Sometimes I will stroke up my partner's spine with my hand or he will stroke up my back as we are beginning to go into the resting phase. This gives us both the clear sense that we are directing the energy up. Sometimes we touch each other's heads on the crown, and this helps focus the energy there. The energy then begins to shower down. One of the most delicious and exquisite qualities of the Valley Orgasm is that the energy moves up the whole body and through the crown, sometimes moving out of the body, and then showers down like an exquisitely delicious nectar showering down through all the cells and all the atoms of the body.

Question: Have you found the practice has increased or decreased your sexual desire?

Answer: My sexual desire is about the same, but I feel much more satisfied. Also, my perception of sex and sexual relationships has continued to expand. I feel I am very slowly moving toward my goal of being totally alive, making love with the whole universe in every movement. I feel immensely grateful to have a partner with whom to practice loving.

We feel that we are always together, and whether we are physically together or apart, we can make love and share our energies. Our transformed sexual and emotional energies nourish our spirits and are shared with others as love.

NOTES

1. Originally the Taoist sexual exercises were called "Ovarian Kung Fu." Some students feel this sounds too violent or too much like martial arts. The term "kung fu," however, means discipline or intensive work, referring to one who puts time into practice. Ovarian Kung Fu implies an expression of power and control, of the ability to take command of one's body and sexual life. (Mantak Chia)

2. The Jing (principal) energy of a woman provides her with life-force energy. This life-force energy is contained to a large extent in the ovaries. It is here that the hormones are produced that determines a woman's breasts, voice, etc. The ovaries constantly produce sexual energy. The Ovarian Breathing Process releases the energy produced by the ovaries, and makes it possible to store this energy, which has a Yang (active) quality, in the woman's body. After ovulation and before menstruation the energy is milder, as the properties of the energy change from Yang to Yin (passive). Also, during this part of the cycle the energy is at its highest stage of development for absorption and transformation.

Ovarian Breathing, if practiced every day, can start the absorption process and conserve the life-force energy that otherwise would be lost through menstruation. This is the process by which the sexual energy is transformed to CHI. (Mantak Chia)

3. In this practice of internal alchemy, the student learns to transform the negative emotions of worry, sadness, cruelty, anger, and fear into pure energy. This process is accomplished by identifying the source of the negative emotions within the five organs of the body. After the excessive energy of the emotions is filtered out of the organs, the state of psycho/physical balance is restored to the body. Freed of negative emotions, the pure energy of the five organs is crystallized into a radiant pearl or crystal ball. The pearl plays a central role in the development and nourishment of the soul or energy body. The energy body is exclusively nourished with the pure energy of the five organs (the virtues). (Mantak Chia)

4. Unlike the ordinary quick orgasm, or peak orgasm, whose thrilling moment is confined primarily to the genital area, this orgasm will deliver to you a new sense of equilibrium that will be stored in your body long after your pleasure has become a fleeting memory.

Taoists advocate the Valley Orgasm as a continual rolling expansion of the orgasm throughout the whole body, prolonging inward orgasm to a half-hour, one hour, two hours, or longer in a gradual, but ultimately greatly heightened ecstasy. You can enjoy this form of sexual love indefinitely without paying for your pleasure with your life-force.

During the Valley Orgasm, lovers can relax and have all the time in the world to share their tenderness. There is no frenzied explosion, only wave after wave of higher subtle energies bathing the entwined man and woman. The Valley Orgasm is not a technique, but rather a certain kind of experience that the lovers allow to happen to themselves, encouraged by a time-tested process. (Mantak Chia)

5. By far the most powerful energy exchange between two partners occurs at the level of subtle energy. The Taoists have been studying the circulation of subtle energy through certain energy points in the body for thousands of years and have verified, in detail, their importance. These energy points form the basis for acupuncture. Although Western medical research has acknowledged acupuncture as being clinically effective, scientists admit they cannot fully explain why the system works. The circulation of energy through these energy points, or meridians, is called the Microcosmic Orbit. (Mantak Chia)

6. The Taoist masters started to notice the flow of something in the body. The flow began in the navel, traveled down to the perineum and up the spine to the head, down the front through the tongue, to the throat and then down to the navel. The circulation of energy through this route came to be known as the Microcosmic Orbit.

The more they were able to still their minds and bodies, the more intense the flow would be. As they continued to still their minds, they began to discover more paths opening and to feel the energy flow in a straight direction, up and down. From the perineum up to the head, the flow was then felt passing through the major organs in three channels, which later became known as the Thrusting Channels. As their practice continued, they felt the energy start to flow in a circular motion, similar to a belt, around a major energy center that they discovered in the navel, the Belt Channel. (Mantak Chia)

7. We are all born with an abundance of energy that the Taoists call the principal energy, or "Jing." The Jing energy also converts into life-force energy for the organs, which energy is called "Chi."

Sexual energy (creative energy) is the only energy that can be doubled, tripled, or increased even more. Therefore, if we want to conserve or restore lost principal energy, sexual energy provides the means to create that extra power, if we conserve, recycle, and transform it back into principal energy. We then will have more energy available to transform into Chi, which in turn becomes transformed into another type of energy called "Shen." The word "Shen" means spiritual energy. (Mantak Chia)

PART THREE
Alternatives Within Erotic Spirituality

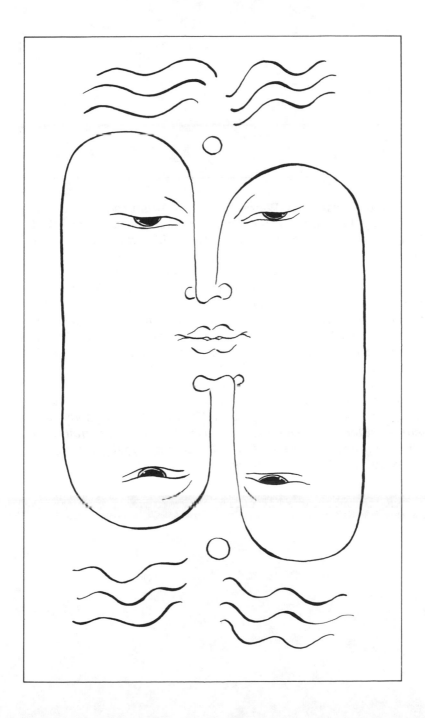

"Christ and Tiresias: A Wider Focus on Masturbation" is co-authored by David Schulz, who is well known for his sexological writings, and Dominic S. Raphael, who is obliged to publish this watershed essay pseudonymously. Masturbation for personal pleasure is condemned by official Church dogma, yet actual pastoral practice tends toward a more tolerant view. Schulz and Raphael argue that Church dogma limps behind both contemporary sexological and spiritual practice. They carefully distinguish between mere self-stimulation and self-pleasuring, reminding us that the word "pleasure" means "that which stills" and not "that which excites." Self-pleasure in this sense is erotic delight in which genital orgasm is transmuted into whole-body bliss or communion with Being. Again, Tantrism is used as an example of a body- and sex-positive approach. This very courageous and timely consideration will hopefully do much to alleviate guilt and encourage greater tolerance toward pleasure, bodily existence, and sexuality in Christian circles.

CHRIST AND TIRESIAS:
A WIDER FOCUS ON MASTURBATION

By David A. Schulz, Ph.D.
and Dominic S. Raphael

Millions of human beings are alienated from the Church on account of its teaching on sexual morality. For many people this alienation starts during puberty and is triggered by Church sanctions against masturbation. The Church's official condemnation of masturbation has cultural roots. It is not rooted in the teachings of Jesus Christ. Yet, in people's mind today it is closely associated with the Christian message. So closely that they are apt to reject together with this offensive piece of cultural baggage all the Good News, sometimes for the rest of their lives.

A closer look shows that this issue concerns not only Christians. Western society as a whole suffers from a blind spot in the area of sexuality for which the issue of masturbation is symptomatic. The classical myth of Tiresias sheds light on this area, helps us to widen our focus, and shows unexpected aspects of sexuality in a spiritual context.

For technical reasons we decided not to melt the sections which each of us contributed into one continuous whole. We let them stand side by side, marked with our initials. This may mean a loss of eleganoe, but we hope that it will also mean a gain in freshness.

THE CASE OF SELF-PLEASURING (by D.A.S.)

Of all the aspects of human sexuality none seems more difficult to celebrate in a body-positive sexuality than masturbation. This is particularly true when approached from a Christian perspective.

Literally meaning "to defile by hand," the word *masturbation* itself carries the disapproval of centuries. Yet it is now commonly recognized that there is no scriptural basis for this condemnation. Passages in the Old Testament once thought to prohibit masturbation are being reinterpreted. Jesus himself said virtually nothing about sexuality and nothing at all about masturbation. Nevertheless, Christian condemnation of this practice persists. In the past it was most often directed against male masturbation because of the "loss of seed." Female masturbation has often been winked at by moral theologians, while nineteenth-century physicians tried to stamp it out to the point of cauterizing or removing the clitoris.

Modern attitudes toward the subject are changing. While the Victorians spoke of "self-abuse" and attributed everything from pimples to a shortened life span and insanity to masturbation, we are inclined to speak of "self-pleasuring."

Where once psychoanalytic theory—with its view of masturbation as an immature form of sexual expression—dominated clinical thought, sex therapists now claim that masturbation is an important part of sexual behavior throughout the life cycle. When once it was widely considered to be a form of antisocial behavior, some feminists now declare it essential to the establishment of an authentic feminine power base. While not everyone agrees, there does seem to be widespread acceptance of the practice as a good and healthy part of life. Yet its spiritual possibilities have hardly been recognized. How could this behavior—considered at best superficial pleasure—open up the depths of human experience?

In considering its spiritual possibilities, it is impossible to use the word masturbation, because of its pejorative meaning. How can we see the depth possibilities in this practice if we are uncomfortable with the word describing it? "Self-satisfaction," a word sometimes used in Europe, seems too turned inward. If "self-pleasuring" can be seen as something more than mere stimulation, then this term may be our best choice. By self-pleasuring we mean the enjoyment and fruition of our own sexual arousal.

Some readers may feel that we belabor the obvious when we stress the enjoyment of our own sexual arousal, but this simple pleasure is rarely affirmed in Christian writing. Indeed, for most of Christian history, the pleasure of sexual arousal has been seen as a form of pagan hedonism. Many Christians, therefore, find it a great liberation to finally be able to affirm this pleasure in sexual intercourse. How many are genuinely able to do so when self-pleasuring?

The specification of what the fulfillment of our own sexual arousal might mean is the main purpose of this essay. Here it simply can be said that we see it as nothing less than the experience of wholeness—the experience of communion with Self, all other people, with the cosmos, and the divine Ground of Being. Thus, self-pleasuring is to be distinguished from self-stimulation—the simple enjoyment of genital stimulation.

A CENTRAL SCHEMA (by D.A.S.)

The official opposition of Christian churches against self-stimulation stems from a central thread of thinking about sexuality. A major locus of this thought is the *Summa Theologica* of St. Thomas Aquinas, though the roots go back at least to St. Augustine. This view declares that the purpose of sexual arousal is [read: "ought to be"] reproduction. Aquinas believed that sexual intercourse was moral only when it occurred between husband and wife, for the purpose of procreation. He even argued that the only moral position was husband on top in the "missionary position." In this century another purpose has gradually been acknowledged: the unitive. Protestants have been quicker to recognize this function than Catholics and some Protestant churches have even extended it to non-marital— particularly pre-marital—intercourse as well.

Given this emphasis, it is easy to see why self-stimulation has been condemned. It is non-reproductive and non-unitive. Not even Protestant theologians have extended the unitive function of sexuality to self-stimulation. Self-stimulation, even for women, is seen as at best a second-rate form of sexual behavior to be ignored in adolescence but condemned in adulthood: something, in any case, to be "struggled with."

In making such broad generalizations about official Church attitudes, it may seem that there is total rejection of self-stimulation, but in pastoral practice there is not. It is widely acknowledged that self-stimulation can not be evaluated simply on the basis of observable behavior. The internal state must be considered in making moral judgements about the act. The character of the fantasies associated with the behavior is often an important clue to this interior state.

Likewise, the social situation in which the act occurs must be understood. Thus, some churches acknowledge that self-stimulation for the purpose of producing semen for laboratory analysis may well be considered a moral act. It may also be morally correct when husband or wife self-stimulate rather than choosing another partner for intercourse when their spouse is unable or unwilling to engage in coitus for a long period of time.

Other qualifications might be considered in order to declare self-stimulation a moral act. But, for all of this, the spiritual possibilities of self-pleasuring are not—to our knowledge—explored by Christian theologians. This is not true of other religious traditions. In any case, we will argue that self-stimulation can fulfill the unitive function of human sexuality, in which case it is better called "self-pleasuring."

DISCOVERING THE SEXUAL INSCAPE (by D.S.R.)

Is sexuality exclusively partner-directed? Is not sexual arousal a unifying force within ourselves? Why is the "unitive function" of sexuality acknowledged only in the unity between partners? Why so many other aberrations from Common Sense in Western views on sexuality? A historic overview suggests a general answer. In Western society, ethics has consistently maintained as it were an outsider's perspective on sexuality and has thus gotten only half of its field into view. It seems high time to complement the one-sided picture which resulted. Ethics must look at human sexuality from the inside, too.

St. Augustine (354-430 C.E.) and St. Thomas Aquinas (1225-1274 C.E.) are the two thinkers who most influenced the sexual ethics prevailing in the Western Christian churches up to our own time. It was St. Thomas' great merit to integrate the world view of Aristotle (384-322 B.C.E.) into medieval scholasticism. Yet, there was a drawback to this achievement. Aristotle had been first and foremost a naturalist, an observer of nature in the sense of an outside observer. Not only scholasticism but typical Western science adopted Aristotle's stance: You set yourself over against your object and study "how it works." This yields results, but only on the level of purpose (*uti* or "usefulness," Aquinas called it); the level of meaning (*frui* or "fruition, enjoyment") is deliberately ruled out. Meaning cannot be observed from without, it can only be experienced from within. We are rediscovering today that there is more to life than science gets into focus. We are also rediscovering that there is more to human sexuality than its procreative purpose, or even its unitive function. It is the inner meaning which we experience in our sexuality that any future ethics, Christian or otherwise, will have to take into account.

More influenced by Plato than by Aristotle, St. Augustine would have been in a better position than St. Thomas to discover the ethical implications of viewing sexuality from within. All the more so as Augustine was intensely concerned with his own inner experience. His *Confessiones* are the first introspective autobiography in the West. They give us many hints at what today we would call his "hang-ups," which, through his enormous influence, became for more than a thousand years the hang-ups of Western society. Still, the most severe damage did not result from St. Augustine's personal problems but from the influence of Mani on his thought. Although Augustine later rejected the Manicheism of his youth, he remained a "carrier" and infected the Christian tradition with its germs.

By now the Manichean error (rarely identified as such) is widespread and well known. It consists in confusing the biblical notion of "spirit" with mind and the biblical notion of "flesh" with matter. The Bible, however, means by "spirit" (divine) aliveness and all that leads to fullness of life; "flesh" (originally, meat no longer alive) connotes all that is bound for corruption, including "jealousies, resentments, disunity" (Gal. 5:20)—certainly attitudes of the mind, not matters of the body. What St. Augustine's dichotomy between mind and body has done to denigrate sexuality and to make Christian sexual ethics un-Christian can still be felt today, 1,500 years later.

There is, of course, another side to this story. St. Augustine was a passionate lover, a great human being. In his heart he knew that love on all its levels is of one piece. Once, preaching on the highest reaches of divine love, he suddenly interrupted himself. "Show me a lover!" he cried. "Any lover will know what I'm talking about!" In his heart he knew a wholeness which his intellect kept shattering. [1]

Aquinas, too, was a towering mind with a world-wide horizon. His vision was not as restricted as his narrow sexual ethics. He was a poet. All through history the poets knew not only the outer but also the inner landscape of Eros.

The Bible itself contains keenly erotic poetry in Solomon's *Song of Songs*. Yet, though they sang in its power, they never thought reflectively about the inner wholeness that erotic excitement effects within our psyche. Only the partner-related outside of the erotic experience had come into focus so far.

Even in our own day, when all partner-related aspects of sexuality have been closely examined and broadly discussed—often ad nauseam—its self-related side is seriously neglected. This neglect seems to spring from a powerful resistance which our society—and by no means only the Church—puts up against facing this unexplored dimension of human sexuality, its "inscape."

This resistance seems to be getting ever tighter. The best book I know on the subject was to come out in its third edition, when the printer who had no problem with its content seven years ago and four years ago, now told the publisher: "We aren't printing that sort of thing any more." Here is a key passage from that book by Jack Mozin (abbreviated for lack of space) and two shorter ones by other authors to complete the picture.

> Every sexual experience has an inner realm which no one, not even the closest lover, can share completely; it is ours alone. Some people, however, lose sight of the inner side of the experience, and are thus convinced that sexual excitement is "caused" by others. Western cultural tradition encourages people to value and develop awareness of the outer world and to devalue and suppress awareness of the inner world. The pressures toward extroversion appear to be stronger yet in matters of sex.
>
> As a result, some people are reluctant to acknowledge and enjoy the internal dimension of sex. Self-sexuality is, essentially, a way of enjoying the private side of sex by oneself or with a partner present. Masturbation is by no means required for this awareness. Nonetheless, masturbation is one obvious mode for exploring the inner aspects of one's sexuality. When a person devalues the private side of sex or considers it to be in conflict with the outer, partner-oriented side, self-sexuality may be considered worthless or selfish. Often, though, greater self-awareness brings with it a sense of autonomy which makes intimate sharing less predictable and more fun. Exciting encounters with a partner intensify awareness of the inner side of sex, and vice versa. Each dimension increases enjoyment of the other. [2]

> . . . making love with oneself successfully, learning that we can achieve ecstasy alone as well as with a partner, is a very powerful discovery. Most of us are waiting around for prince or princess charming to come and kiss us on the lips and wake us from our emotional and physical slumbers into the vital, passionate beings we know we truly are. Unfortunately it doesn't work that way. We become passionate beings by turning ourselves on, by opening our sexuality ourselves, by reversing the conditioning that closed it all off in the first place. And then when our energy is flowing, when we know how our own bodies work, we are ready for a partner. [3]

> Masturbation is our first natural sexual activity. It is the way we discover our eroticism, the way we learn to respond sexually, the way we learn to love ourselves and to build self-esteem. [4]

Every new insight needs to crystallize in a myth. Only then does it become accessible. Oedipus and Narcissus exemplify this fact. But is there a mythical figure in whom the insight that concerns us here has found expression? When I asked myself that question, Tiresias came to mind, the blind seer celebrated in Greek myths and tragedies. The name of Tiresias means "He-who-delights-in-signs," and his story begins with a sign, a symbol of the infant's self-sufficient delight: On Mount Cyllene the child sees two serpents entwined in the act of coupling—

primordial power in perfect balance. Yet, frightened, the child shatters the harmony of this power circle. He strikes one of the serpents, the female, and in an instant turns female himself. (By an inexorable inner law we become what we attempt to suppress or deny.) But the vision of wholeness persists. Seven years later, Tiresias sees again the sign of the two serpents coupling. Again he strikes out, this time wounding the male, and becomes a man.

We shall take up and continue this story later. For now, let us pause and consider the message of its beginning. It is the message of the child's primordial wholeness—"Heaven lies about us in our infancy!"[5]—but also of the loss of that wholeness. On one level it may be inevitable that our primordial blessedness be shattered by our own hand. But on a deeper level the sign of those two serpents entwined must retain its power throughout our life.

We must continue to draw from its power, for our hidden wholeness is androgynous. This is the reason why the rabbis interpret Genesis 1:27 to mean that Adam was created as hermaphrodite. The Babylonians, too, held the primeval human being to have been androgynous. And to the First Adam—created "male and female" in God's likeness—correponds in Christian tradition the Second Adam. St. Paul says of him "in Christ there is neither male nor female" (Gal. 3:28) but the fulness of both which transcends the limitations of either. "The suppression of half of our natures leaves us crippled, dissatisfied, and dependent upon our partners to provide us with our other halves."[6] But Christ represents the primordial wholeness, the Child within us, of whom Paul says "I live, yet no longer I, Christ lives in me." (Gal 2:20). This is the goal. It is our task, therefore, to care for the androgynous Christ Child within us, to cultivate the Tiresian dimension of our sexuality.

To cultivate the autoerotic inscape of our sexuality does not mean retardation on an infantile level. On the contrary, it means growth. It implies the challenge to live with creative tension rather than striking out at either the male or the female pole of original unity. It means the lifelong task of spanning, again and again, the abyss between opposites by bold arches.

> As once the winged energy of delight carried you over childhood's dark abyss, now beyond your own life build the great arches of unimagined bridges. [7]

A PHENOMENOLOGY OF SELF-STIMULATION (by D.A.S.)

In order to better appreciate the complexity of the matter, a brief description of the varying significance of self-stimulation through the life cycle might be helpful.

An infant's persistent touching of the genitals—if it is not interrupted or restricted by condemning adults—must surely represent as pure a form of self-stimulation as can be found. It represents primordial bliss—undisturbed by erotic fantasy or the urge to achieve orgasm. It is now widely recognized that it is unwise, perhaps even harmful, to condemn this behavior in infants although this used to be commonly done.

In other cultures less restricted by tradition, parents even encourage self-stimulation by playing with the genitals of infants. The medieval printmaker Hans Baldung Grien,[8] shocks many Christians today because he incorporated this custom into his portrait of the Holy Family. In his picture, St. Anne stimulates the genitals of her grandson, Jesus, while his mother and father look on.

Adolescence is normally the time for the awakening of sexual fantasy and the linking of sexual arousal to power through concerns about sexual dysfunction. It need not be a traumatic time in human sexual development (as many ethnographers have shown), but it frequently has been in our culture. Until recently, the United States was one of the tiny minority (4 percent) of societies in the world that had a general taboo against sex. We were almost alone in the world in our belief that sexual arousal itself was in need of strict regulation because of its inherent destructive tendencies.

This belief was encouraged by churches which taught that sex was sinful and self-stimulation a form of self-abuse. To be told as an adolescent that the one form of sexual pleasure over which one had some degree of control was inherently sinful was to place the immediate positive experience of pleasure in direct conflict with the Church's teaching. The individual loses, whatever conclusion is drawn. Either the Church is wrong because the experience feels so right, or the experience must be wrong in spite of the pleasure it provides.

Self-stimulation is yet another thing in the context of marriage. It should not be assumed that sexual intercourse is either a mutual or a moral act just because two people are married. The persistent stance of common law is now being challenged. Courts are declaring that a spouse—particularly a wife—can be raped by the partner in marriage. Likewise, it should not be assumed that self-stimulation in marriage is a solitary act. The spouse can be caringly included in the fantasy or present when the activity occurs. Self-stimulation might be morally appropriate as a form of love play with one's spouse, as a means of better matching sexual desires, or as an appropriate form of self-expression in the spouses absence. All of these activities are widely advocated by sex therapists and, from the clinical evidence available, seen to be common practice. In the past, our tradition assumed that it was the husband's responsibility to initiate sex and, if it was acknowledged that women enjoyed sex (which, Victorians contended, good wives did not), to satisfy his wife. Now we are coming to see that each partner must assume responsibility for his or her own orgasm. It should not be left up to the partner to discover how, on this particular occasion, an orgasm can best be achieved. Usually this is done by clearly communicating what one enjoys and when one enjoys it. In order to do this we must genuinely enjoy sexual stimulation and know how to achieve our own orgasm. A positive attitude toward self-stimulation is thus a precondition for satisfying sex—even in marital intercourse.

Self-stimulation can also play a positive role in old age. Research suggests that people over 65, who stimulate themselves to orgasm, are more likely to be socially active, concerned about their personal appearance, eat better, are physically and mentally healthier and more involved in meaningful social relationships than those who do not self-stimulate. Contrary to past convictions, evidence shows that self-stimulation increases self-esteem and thereby increases the probability of the occurrence of other desirable behavior.

Thus, in general, sex therapists have concluded that self-stimulation is a variation of healthy sexual behavior throughout the life cycle rather than a form of immature behavior or a pathology.

AUTHENTIC SEXUALITY AND THE AUTHORITIES (by D.S.R.)

As soon as we begin to evaluate sexual experience from an insider's perspective—and how else could experience be understood?—we see that its autoerotic inscape clearly belongs to authentic sexuality. Why, then, have the authorities—preachers, teachers, physicians, psychiatrists, parents, and even politicians—joined forces and battled against "the secret habits of sex . . . the evils of solitude and its seductive temptations to the young who are premature victims of a pernicious passion . . . entailing disease and death"? This is from the title of a book on masturbation by Jean Dubois in 1848. Why this two-hundred-year war on masturbation, a war in which Common Sense is only beginning to win a victory? My friend Roger Grandy gave a one-sentence answer: "Sex is about power."

On many levels and in many different senses, sex is about power. The power which concerns us here is the self-esteem that comes to a person through accepting, activating, and enjoying one's own sexuality. The autoerotic side of sex has a particularly important function for personal empowerment. An exclusively partner-directed sexuality means dependence, enslavement. The healthy opposite of dependence is not independence, but inter-dependence. (Independence would merely be a different kind of enslavement: enslavement to illusions. No one is independent.) But inter-dependence, the free and willing give-and-take between equals, means that I do not make my partner responsible for giving me what is in my own power (e.g., orgasm). "When I no longer come from need, I can come from love." Self-sex is therefore, not merely a transitional phase of human sexuality, but remains always a firm base for healthy human self-acceptance, self-enjoyment, and self-love.

Why should this God-given personal power threaten any authority? In order to answer this question, we have to make a distinction. Genuine authority is never threatened by authentic sexuality; only authoritarian authority is. "Authentic" is the perfect adjective to characterize the kind of sexuality we are considering here. The word comes from *authentes*, the Greek term for "one who does things for himself." (Only inauthentic sexuality expects from a partner what one can do and ought to do for oneself.) Among the things humans can do for themselves are thinking, judging, and deciding. These authentic human rights are the wedge that divides genuine authority from authoritarianism.

The word "genuine," too, has Greek roots. It is related to *gignesthai*, which means "to be born." A born leader has genuine authority. One who has been invested (i.e., "is robed") with authority may or may not have genuine leadership qualities— may or may not be a reliable source of information or advice. Originally, authority was founded on charisma. A person known to be a reliable resource for knowing or acting was put in a position of authority by the community. Once put in such a position, however, human beings tend to hang on to it long after they have run dry as sources of information or advice. And once an authority position is created, people unqualified to fill it, sometimes obtain it.

It is usually easy to tell the difference between the two kinds of authority figures. Here is the acid test: Genuine authorities build others up; authoritarian authorities put them down. That is why authoritarianism is threatened by authentic—self-reliant—humanness, and has to attack its powerbase of authentic sexuality.

In fairness, we have to mention a different side of the authority issue. Not every conflict with an authority is revolt against an authoritarian use of power. Authorities bear responsibility for peaceful and just relationships among people. Not everything that "feels good" is as harmless as masturbation. Selfishness also easily creeps into sexuality. And where selfishness becomes a threat to the community's well being, genuine authority will step in. In its intimate domain, sexuality is not subject to external authority. It reaches, however, into an external realm and there its manifestations have to harmonize with the good of the community.

For the sake of fairness, it should also be admitted that even authoritarians occasionally wink an eye at harmless though forbidden sexual activity. For most of Christian history there was, in fact, a wide gap between what was "on the books" and what was actually enforced. In one way this constituted the ultimate authoritarian putdown: It gave you space to do your thing as long as you felt sufficiently bad about it. Nothing undermines self-respect more thoroughly. But then, the authority figures themselves were caught in a predicament. Their Common Sense told them one thing; the great lie of society enforced the opposite.

Were not our parents often in that position? They would remember the sufferings of their own childhood; yet, they were afraid of what the neighbors might say. And so: "If you touch that thing one more time I'm going to cut it off." Then again, "I remember my father telling me the joke of the thrifty Scotchman who wanted to give his son a toy for his birthday, so he cut a hole in his pocket." An exemplary priest, who sent me this account added: "My father liked slightly startling stories, but I think he was also implicitly trying to teach his son: 'Don't worry excessively about some self-exploration and self-enjoyment.' If we all are Church, these were perhaps ecclesial teachings also."

Many children handled the matter with Common Sense, like Eric Gill, "child of a nonconformist parson in nineteenth century England," who writes in his autobiography:

> My experience was typical of that of millions of children of my generation, I suppose. In the matter of sex the only thing I was properly taught as a child was that it was a secret. We were given no responsible advice and had no access to reliable reading matter; we were only put off with vagueness and sentimental nonsense about not tampering with sacred things. Why "sacred" we were never told, for the very things which, up to then, we had been brought up to suppose had no relation to anything but drainage and which were therefore more or less despicable, were now vaguely hinted to be objects of sanctity! So we were undeterred; for when your parents and teachers are quite obviously being unreasonable and even ridiculous they seriously undermine your respect for their admonitions.[9]

That's Common Sense. But this term suggests a much deeper meaning than we give to it in daily parlance. Common Sense is the world view that flows from our original wholeness. We are whole when we are in communion with ourselves, with the cosmos, and with the divine Ground of Being. Common Sense is the sense we make of things when we take a firm stand on this common ground. It is the understanding that flows from the sign of Tiresias' entwined serpents, from the experience of primordial harmony. There rests the power of the child within us, the power that threatens the very foundations of authoritarianism. For Common Sense cannot be denied; it can only be defied, punished. This, too, the myth of Tiresias tells us in its continuation.

This time it starts not with Tiresias, not with the child, but with the authorities that put all others down, with the gods. In fact, it starts at the top with the two super-bosses, Zeus and his consort Hera, male and female divided. They are quarrelling about a question whose answer belongs to the inscape of sex, from where they have locked themselves out through their dividedness. Thus the divided authorities have no choice; they have to appeal to undivided authority, to the Common Sense of the child who saw the sign of the serpents and "knows the secret of the gods."

Hera and Zeus are quarrelling about who gets more pleasure from sexual union, woman or man? Hera says the male does; Zeus claims the female does. Both suspect that they are getting only part of the whole pleasure. Each thinks the other gets more. (That's inevitable once we start dividing.) What choice do the Olympians have but to appeal to Tiresias (more precisely to the undivided child within him) the only one who knows from his own experience both sides and so can arbitrate. They ask and he answers:

> If the parts of love—pleasure be counted as ten, thrice three go to women, one only to men.[10]

An indisputable answer. Indisputable, because it comes from that undivided realm where the very dispute can never arise. As with the reply to a Zen koan, the opposite answer would have been equally indisputable. But this way or that, one of the divided authorities will be displeased; and that one will take vengeance. Whenever opinions clash, Common Sense suffers. Whenever adults are divided, the child bears the brunt.

Hera is displeased both with Tiresias' answer and with the smirk on Zeus's face. Unable to revenge herself on Zeus, she strikes Tiresias with blindness. A vicious projection: unwilling to acknowledge her own mental blindness, Hera inflicts physical blindness on Tiresias. Zeus in turn grants, it is said, inner vision to Tiresias. But does he grant it in the sense of bestowing it or in the sense of admitting it? Even Zeus could hardly bestow on him what he already possessed. And that he possessed inner vision was proved by his verdict, at which he never could have arrived by observation from the outside. We wonder how Zeus would have punished Tiresias, had he given the opposite verdict and what Hera would have "granted" him.

Struck by authoritarian vengeance, Tiresias resembles Jesus Christ. Both speak with authority and both get in trouble with the authorities. We have no space here to show the central position of Common Sense (in its full meaning) in the teaching of Jesus. Even a cursory study of the Parables, Jesus' most typical teaching device, proves that he bases his argument not on his own authority, not on an appeal to divine authority, but invariably on Common Sense, the divine authority in the hearts of his hearers.

Thus, he builds them up, empowers them, makes them stand on their own feet. And at once he is in trouble with those authorities who keep themselves in power by putting others down, with religious no less than with political authoritarians. They cannot refute Common Sense, but they can suppress it—for a time. Jesus is put to death in punishment for making others come alive; Tiresias is blinded in punishment for seeing and (by his verdict) making others see. A last parallel between Jesus Christ and Tiresias is subtle: only in the ultimate struggle, only in being overpowered, do they come to fully own their power. Jesus becomes the Wounded Healer, Tiresias the Blind Seer.

Authoritarians have an almost seismographic sensitivity for subtle threats. And nothing threatens them more than human wholeness. Plato's *Symposium* tells how the gods felt threatened by the primeval humans, still whole as androgynous spheres. So, Zeus "cut them in two, like a sorb—apple which is halved for pickling, or as you might divide an egg with a hair..."[11] Be they olympian or human, autocrats will always try to destroy that androgynous wholeness which is the basis for overcoming social ills by Common Sense.

Referring to Plato's myth of the androgynous spheres, the poet Rilke sings of regaining wholeness not by looking for external complementation, but on the solitary path of authenticity.

> ... the gods long ago learned to dissemble halves ... nothing could ever again help us to fulfillment, except our own solitary course over the sleepless landscape.[12]

SELF-PLEASURING IS MORE (by D.A.S.)

While we now recognize that self-stimulation can play a very important role throughout our lives, self-pleasuring—as we conceive of it—is a much fuller expression of our sexual arousal. Indeed, we contend, it is its fulfillment.

It is rare in our tradition that any aspect of human sexuality is considered to have a spiritual dimension. Yet, in other traditions, this is not so seldom the case. A young friend spoke exquisitely of his experience after six years of Tibetan Buddhist practice. Although he was personally disinclined to call his experience "spiritual" or "religious" because of his negative association with these terms, what he described has often been so characterized. He was able to sustain a high level of sexual arousal for several hours during which time he felt he was in complete harmony with the cosmos, at home in the universe, and united with all other people on earth. He was able to continue this practice for several years.

That orgasm, however achieved, is an altered state of consciousness few would dispute, but that this state is—or can become—a spiritual experience, is a new consideration for most people in our tradition. Yet, some are willing to experiment. A young man writes of his attempts at self-pleasuring, "I try to harmonize mind and body . . . try to 'bring the identity stream into the body,'as Baker Roshi puts it. After all, I play with my penis, so why not take masturbation one step further?" Betty Dodson, an erotic artist and feminist, pursued the matter more rigorously. Together with researchers at Rutgers University, she discovered that the brain waves she emitted while self-pleasuring were identical to those emitted during meditation. She contends that masturbation is for her a form of meditation.

LESSONS FROM TANTRA (by D.A.S.)

In his analysis of Tantric Yoga, Alan Watts has some helpful insights on how it is that sexual arousal can be a means of achieving spiritual fulfillment. Perhaps these insights will apply to self-pleasuring as well. Watts contends that the major difference between orgasm as tension release and orgasm as spiritual ecstasy is the recognition and reception of the orgasm as a gift. As Watts observes:

> In Tantra the final release of orgasm, neither sought nor restrained, is simply allowed to "come" as even the popular expression suggests, from our intuitive knowledge that it is not a deed, but a gift and a grace. When this experience bursts in upon fully opened feeling, it is no mere "sneeze in the loins," releasing physical tension, it is an explosion whose outmost sparks are the stars . . . Only prejudice and insensitivity have prevented us from seeing that in any other circumstance such delight would be called mystical ecstasy.13

Orgasm as the result of self-pleasuring is also experienced as mystical ecstasy, but it is, perhaps, even more difficult to acknowledge because we think of such activity in terms of "grasping desire." The hand is ordinarily actively involved in the pursuit of such pleasure. We are physically straining to achieve orgasm—often under hurried circumstances. But does this have to be so? Ideally, in the classic Tantric posture the couple do nothing—aside from making contact with their genitals—to facilitate either intromission or orgasm. The penis erects, the vagina lubricates, and the two merge when both are ready. In some Tantric tradition, orgasm for the male is not encouraged—since this would spend his psychic yang energy—and so he strives to avoid orgasm or postpone it as long as possible. She, on the other hand, may be encouraged (as in Tibetan Tantra) to enjoy as many orgasms as possible (with a partner or through self-pleasuring) because it is thought that this will increase her yin energy.

In either case, the objective is not tension reduction, but the experience of mystical ecstasy orgasm that transcends itself. In Watts' view, this comes about when the pleasure of the experience is not grasped but received as a gift. The Tantric partners are then—for each other—the Goddess and the God. They enter—through their sexual union—into a much higher state of consciousness than they could have achieved through their individual and separate efforts.

The same experience of having received a gift can occur during self-pleasuring. The very limited accounts that we are free to draw upon suggest that self-pleasuring is, in fact, a means of experiencing mystical ecstasy for some people. We have no way of knowing how widespread this experience is. For the moment, it is enough to know that it is possible—if we believe our respondents.

PRIMAL SEXUALITY, MYSTICAL RAPTURE, AND ASCETICISM (by D.S.R.)

Throughout all phases of life, sexuality in all its forms retains an echo of our primordial bliss as body conscious infants. We might call this ingredient primal sexuality. It is primal not only biographically, being the first aspect of sex we experience, but it continues to be primal or basic in all sexuality. Partner-directed sexuality is secondary relative to this primary one, because one cannot relate to another before one has a home base from which to reach out. Most children learn first to play by themselves with a ball before they can join in ball games with others. Even those who would insist that balls are made for playing with others will hardly insist on making solo ball playing illicit. People who enjoy ball playing at all get a great deal of enjoyment from just handling and tossing and catching the ball, both with a partner and alone. To the extent to which sex can be play in the best sense, this ball playing metaphor applies. Self-sex is our primal sexuality and remains primal.

Why then are most people so reluctant to speak about self-sex, even with intimate friends, often even with their sexual partners? There seem to be several reasons. We fear to appear infantile in this adult society; we have internalized parental disapproval of "playing with ourselves;" we have been programmed by public opinion to consider only the partner-directed side of sex "real" sex. But there is a deeper and more valid reason, I believe: A caring shyness guards our inner sanctuary from profanation, veiling it with silence. Primal sexuality and mystical rapture are nearly indistinguishable in the darkness of that sacred inner space. Both are represented by the Tiresian snake emblem.

Not by chance do all accounts agree that Tiresias saw the coupling snakes on Mount Cyllene. That mountain in Acadia is the reputed birthplace and earliest sanctuary of Hermes, the Olympian messenger. We all know his herald's staff (Hermes is later the Roman Mercury) with its two entwined serpents. On his *hermae*, phallic pillars erected in honor of Hermes as god of fertility, one finds those same serpents. They are related to the symbolic representation of kundalini as a snake coiled up upon itself in the form of a ring (*kundala*) at the base of the spine. This serpent ring takes also the archetypal form of the Ouroboros, the snake eating its own tail, "symbolic of self-fecundation or the primitive idea of self-sufficient nature. In Gnostic manuscripts, the Ouroboros expresses the unity of all things and sometimes bears the inscription (*Hen to pan*, 'The One, the all')."[14] When I think of kundalini representing all this cosmic power as lying coiled up within myself, waiting to be actualized, I begin to feel the way I felt as a child when passing by one of those high-voltage switchboxes marked with a red lightening bolt and the word "Danger!" The difference is that now I myself am that switch box.

Our sexual inscape reveals not only primordial bliss, but also primordial terror. This is expressed in graphic form in the Gnostic Ouroboros.

> Half of this mythic being is dark and the other half light (as in the Chinese Yang-Yin symbol), which clearly illustrates the essential ambivalence of the snake in that it pertains to both aspects of the cycle (the active and the passive, the affirmative and the negative, the constructive and the destructive).[15]

No wonder we tremble before the mythic monster in our own inner depth. Norse mythology knows that the serpent Midgardsormr encircling our world may at any moment awaken and destroy the universe. No wonder we are afraid to stir it, to speak of it, to even think of it. But are we to fear our inner snake-power itself or rather its abuse? And is there a more perilous danger than repressive rejection from consciousness?

Our perplexity finds expression in the complex term "lust." Fascinating discoveries await us when we begin to disentangle its conceptual knot and trace its threads to their linguistic origins. When we use the word "lust," that "question-begging word,"[16] as Alan Watts calls it, two notions tend to get confused in our minds: pleasure and wantonness. The word "lust" used to mean delight and relish as it still does in German, but its meaning kept sliding towards lewdness and lechery. Why? Lust is desire; but desire can miss its mark. To desire means literally "to long for a star (*sidus*)"—the star of your unique identity. Behind this stands medieval cosmology. Every plant was thought to have its star, the one to which its seed responded, the star whose light made it grow into its unique shape. The seed within us desires to respond to our star, yet we may be mislead by a mirage.

Wantonness goes astray for lack of guidance. That is exactly what the word "wanton" means. Its "wan" part indicates a lack. (It is related to words like "vacant, waste," and "void"). The syllable "ton" indicates what is lacking, namely guidance, a tug in the right direction. (Cognate words are "tug, conduct," and "educate.") Thus, lust is neither vicious nor virtuous. It desires pleasure, it can stray into wantonness. What it needs in order to reach its "unreachable star" is guidance.

What shall guide our innermost desire? The answer is obedience. But let me quickly add that obedience does not simply mean following orders. That is merely a "method" by the same name, a means by which, if all goes well, one learns that real obedience which is the goal. And all goes well only when those who give orders use their authority to build up those who follow orders. To build them up means to encourage them to listen ever so carefully both to their own deepest desire and to the circumstances through which "the star" speaks. For this is obedience in the full sense; the literal meaning of the word is "thorough listening." To listen thoroughly means listening in two directions; inward, to find ourselves, and outward, to find the way. If we miss the one or the other, let us not blame lust, but our lack of alertness in guiding lust through obedience. The world we humans have created is full of mirages; let's face it. We need to be alert. But the word "lust" keeps perpetuating the confusion between pleasure and wantonness, between the star and the mirage. Both the star and the mirage, both our goal and our trap, are on the outside. Within us is the snake-power of desire longing for the star, for that true and ultimate pleasure which, as the Latin root suggests, stills our desire. The word "lust" deceptively insinuates that our desire itself is to blame, that it is necessarily disobedient, deaf from birth. And so it incites us to kill our desire, the driving force of our quest, instead of guiding it. That would be like blaming your feet for going astray and cutting them off.

Christian tradition at its best has always upheld the original goodness of our innermost being, which gets tempted from the outside, gets wounded, and weakened by going astray, but deep down there remains good. Jesus appeals to that innermost goodness. Only preachers sometimes taint us with innermost rottenness.

The more we accept the original blessing that we humans are alive with God's own lifebreath (Gen. 2:7), the more we will be ready for both the mystical experience and primal sexuality—indeed for the possibility of mystical rapture through primal sexuality. There exists a close link between pushing mysticism out of reach for "ordinary people" and repressing authentic sexuality. To affirm "the antecedence of the couple over the individual"[17] as a translation of the Otherness of God into ethical terms, springs from absolutizing that Otherness. God is not only the transcendent Other—the Star beyond all stars of our desire—but God (as immanent) is "closer to me than I am to myself."[18] We owe this expression of mystic insight to no other than St. Augustine.

It is true that partner-directed sexuality can become mystically transparent for our relationship to God as the altogether Other. But it is equally true that primal sexuality can become mystically transparent for the divine Self-awareness within us. Love is our existential "yes" to belonging. This "yes" addressed to God embraces not only all others, but myself.

Self-love of this kind is not narcissistic; it is Tiresian, if you wish. Narcissus and Tiresias are mythic counterparts. The mother of Narcissus, Leiriope, is the first one ever to consult Tiresias for an oracle. (Such firsts often underline importance in a myth.)

Tiresias completely comprehends the entanglement of the boy, for he himself has pulled through. "Narcissus will live to a ripe old age," the Tiresian oracle pronounces, "provided that he never knows himself." We have to choose between knowing ourselves, knowing our true Self, or not knowing at all. Not knowing, we are dead; knowing (merely) ourselves kills us; knowing our true Self, we die—into fullness of life. Water is here,

as so often, the symbol of life (and death; for they are insepa-
rable).

Narcissus owes his very conception to water, when the
River God Cephissus ravishes the blue Nymph Leiriope in an
embrace of rushing water. The spring water, on the surface of
which Narcissus sees himself mirrored and falls in love with his
own image, becomes his doom. Yet he does not drown. He never
plunges into the death- and life-giving water. He plunges a
dagger into his own heart, and his blood splatters on dry
ground, making narcissus flowers spring up. Tiresias also dies
at a spring. In flight from Thebes, the old man pauses to drink at
the spring of Tilphussa. Day is dawning. Drinking he dies.

It opens new vistas if we dare to see in this drinking from
the spring Tiresias' final and complete acceptance of primal
sexuality and mystical rapture, both in one. But our age has no
eyes for the inscape of sex, only for its outer landscape. Not
Tiresias but Hercules is our model. Flaunting his brute, macho
strength, Hercules seeks immortality though prodigious labors.
In his infancy, he too, encountered the two serpents. But at once
Hercules strangled them both.

Is it too far fetched to see in Hercules the man who cannot
accept his primal sexuality? Thus, he goes from one amorous
adventure to another, like us. He kills his wife and children in a
fit of madness, like us. And to get out of his burning skin which
he cannot stand any longer, he has himself burnt alive. Like us?
One of Tiresias' last oracles concerns Hercules, just as his first
one concerned Narcissus, and his most famous one, Oedipus.
The question is: what shall be done with the two serpents the
child has strangled? The serpents are to be burnt (as Hercules
will burn), and the place is to be purified with water from the
spring.

Fire transforms. The serpent, too, is a symbol of transformation. Those who do not yield to the inner serpent-power, will
be transformed by fire.

"We only live, only suspire / consumed by either fire or fire,"
says T.S. Eliot in a passage behind which stands the mythic
imagery which we have been invoking here.[19] Transformation in
the realm of our primal sexuality is both discovery and ascetical
task. Lack of space allows me to offer only a few illustrations;
First, transformation through discovery:

> How shall I ever forget the strange, inexplicable rapture of my first
> experience? What marvelous thing was this that suddenly trans-
> formed a mere water tap into a pillar of fire—and water into an

elixir of life? I lived henceforth in a strange world of contradiction: something was called filthy which was obviously clean; something was called ridiculous which was obviously solemn and momentous; something was called ugly which was obviously lovely. Strange days and nights of mystery and fear mixed with excitement and wonder.[20]

I discovered masturbation accidently when I was thirteen, up in a tree, of all places. It was totally unexpected. From the beginning, I have accepted masturbation simply as an exciting thing to do and, luckily, I have never suffered any qualms or guilt about it. You could say it's a spiritual thing, going beyond the usual confines of consciousness. Sometimes this is most powerful when movement is kept to a minimum, allowing awareness of more subtle sensations to build. At its most intense, there is a feeling of being united with the cosmos, that fundamental whatever-it-is which keeps us all going. The wonderful thing is that I can do this for myself.[21]

The question is, how? Not every orgasm is a mystic experience, just as not every liturgy is. Nonetheless, like liturgy, it points toward that possibility. Whether we reach the unreachable star depends on our inner attitude. The gift we try to clutch and grasp dies in our hands like a fragile butterfly. The gift to which we respond in gratefulness, never ceases to grow and to make us grow.

How are we to translate this attitude into practical action? Margo Woods says in simple terms what seems essential. It appears grotesque that our ancient celibate tradition in the West did not come up with anything but prohibitions that cause inhibitions, not even with the most basic advice of this kind.

Raising the body's sexual energy almost to the point of orgasm, instead of letting the energy go out into the orgasm, allow it to come up in the body, up to the heart. If you rest at that point and put your attention in your heart, the energy which has been generated will flow naturally upwards toward the heart. You don't have to do anything; it just happens. Turn yourself on. Then raise the sexual energy up in your body—to the heart. This path to ecstasy is natural and simple and available to all human beings. It is like a water faucet that has been shut off so long it has rusted. It may take a bit of effort at first to turn it on; but the water is still there, just waiting to be released. When the heart is open, when love is flowing, the possible evils of a strong sexual drive are eliminated because the heart listens. It is stronger than the sexual drive and directs it toward the highest good.[22]

The heart listens. That is the essence of obedience. The heart stands for the whole person; not only our emotions but also our will and our intellect; mind and body. Obedience as heart-listening is, therefore, the same as mindfulness—with emphasis on fullness. It takes our undivided effort to reach our star. Only the mindfulness of this wholehearted listening is able to direct the serpent power of primal sexuality towards the highest good.

But where does the power to listen originate? It is God's gift, I as a Christian say with conviction. We must distinguish the gift (*gratia*) of this listening-power from the serpent-power of our inborn vitality (our *vigor naturae*); Augustine was right in this and the fouth-century British ascetic Pelagius was wrong. Yet we must never separate the two. And in this regard Augustine was wrong and Pelagius was right. By God's pure grace our inborn vitality is graced with listening-power, if only we will show ourselves grateful for this gift by using it. The Ouroboric serpent ring is half light, half dark. The snake is credited with power to both kill and cure. It is at this asymptotic point that the parallels of Christ and Tiresias converge in mystic paradox.

Plague has descended upon Thebes. The Delphic Oracle, consulted how the plague can be stopped, replies: "Expel the murderer of Laius!" Oedipus pronounces a curse on Laius' murderer and sentences him to exile. But who is that guilty one? All are expecting the answer from Tiresias. It is the climax of his career. At this point Athena takes the serpent Erichthonius from her aegis and commands him: "Cleanse Tiresias's ear with your tongue!" In archaic pictures, this is a serpent-child peeping from under the goddess's shield. It is in the power of the serpent-child, then, that Tiresias listens and speaks. But this power is here mastered by the command of Athena Parthenos, the virgin goddess of wisdom. This mastery constitutes asceticism at its best.

The essence of asceticism is obedience. In Biblical terms: "Obedience is better than sacrifice" (1 Sam. 15:22). The Psalmist replies with a verse which tradition has put on the lips of Jesus Christ: "You, who wanted no sacrifice or oblation, opened my ear . . . . I am coming to obey" (Ps. 40:6 and 8). Obedience is the chief characteristic of Jesus Christ, the New Adam, in contrast to the Old Adam. The Serpent in Paradise suggested to Adam a usurpation of the godlikeness he held already as a promise that would unfold in good time. Adam is presented like a child that will not wait for the bud to open, but spoils it by pulling the petals apart. He was not obedient. He did not filter the voice of the Serpent through a listening heart. The New Adam did, as we learn from Phil. 2:6ff.

The choice between these two attitudes always challenges us. Life, real aliveness, is not something we automatically have by being born. We have to "choose life" (Deut. 30:19). The Circled Serpent is two-colored; it represents both life and death. To choose life means, paradoxically, readiness to die—into ever new dimensions of aliveness. One cannot remain in the original equilibrium of ouroboric bliss. Not to clutch and grasp at pleasure, but to give ourselves willingly to life in its fullness means "obedience unto death, death on a cross" (Phil. 2:00)—whatever our personal cross may be.

The polar opposite to the serpent circle is the crucified serpent; the broken ring, stretched out on the two intersecting cross beams; the circle cancelled by the X of contradiction. We know this figure from the Bible as the bronze serpent (Num. 21:4-9.) It is, like Athena's Erichthonius, the snake empowered to both kill and cure. "As Moses raised up the serpent in the desert," so Jesus will have to be raised up (John 3:14). "But when I am raised up from the earth" (on the cross), "then I will draw all things to myself" (John 12:32), restoring the original harmony on a completely new level.

Erich Neumann has shown how the great life task of personal unfolding follows this universal pattern. From ouroboric pre-consciousness through differentiation and polarization, culminating in the life/death struggle of the hero, to a psychic synthesis in the second half of life, "frequently accompanied by symbols representing the new unity of opposites. . . . The hermaphroditic nature of the ouroboros reappears here on a new level."[23]

In the last stanza of the poem that started with childhood's "winged energy of delight," Rilke places the life task of uniting opposites squarely into the context of mysticism:

> Take your practiced powers and stretch them out until they span
> the chasm between two contradictions . . . For the god wants to
> know himself in you.[24]

This is the goal of asceticism.

A NEW KIND OF ASCETICISM (by D.A.S.)

It is evident that self-stimulation is not automatically a means of grace. As most often experienced, it is probably simply tension reduction—"a sneeze in the loins." For self-stimulation to become self-pleasuring—the enjoyment and fulfillment of our own sexual arousal—it must be properly celebrated. To do this we must be trained to appreciate the depth dimension in such an earthy act. Tantric Yoga can offer helpful insights for such training, but a different orientation to self-stimulation is required.

At minimum such training should include practice in defusing the state of arousal from the genitals to the entire body. A whole-hearted commitment to the enjoyment of our embodiment is required. Rather than simply tolerating our bodies as prisons of our souls, or at best as dull tools for working in the world, we can learn to celebrate them as sensitively tuned instruments for the expression of love incarnated. Guided imagery might be useful in shaping genuinely erotic (as opposed to simply pornographic) fantasies that explore our appreciation of loving.

The experience of wholeness—of mystical ecstasy—should become a source of strength and energy for going out into the world and living out of a sense of greater abundance in our daily lives. Many of the problems of the sexual revolution arise from increased sexual activity without a commensurate understanding of the nature and source of erotic love. Relationships based on the need for sexual gratification are based on a feeling of scarcity rather than an awareness of the abundance of this form of love. Self-pleasuring can help to restore a sense of abundance.

In so far as self-pleasuring can increase self-esteem, it reduces our dependence on status—enhancing conspicuous consumption and, therefore, can assist us to live more lightly on the earth. Such self-pleasuring is a genuine form of sexual liberation—a freeing of the human spirit for more creative, caring involvement in the world. As such, it is genuinely Christian—though not yet recognized as such.

TOWARDS LIBERATING THE
SEXUAL REVOLUTION (by D.S.R.)

These few concluding remarks presuppose all we have said before. They want to point in the direction of a task to which our insights challenge us. As Margo Woods observes:

> We are not an erotic society no matter how many half-clothed women are displayed on billboards, no matter how many fortunes are made in sex magazines . . . In so far as you don't like your body, you freeze your sexual energy . . . Relearn your own body. The pleasure you experience will do more to work against your negative

> conditioning about your body and your sexuality than anything else you can do or think . . . The Sexual Revolution has taken place. What remains is to connect the genitals to the heart; to bring sex and love together . . . . The secret of opening your erotic nature is to make love to yourself.[25]

As our primary sexuality, self-sexuality is a psychological dimension of every sexual activity and unites all sexual persuasions. Genuine sexual liberation stands and falls with autosexuality.

The highest level of sexual experience is wholeness, mystic communion with self, with all others, with the cosmos, and with the divine Ground of Being. This experience is not restricted to sex with a partner, nor does the presence of a partner assure openness for it. Openness for this gift depends on discovering and cultivating ones' sexual inscape through psycho-physical training. The need for training of this kind is especially urgent during adolescence and in celibate life. This calls for developing methods, which in Western society are still almost completely lacking. Not only have we failed to raise sexuality methodically to higher spiritual levels; we have instead multiplied prohibitions that inhibit this development.

But, as St. Paul explains, "for freedom Christ has set us free" (Gal. 5:1a). There is a great deal more at stake in sexual liberation than taking away the stigma from autosexuality. Yet, historically this issue has become a pivotal point. Here, public opinion, shaped by medical, ecclesiastical, and pedagogical authoritarians is most at odds with Common Sense. Here self-hatred, rooted in that contempt of our bodies drummed into us from infancy, has its strongest foothold. That is the reason why the next step forward in sexual liberation must be made here. Authoritarian repression may be expected to increase, however, according to the measure in which genuine freedom gains ground.

Because autosexuality remains a pivot of psychological oppression, it must be the concern of Christians whom Christ has set free and whom St. Paul alerts: "Stand fast therefore, and do not submit again to a yoke of slavery." (Gal. 5:1b) And because autosexuality is the starting point, if we want "to connect the genitals to the heart, to bring sex and love together," it must be a concern of every religious person. As Alan Watts reminds us:

> Without—in its true sense—the lustiness of sex, religion is joyless and abstract; without the self-abandonment of religion, sex is a mechanical masturbation.[26]

NOTES

1. Aurelius Augustinus, *In Joannem* 26:4.

2. Jack Mozin, *Men Loving Themselves* (Burlingame, Calif.: Down There Press, 1988), 93.

3. Margo Woods, *Masturbation, Tantra, and Self Love* (San Diego, Calif.: Omphaloskepsis Press, 1981), 31.

4. Betty Dodson, *Self love and Orgasm* (Published privately, 1983), 22.

5. William Wordsworth, "Ode: Intimations of Immortality," line 66. Note this whole section of the ode.

6. Margo Woods, op. cit., p. 44.

7. R. M. Rilke, "Da Dich das geflügelte Entzücken," in *The Selected Poetry of Rainer Maria Rilke*, edited and translated by Stephen Mitchell. (New York: Random House/Vintage Books, 1984), 261.

8. In Alan Shestack et.al., *Hans Baldung Grien: Prints and Drawings* (Washington, D.C.: National Gallery of Art, 1981), 131.

9. Eric Gill, *Autobiography* (New York: The Devin-Adair Company, 1942), 46.

10. Robert Graves, *The Greek Myths* (New York: Penguin Books, 1986), Vol. II, 11, #105j.

11. Plato, Symposium, #190, in *The Dialogues of Plato*, translated by B. Jowett. (New York: Random House, 1937), Vol I, 317.

12. R. M. Rilke, "Elegie," in *The Selected Poetry of Rainer Maria Rilke*, edited and translated by Stephen Mitchell. (New York: Random House/ Vintage Books, 1984), 291.

13. Alan Watts, *Nature, Man, and Woman* (London: Abacus, 1976), 154.

14. Juan Edwardo Cirlot, *A Dictionary of Symbols* (New York: Philosophical Library, 1962), s.v. "Ouroboros," 235.

15. Ibid., s.v. "Serpent," 274.

16. Alan Watts, op. cit., 153.

17. "Biblical tradition translated the revelation of the otherness of God into ethical terms by affirming that it signified the antecedence of the couple over the individual as a sexual being." Eric Fuchs, *Sexual Desire and Love: Origins and History of the Christian Ethic of Sexuality and Marriage* (New York: Seabury Press, 1983), 176.

18. Aurelius Augustinus, *The Confessions*, Bk. III, ch. 6.

19. T. S. Eliot, *Four Quartets* (New York: Harcourt, Brace and World, Inc., 1971), "Little Gidding," IV:212f.

20. Eric Gill, op. cit., 47.

21. Jack Mozin, op. cit., 39f.

22. Margo Woods, op. cit., 27, 107, and 103.

23. Erich Neumann, *The Origins and History of Consciousness* (Princeton, N.J.: Princeton University Press, Bollingen Series XLII, 1972), 414.

24. See R.M. Rilke, op. cit.
25. Margo Woods, op. cit., 106, 27, 28, 102, and 107.
26. Alan Watts, op. cit., 154.

If masturbation is deemed controversial by some, homosexuality is an even riskier subject for the clergy to address. Theologian Dody Donnelly, however, has done just that in her compelling book Radical Love, from which the essay "Homosexuality and Radical Love" is excerpted. In her outspoken way, she sums up her position as follows: "I suspect that God is not upset about homosexuality; but we are. Nor does God, though responsible for sexuality itself, seem a bit guilty about it. The embodied, ensexed human models keep right on coming into this world." It is impossible to do justice to the enormously complex issue of homosexuality in the context of this anthology. But in this piece Donnelly reminds us that "radical love" is nonexclusive and unencumbered by a society's preferred historical forms of behavior. In our quest for spiritual enlightment, we must inevitably examine the psychological roots of our sexual preferences and also overcome our sexual and emotional neuroses — all those self-limiting, egoic patterns that prevent us from being real and whole. Homosexuality, like heterosexuality, can turn out to be just such a neurotic trait. It can also turn out to be part of who we are when we are not neurotic. Regardless of our preferred or destined sexual character, however, we are all challenged by those spiritual traditions that ask us to convert sexual pleasure into erotic ecstay and enlightenment.

HOMOSEXUALITY AND RADICAL LOVE †

By Dody Donnelly, Ph.D.

As he picked up the teacup, Tony's hand shook a bit, and his voice was too loud in a nonstop stream of talk. I had been his friend and counselor for three years, so I plunged in. "Tony, what's on your mind?" The cup bounced as he set it down hard with a relieved sigh and blurted, "I thought you'd never ask!"

I laughed in reply and he went on. "You know, ordination is three weeks away, and I need to talk to somebody about this, because I can't keep going over it in my head." He hesitated; then: "I'm gay and I haven't been able to share that with anybody on the ordination committee, and now I don't know if that's dishonest or not. If I do come out of the closet, they won't ordain me, I'm sure." Tony's words poured out in a painful torrent, and the tears weren't far behind.

Why would this thirty-year-old have to hide his sexual orientation from even his closest friends and mentors? Because of society's fear of a sexuality that might be "different." Ministers and priests are supposed to be "holy" people; a sexual preference other than heterosexual is inappropriate for them, though intercourse in heterosexual marriage is permitted for ministers. But many Christian theologians hold that it belongs only there in marriage, with no extramarital activity if we are to be "moral." And as for the gay-lesbian orientation itself? Not "normal," especially for people thinking of the ministry. How could they possibly help others with their sexual problems?

Tony was ordained after a painful encounter with the ordination committee, and he later found the counseling he wanted. But when he met his parish they couldn't accept a gay minister, so he had to leave the congregation. Today he's on the national staff of his denomination.

Behind his story lie all the old questions: What is sexuality? What constitutes "normal" sexuality? What does sexuality mean for becoming a complete human being? What does God think about sex? And, especially, what's the purpose of it all: sex, spirit, thought, labor? What's it all about, Alfie?

---

† Chapter six from *Radical Love* by Dorothy Donnelly. © 1984 by Dorothy Donnelly. Reprinted by permission of Harper & Row, Publishers, Inc.

What fascinates me about Tony's story and its outcome are the strong feelings and the violent actions provoked by his gay orientation, as if we had neatly packaged, adequate answers to those stiff questions above. Alive and well was a "theology of arrogance" that decided and acted with absolute surety about matters that still perplex the best scientists—and saints!

Examining the assumptions of that theology, we find a distortion of the importance of heterosexual genital married activity that turns it into a mechanical performance of the only permitted kind. We thereby sin against truth and tolerance because we don't have all the data in on what constitutes "normal" sexual conduct; we don't know enough to make a definitive moral judgment about *all* forms of sexual conduct. So we end up exploiting, manipulating, and misusing sexuality, strangling its coflowering with the spirit. Idolizing heterosexual intercourse as the sole criterion of normal sexual relationship is another instance of the pornographic mind because it emphasizes one expression of sexuality as the only valid vehicle for love.

In selecting and living out a sexual lifestyle, how can we avoid this arrogance and still evaluate critically the various styles available to us today? Tony's congregation, for instance, saw his orientation as immoral; Tony himself did not. What criteria were used? How can we decide among so many conflicting opinions, dogmas, and pronouncements, often made with fierce certainty?

In our time, sex is often a matter of jokes, fear, and guilt, rather than an expression of joyful, caring love. We know, too, that the misdirected power of sexual feeling can explode into anger and panic rather than be released as liberating, sensuous enjoyment. So the questions and the answers are pushed by the pressure of actual crises, difficult decisions, and the need for certainty.

Consequently, many of us have learned not to rejoice in the ecstasy of oneness that sexuality can bring, not to understand it as training in becoming a feeling, loving friend, as Jesus is. Sexuality is an education in how to be human, how to be open and vulnerable, not hiding behind façades and pride; it opens us to growth and learning how to love. Yet some writers have, through their pronouncements, made it into a most dangerous activity. Books of moral theology (ethics) are still often about what not to do in order not to sin.

Moral decisions are often made in the name of religion. Yet valid religious experience is, first of all, human experience.

Historically, we've learned to call religious those parts of life that are mysterious, beyond comprehension, because they are so other. They send us in search of the sacred and the transcendent. Calling ourselves religious but denying these dimensions of life makes us the opposite. And in the opinion of Anthony Padavano, if one responds to these aspects of life, even if not as a member of a formal religion, one thereby becomes religious.

All valid religious experience sends us on a search for two precious jewels: freedom and fidelity—excellent criteria for judging the worth of our decisions. Freedom is the right and ability to do what we feel we must do to be human. Fidelity finds us using freedom to be what we choose to be even though others may not agree with how we interpret that choice.

Freedom and fidelity serve our goal of becoming radical lovers. The agony and ecstasy of good decision making means using freedom in search of a commitment to what makes our life meaningful. Chosen commitments free us and allow us to stop thrashing about, never arriving at God's heart within our own. Commitment centers our energies and releases them for action.

Radical love implies a use of faithful freedom with these criteria in mind: presence to and respect for our friends, caring for their integrity, and the giving and receiving of self in concern in order to live as Jesus did. These criteria for faithful, loving decision making would seem to apply to any lifestyle, any sexuality. Love is the central tenet of Christianity. Are we to assume that homosexuals/bisexuals don't or can't so love? Can't, then, be Christian?

Love as humanizer can make sexuality a powerful aid for living in faithful freedom, just as love must sometimes humanize spirit to integrate its kind of response to God's call. Here the possible meaning of our individual uniqueness, our See-Levels, becomes clearer. God seems to be in love with difference; He makes so much of it! Not one of us is like any other. Our God is not threatened by different ways to express his gift to us of human sexuality. Our God is so messy. He so loves variety!

But a difference in sexual expression can threaten us; we don't have a God's eye-view just yet. In fact, one sign of growth in breadth of personality is that ability to include more and more different others in our acceptance range. The size of our character thereby grows, and so does our capacity to love. Jesus was a totally actualized person with a full-size personality. He could tolerate incredible differences and uniqueness; he seemed to thrive on it, for in it he saw his Father's hand, his endless creativity: endless varieties of lovers in our endless varieties of human personality so that we can uniquely care for one another.

We can relate God's tolerance for difference to the question of the morality of homosexual orientations. We're persons with particular sexual orientations, preferences, and types of activity. Gay-lesbian *orientation*, then, does not mean inordinate, subnormal sexual activity any more than does heterosexual. Each of us loves uniquely, shaping our sexual-spiritual lives with our God-given powers. To respect that variety, we need to say "homosexualities," because differences are just as prevalent among gays and lesbians as in the "straight" community. Some gays are faithful, some are not; some gays are wanting in commitment and faithful freedom, some are not. So also for the lesbian orientation.

As our homosexual brothers and sisters publicly declare their orientation, church and society must come to terms with these issues of justice, love, and respect for difference. We need an ethics and a moral theology based on the actual sexual human situation and not on assumptions and mythology from the past. In the light of our ignorance of what constitutes normal human sexuality, can we continue to make definitive moral judgments about what we don't completely understand?

For example, biology and genetics still debate over sex differentiation and no one knows definitely if homosexual tendencies are innate, learned, or induced by hormonal triggers.

For more data for the study of psychospiritual life we may look to brain research in the nineties. Yet the psychological researchers still give differing answers to questions basic to decisions about sexuality. Is the brain different in men and women? If so, at what stage of development does it become so? Is sexual orientation a matter of nature or nurture? Are people gay or lesbian because of how nature shaped them or because of conditioning?

The hypothalamus is differently sexed, according to Prof. Diane McGuinness of the University of California, Santa Cruz. She feels it's almost certainly differently stamped before birth by sex hormones that develop at puberty. We also know from Stanford University researchers that some sex differences seem to be independent of culture—for example, the ways information is gathered and problems are solved. In the brain, they feel, from the beginning are woman's sensitivity to sound and people and man's interest in objects, spatial dimension, light, and patterns.

Yet research indicates that these statistical differences between males and females are extremely minor compared with differences among people of the same sex. In fact, eighty to ninety-five percent of all variations observed among people occur among men as a group, and among women as a group.

If we apply this information to the question of gay-lesbian orientation, cut-and-dried statements or decisions do not seem to fit that orientation—any more than they fit heterosexuals' activity sexually. Some counselors say that their gay-lesbian clients are merely confused; others, that they have "castration anxiety" or fear of female genitals. Yet many homosexual people also engage in heterosexual intercourse. They have, perhaps, then, a bisexual orientation, one that may someday prove characteristic of many people—depending on how we as a society and as church develop our attitudes about the purpose and meaning of sexuality.

Trying to gather some fairly reliable data, then, is the first step in making a moral judgment about anything, not just sex. And clear data seem hard to come by, since some scientists claim homosexuality is a disease; others, a brain-induced condition; and still others, arrested development, hormonal imbalance, or just plain conditioning.

However, the 1981 Kinsey Report from Indiana University shows that homosexuality may be determined at birth by biology and that about ten percent of all children are born with a strong "gender nonconformity," a failure to like what others of their sex like. It's not learned, contrary to the findings of the 1979 Masters and Johnson study.

The Kinsey group found that homosexuality cannot be traced to a psychological social pressure but is a "very deeply rooted set of impulses and yearnings . . . needs and feelings," with the signs showing as early as four years old.

Important for the moral question is the 1965 Kinsey Report on sex offenders, however. It found that the use of force is rare among gays and lesbians; it seems to be a prerogative mainly of heterosexuals.

These findings work against our tendency to lump all of humanity into polar opposites: homosexual and heterosexual. Yet an early Kinsey Report in 1948 on sexuality among American males showed a wide continuum from exclusively heterosexual to exclusively homosexual behavior. Sexual preference can be rated on the same scale as behavior. But the two are not always in line. All of us need to restore wholeness and consistency between what we really prefer and how we behave sexually. The old performance-syndrome really operates here. That's why a number one question in counseling always is: "What do you really want?" Seeing all sexual lifestyles along a wide continuum of preference and behavior, and not cut into two varieties only, can eliminate ideas that gays and lesbians are wholly different from everyone else, a "they" as opposed to "us." Christianity, in its finest hour, knows no stranger, no "they." Our present period could be one of those hours for the churches and society as well, a chance for growth and understanding through permitting what we now call "difference," allowing for a pluralism in sexual lifestyles in a nation committed to pluralism, and thus not judging before the time.

Yet church people along with the general population are afraid of the gay-lesbian lifestyle and ask, How can gays and lesbians live their love of God and neighbor in a holistic spirituality? In a church? Yes, of course, they can and they do. Many of them are, of course, open, generous, compassionate, kindly people serving church and society every day. They have been for years, and centuries!

A few criteria for determining sexual right and wrong in a given situation may help. Long ago Thomas Aquinas summarized centuries of moral thinking in a threefold standard for judging behavior: (1) done for the right purpose; (2) done with the right person (spouse!); (3) done in the right way (heterosexual intercourse). On December 1, 1983, the new Vatican statement on sex appeared, repeating over and over that love is to be the characteristic of authentic sex, with personal maturity the goal of "rightful sexual communion." "Sexuality, oriented, elevated and integrated by love . . . is achieved in the full sense only with the realization of affective maturity."

The document shows some real changes since Aquinas's position above. For him, sex "for the right purpose" meant just one thing: procreation. But the 1983 document feels that sexual intercourse has a twofold value: an intimate communion of love between the couple, and the fostering of children, with unity ahead of fecundity this time! It recognizes, too, the great challenge involved in integrating one's sexuality and spirituality, the demanding work of fusing genitality, eroticism, and love.

Homosexuality, however, is still described in the document as impeding the person's acquisition of sexual maturity, and not a likely path to sexual integration. So the documents come and go in a long line of statements about how to live our sexual, moral lives. We respect their wisdom, but we are left with our conscience in our hands, as Thomas More put it, and we are responsible for deciding.

So, back to decision making! We should remember one point exemplified above: there are no "pure" facts; the facts are always somewhat inadequate. Waiting until one is absolutely certain is fruitless and frustrating; it can also be avoidance, for not to decide is also a decision. Every moral judgment and decision is an experiment. So we gather what data we can humanly obtain, then we ask about the *motive*: Why should I do or not do this? Then comes my *intention*: What do I desire to attain in this act? And, finally, the *results*: What will be the consequences and how am I responsible for them? So we can bring sexual intercourse into some focus by evaluating it according to these three questions and the always relevant question: How does this act fulfill my commitment to live Jesus' value system? How just is it? How loving?

Another listing of questions can throw light on the dark areas of our decision in a given situation:

- What is the *normal* behavior about this question in this society? Is it changing now? What data do we have? What biases and prejudices exist? Input from culture, science.
- What do the *laws* say about it? Are they changing? Input from codes.
- What does our own *conscience* have to say about it? Consulting with others?
- What does *God* seem to think about it when we ask in prayer? When we are still and listen? In Scripture?

Applying these questions for ethical decisions to sexual orientation or activity can be helpful, for they push us to be honest—the bottom line, the real pain level in trying to decide. We try to see the truth as best we can, after thought, consultation, prayer, looking into God's eyes to see if we can borrow some of his enormous tolerance for difference—even our own! We use in adult fashion that conscience of ours, the meeting place for ethics and morality. It brings intuition and reason together with contemplative listening to God, and that is the best try we humans can make. But that best try presupposes the daily habit of asking God for the gift of discernment or right decision, a gift of understanding God wants to give us.

Getting our conscience in shape through consulting God daily about everything, not just sexual decisions, enables us to operate in the new, truly pluralistic world that's being born. Tolerant of difference, prayer deepens a radical love that embraces the lover's uniqueness and holds us to a commitment to faithful loving. It teaches us how to select and live our sexual orientation with justice and love. It leads us to examine any theological basis that works against acceptance and tolerance for the orientations of others—especially because radical love accepts my neighbors as the actual persons they are. It takes a firm position of accepting their otherness, their right to be themselves, with a different See-Level from mine, a different way to see and interpret the world. It is radical because it cuts to the root (radix) of my unconscious demand that the neighbor be like me! Radical, too, because it allows them to be radically who they actually are, God's idea. To that we say Yes, no matter how hard that idea might be to understand—or embrace! No wonder Jesus was the truest of all revolutionaries: he taught radical love!

Practicing such a love begins with accepting where others really are. It means that some Christian theological teaching about homosexuality may need reexamination. The 1976 Catholic Bishops' letter "To Live in Christ Jesus" says, "Homosexual activity, however, as distinguished from homosexual orientation, is morally wrong." Activity is declared morally wrong because it's assumed that some kinds of homosexuality are curable. This attitude seems to ignore some of the data we've looked at above.

The letter says further that homosexual activity is not *natural* for anyone and is therefore not morally justified. Basic assumption: because "they lack an indispensable finality (biological procreation potential) these acts are intrinsically disordered and can in no way be approved." Yet in Catholic teaching since Vatican II, including the new 1983 letter, more than procreation may be intended in sexual activity: "an intimate communion of love between the couple." So why not a loving gay or lesbian couple?

Luther said well that the church is always having to be reformed, especially its theory of self and God. When they wrote their letter, the Catholic bishops started with an unproven assumption: that the only morally acceptable way of living one's sexual love was heterosexual and in marriage—because it's open to creating new life. They assumed they knew what "natural" sexuality was.

In an overpopulated world how strange is this emphasis on procreation! The Hebrew proscription of homosexuality implied that it was immoral because it did not provide new lives for the tribe. Implied in the bishops' letter, too, is a view of marriage as the only acceptable expression of genital sexuality, yet marriage is a social form rapidly changing today. More important, the letter seems to assume that *within* marriage moral violations of love are unknown: rape, physical abuse, spiritual and psychic violence. Are these moral aberrations to be preferred to sexual relations expressing love and commitment between loving persons of the same sex?

A more pluralistic spirituality needs an intelligent and humble theology that is aware of all available data, critical of its own historical assumptions, designed to promote love in the church community, and concerned about whether or not people are caring for one another. That theology will mean educating all of us through pulpit, radio, and television to speak out against the injustices rampant in sexism—including attacks against the homosexual person. Theology is finally beginning to be aware of the plight of women in the churches—another rampant form of sexism. But this skirmish is a fine preparation for taking on a bigger one: *all* sexual intolerance.

We need to say clearly that homosexuality is not sexual depravity freely chosen. Nor is it an infection passed on to young people. We must deny that all homosexuals are violent and given to crime. We need to welcome the homosexual sister or brother into Christian communities with the same social rights and privileges as any other member. Why are they forced to found their own "Christian" churches? Since when is one's sexual orientation the prime criterion for church membership?

Part of the agenda of all Christian churches struggling with shaping a theology of sexual love will have to be a close look at the present form of marriage—surely not the totally "Christian" lifestyle it's presumed to be. The report "Human Sexuality" of the Catholic Theological Society of America considers other morally acceptable expressions of the sexual-spiritual life besides today's heterosexual marriage form.

Again, such a critique needs valid criteria, whether we are examining a social form like marriage or a disease like sexism. The deepest criteria remain justice and love in the relationship, no matter which genders are involved. Truly moral relationships express mutual, non-coercive love, care, and respectful concern for growth in the integrity and personhood of the beloved. These form the basis for friendship and foster mutuality to help both partners grow more human and, so, more holy. The Society's report emphasizes the quality of the relationship as crucial: "Christian morality does not require a dual standard. Gays and lesbians enjoy the same rights and incur the same obligations as the heterosexual majority. They are required to examine and evaluate their behavior in the light of the same values and characteristics of wholesome human sexuality."

Some of these values and characteristics we've seen above, but we don't assume that we've got them all in a box. More work needs to be done: What is the purpose, the goal, the meaning of our being embodied, ensexed? Let's keep that open. Science can help us with data to reshape theology's basic assumptions; we've seen this in the change in Catholic thought from Aquinas to Vatican II. Just as political revolutionaries working toward human liberation in Nicaragua and El Salvador contribute their life experience of trying to live the gospel, so people there must translate the Scriptures for their kind of love story with God, their struggle to be faithful and free, to be human. Such people who try to be honest about what they experience, to call out that the emperor has no clothes, have always been the prophets for the rest of us too busy to notice. So Christian churches are now going through the process of using all these data to reshape their theories of sexual spirituality, marriage, woman's role, and human liberation.

In the past, churches have had to rethink and change their stand on slavery and on divorce. Now churches must rethink the question of war in a nuclear age. Again, we must ask the basics: What does human experience tell us about any sexual practice? What do married people—or singles (the neglected masses!)—tell us about the meaning of their sexual experience? This important data can shape a theology of *eros* to fit real human sexual experience with neighbor and God, not some preconceived textbook concept of what sexuality means. How can each of us take responsibility (move through our conversion experience) for mutual justice and love in our sexual lifestyle, no matter what its form? That is always the bottom line.

Out of the suffering of gay-lesbian communities today may come great insights for all of us. That lifestyle and orientation asks questions that have needed asking for centuries. What is *normal* sexuality? If we don't fully know, why do we beat, kill, or vilify people whose orientation is not ours? Fear? Panic?

Scapegoating? In living a Christian life, isn't faithful caring for another's good a more valid criterion than heterosexual intercourse? Jesus doesn't condemn sexual lifestyle; he is busy with more important things. He seems more interested in justice, care for others, responsible use of freedom, tolerance for difference, openness to risk and sharing, and the ability to recognize our own trapped narrowness, prejudice, and bigotry. Sin to him is alienation from one another and God, refusing to allow anyone different views, customs, lifestyles, refusing to experience life or to grow, change, fail, and meet God in the world. Sexual love for him is part of the gift of life to be used, like every gift, with responsibility for practicing justice and love toward oneself and the beloved.

Today's sexual revolution implies a discontent, in spite of some of its negative features, with the assumptions of sexual right and wrong inherited from 2,000 years of ethical moral decisions usually handed down by celibate males. In a world freezing to death for lack of love, how ridiculous to insist that there is only one legitimate way to express sexual love! Jesus' command to love one another doesn't describe one particular sexual expression. The witness of many faithful, loving relationships of gays and lesbians today, then, may be God's way of making us examine some assumptions about sexuality, love, marriage, and spirituality. If we assume we're here on earth to learn how to accept and give love, their experience can be valuable additional data about what love can mean.

Today many Christian gay and lesbian couples bring to their church communities their desire to make a commitment to one another and to ratify it before a community in a "holy union." Can we assume that God is displeased with that? I suspect that God is not upset about homosexuality; but we are. Nor does God, though responsible for sexuality itself, seem a bit guilty about it. The embodied, ensexed human models keep right on coming into this world.

Gay and lesbian holy unions are a type of marriage expressing the same goals as heterosexual ones—faithful love and commitment in a just, loving relationship. Trouble with this notion may come because we assume that Christian heterosexual marriage has always been as we know it. Yet it was not until the Council of Trent (1565) that the church declared a Christian ceremony necessary for a valid marriage!

We can question the present social form of heterosexual marriage, its roots and evolution: can its troubles indicate its imminent change into multiple forms of expression, and not one solely acceptable form? The roots of marriage lie in the early church reacting to cultural pressures to combine Jewish, Greek, and Indian ideas of marriage. The church preserved the legal familial marriage and made it monogamous. So the church outlawed divorce, and illogically enough, forbade concubinage, combining Jewish insistence on procreation and Greco-Indian ideas of sexual abstinence in a "Christian" form of marriage. We confused the state of chastity (an ideal of the time) with the profane arranged institution of civil marriage. No glue could hold that mixture together forever. As soon as Christian zeal cooled and church became part of state, concubinage and prostitution returned. Marriage as a Christian idea was further transformed in the Middle Ages by the cult of courtly love, which gave birth to some aspects of the romantic concept of marriage we have today.

For Paul, marriage made holy the sexual feelings between spouses. But the church taught that the sacred element in marriage was fidelity of the partners to a contract. And this law of fidelity was supposed to develop one's humanity. Paul got angry at those who would make the law a god, who thought that people could only be trusted to be faithful if there were a law or contract.

But marriage is an historical social form, not an absolute. New roles for women will certainly change it; but no matter how marriage changes, it still needs a friendship-based theology— which it has never had. Modeled on Roman forms, marriage today is an amalgam of different cultural views of both love and sexuality, conditioned by politics and economics always—for example, by the emergence of the middle class and by the Industrial Revolution.

Protestant theologies of marriage have been helpful as antidote to the Catholic variety; they were at least written by married males. Yet Protestant scholars, too, swing from theories of dualism to sexism, to overemphasis on genitality, to personal loving union. No wonder, given the amalgam of historical elements they had to try to incorporate. Today's process theology seems more helpful in its view of persons as dynamic becomings, with God's image in us as our capacity to love. Norman Pittinger's approach stresses love as central to sexual expression, with fidelity intrinsic to the union.

Can we develop—or do we wish to develop—a theology from useful elements of Jewish, Catholic, Protestant, and Eastern views that can transcend those fixed elements: a male-female, sexual-spiritual committed relationship? If person transcends sexuality always, and if it is the union of persons that needs both a new theory and a new social form, then the best of historical theologies of marriage may provide some resources. Although we need always to be aware of today's changing social and sexual conditions, this theology must be based on faithful commitment to live in justice and love in union with God and one another, no matter what the sex of the partner. The way would be open, then, to create forms to incorporate the loving expressions of gays and lesbians into Christian theologies of loving union.

Some questions for analyzing assumptions about today's marriage structures must first be asked:

- What does the marriage form assume about human beings? Is it possibly based on a perfectionist model that insists that one could not possibly be mistaken in this call to marriage?
- Does the present marriage form allow for continuing *conversion experiences* for the couple as God calls? Are persons placing their primary commitment to God's call, which could allow for change, being called to another lifestyle?
- Can we look upon annulment and divorce as sometimes necessary closure forms, and not failure certificates? If so, why are they not done in the spirit of reconciliation, so that these ending experiences will have fitting prayer and liturgy to help people move through such major change?
- Could liturgical, prayerful ending ceremonies help effect the healing so needed after a separation? Why is the religious experience of prayer and healing not used as a person pursues a different call from God?
- Could the churches, aided by separated persons' experiences, regularly provide such public or private ceremonies of healing as valid rites of passage to fit a changing gift-call? Would the healing dimension of prayer and acceptance by a community help a person move through the experience?

Both the woman's movement and homosexual unions call for the reexamination of today's concept of marriage. Subject to change, it needs to move toward structures that can provide the intimacy, the sheltering of love, and the support of commitment that will respect difference, that will recognize women as equally human persons with men, and foster mutual growth in justice and love. Marriage today is an ambiguous label, however. Some marriages are financial or social convenience structures; some merely provide legalized prostitution; others try for full equality of partners and endure the punishment society inflicts for cracking stereotypes of what a macho husband and a motherly wife should be.

In our time when every social form rocks with value change, married people struggle to build a spiritual-sexual life while handling personal value shock. But that shock signals responsibility for reexamining our lifestyles to see if they're serving love. If they are not, changes may be in order. One half of the marriage partnership, woman, may decide to claim her equal humanity, her responsibility to discover and follow God's call to her to use her gifts. If she does, then the church must take that major world change into account in interpreting what shape marriage should take and what is morally acceptable in sexual unions.

An important help for women claiming that equal humanity and responsibility is the fine work of women like Carol Gilligan of Harvard University. Her study in contrasting ways of defining and developing morality, *In a Different Voice*, published in 1982, is required reading for the student of developing sexual morality. She provides the other side of Lawrence Kohlberg's study based on male development and urges women to appreciate their tendency to see the world in terms of *connection*, relationships, and intimacy. Claiming and valuing this tendency is part of the *human* enterprise, not just woman's. It provides psychological grounding for the gospel call to love everyone as potential friend and to see no one as enemy.

Many marriages do not serve justice and love; many new forms of sexual relationship appear to. Woman now claims her right to friendship with her partner. A plurality of differing forms would seem in order to fit these changing developments.

Since Christianity is an incarnational religion which celebrates embodiment, Christians need not hide themselves and their sexuality in shame. Spiritual life begins with self-honesty. Lorna Hochstein shows what this means when one's sexual preference is for one's own gender. In the eyes of this writer, the fact that lesbian love is possible is a sign that the reality of the Divine exists independent of social prejudices or theological (patriarchal) dogmas. Whether one's orientation is heterosexual or homosexual, spiritual practice is in essence the same: it always consists in one's going beyond the self. And for this to be possible, one must first have accepted oneself.

MIRRORING GOD

Lorna Hochstein, Ph.D.

Ultimate Reality must always be encountered in earthly events if it is to matter at all.

D. Austin[1]

God did not create lesbians as a diversion, on a whim, or by accident. There is something deliberate and meaningful about lesbian love, something ultimately and ontologically purposeful. Lesbians bring the Catholic Church, the Christian tradition, and anyone willing to listen a message about the nature of God. We are, perhaps, a minority report, but the lives of lesbian women are God's Word through time, across cultures.

Christianity is an incarnational religion. Christians believe that God became a human person, that through the human presence in Jesus, God was manifested to the world. Through Jesus, divinity entered into a concrete relationship with other created selves. It is in and through that relation that God's nature is revealed to the world. The person of Jesus of Nazareth died, but Christian belief informs us that God continues to be revealed to the world in an on-going way through the lives and relationships of human persons. Jesus, an embodied human man, was God's Word to the world. So each of us, too, communicates something of God to others in and through our body/selves. As we are able to encounter God in Jesus, so we are each able to encounter God and experience the divine most profoundly through our loving relationships with other such body/selves.

All people communicate bodily. I do not live with and love a spirit; I live with and love an embodied flesh and blood woman. As I communicate something of God to my lover through my work, play, and lovemaking, so she reveals something of God's nature to me. This communication, this revelation, is both emotional and physical. God uses body/selves to share God's own self with the world. God *needs* body/selves to share Herself with the world. Finally, God needs lesbian body/selves to share Her own self with the Church and with the world.

Self-disclosure is essential to the life, depth, and growth of any human or divine being. Making oneself known to that same self and to others is essential to the life, depth, and growth of every human–human and human–divine relationship. It is this sharing of personal knowledge and insight with one's own self, with God, and with other persons that allows us to become spiritual women.

First we must share the knowledge of our lesbianism with our own selves. Seven years ago, on a warm June evening, I walked the banks of the Charles River with a friend and we talked. I turned to her, finally, and demanded that she kiss me. She did, and I knew then that I was one of those women we had been discussing so intently. That realization remained clear for the next twenty-four hours, and I was happy. Later, fears and doubts assailed that incredible clarity and I plunged into eighteen months of radical estrangement and paralyzing uncertainty, alienation, and pain. I struggled with this piece of self-knowledge and with a marriage I knew must end. I was twenty-five years old, actively Catholic, married for four years, and beginning graduate work in psychology. I had made a tentative peace with my family and I felt content. I was not expecting the confrontation with truth that began that night. My awareness of my very being changed.

Prior to that time, I was not a particularly spiritual person. Although I was interested in the Catholic Church, in God, and in the Bible, and although I often attended Mass and received the sacraments, my interest lacked passion and genuine connection to that source of creation and sustainer of life that I call God. I lacked a primary connection to myself, and thus, I lacked a primary connection to God.

I had successfully kept my lesbianism a secret from my own self; I had not allowed my soul to speak to my conscious mind. Since I was unable to share this deepest being with my conscious self, I could not share it with others. My unknowing self-estrangement had limited the openness, trust, love, and vitality I felt within myself and so it limited the degree of openness, trust, and vitality I could bring to any relationship with another person or God. I was not, in fact, a spiritual person. The self-deception by which I thought myself a woman who was most deeply fulfilled by loving men limited the potential for connectedness with myself and between myself and others. I could only become a spiritual person when I acknowledged that God had created me lesbian and that because of my primary emotional, spiritual, and physical love for women, I live and love and experience God in a special, particular way. I experience God most profoundly in my love for other women.

Lesbian women become more deeply spiritual women when we acknowledge that God created us lesbian, and that as lesbians we mirror God to each other, to the Church, and to the world uniquely. Our self-disclosure is God's self-disclosure; our silence is God's silence.

The patriarchal tradition of the Catholic Church has erased, denied, and trivialized all women's experience, virtually destroying our attempts at self-knowledge and self-expression. It has thereby kept generations of women in an unspiritual state. By refusing Christian women (especially women-loving women) the means of self-knowledge, patriarchal Christianity has denied itself and the world knowledge of God. But acknowledgement of a woman's lesbianism to her own self is only the first step toward a spiritual life. To be spiritual women, to mediate the presence of God to others, we must acknowledge to ourselves *and to others* that we are lesbian. Such self-disclosure is essential for the continuing growth of God's presence in women's lives and in the life of the world.

A disclosure of one's love of women or, more typically, of one's love for a particular woman, does not always yield "happy" results. I had labelled myself lesbian for several years before sharing that orientation with my parents. I was involved in a committed relationship; my lover and I owned a home and two cats and had a circle of gay, lesbian, and straight friends. Everyone close to me knew of my love relationship—everyone except my parents. I hated the evasions and the withholding of information which seemed to constitute lies. I had never shared with my parents the cause of my deep depression and distance as I struggled through my accepting my lesbian self, and I had never stated that my lesbianism was a major reason for my divorce. I had never explained my obvious closeness to my women friends, my commitment to feminism, or my rage at patriarchal society. So much of what I did and said made no sense without these explanations. Long before my mother directly asked me about my sexual orientation, I knew that, when she did, I would cease the evasions and tell the truth. And I did.

It would have been easier for me not to, easier for them and easier for me. But the pretense was stifling and I knew that the longer I kept silent the more distant I would feel from them, the more contempt I would have for their blindness, and the more anger I would feel at my own cowardice. When my mother asked if I was a lesbian, I said I was. Two years later neither of my parents mention my lover's name. I go to their home alone. My mother (and, presumably, my father) feels that my lover has ruined my life. This self-disclosure has not had happy results.

There is much about my life that I have not shared; there is much they do not wish to know. At least the possibility for such honest sharing is present now. I am only occasionally evasive. In many ways my parents still do not know who I am or what I am about. They do not know because they have chosen not to ask or to hear, not because I have refused to tell them. They have the information they need to know and understand the choices I have made whenever they choose to use it. Painful though this response has been, I am glad that my mother asked and that I told. When I acknowledged my love of a woman, I helped clear space for the possibility of truth, openness, trust, and love; for the possibility of God's presence between us in a new way. God, too, loves women.

Our Catholic Christian belief has informed and influenced the way each of us perceives and experiences our life and our love of women. We each know how Catholic dogma has contributed to our past or present image of ourselves as wrong, sick, sinful, immature, perverse people, as women less valuable to the Church and the world than women who primarily love men. Sometimes we have gotten so stuck in this self-denigrating mire that we have forgotten another fact. That is, that while we are each influenced by Catholic doctrine concerning sexuality, our experience of loving women can inform Catholic Christian belief. Our willingness to believe others' assessment of lesbians has led us to deny a part of ourselves and a part of God. It has allowed others and ourselves to continue to portray God in exclusively heterosexual images. It allows us to deny the basic truth that all of us—female and male, lesbian, gay, or heterosexual—image God. If we allow for the possibility of love between women, we allow for a new image of God. If we deny that love, we create a limited, idolatrous God whose being is mediated only by heterosexual women and men.

What does lesbian love reveal about God? A woman's love for another woman, a woman's serious commitment to relationship with another woman presents a continuing sign that with God all things are possible. Emotional and sexual love between women exists despite all lack of validation, recognition, affirmation, and active fostering. It continues to exist despite strenuous attempts to destroy it or degrade it. The on-going existence of woman-love is a dramatic sign that God's presence is possible anywhere, any time, and that hopelessness is not ever justified. It is a sign that any desire to cease struggling for truthfulness in our relationships with others must not be indulged. God's creative love is sturdier, stronger, more creative, flexible, and enduring than any warrior, judge, almighty, powerful, father God could ever be.

Enduring though this presence is, love between women also conveys the vulnerability of God's presence. Such presence is easily affected by a touch of cowardice; silent lies can stifle its growth. Lesbian relationships remind the world of the price of integrity. Lesbian relationships can embody intense strength and resistance to all attempts at eradication, as well as serious vulnerability to secrecy and ungenuineness.

Love between women reminds us that God calls us to love deeply the most unlikely people. My struggle to accept my physical and emotional love of a woman taught me that I place limitations on whom I would love. I had placed limitations on where I would allow God to be present. I have learned that an act of lovemaking can be as sacramental as the breaking of bread. God does show Herself in unexpected places!

Love between women reminds the world that God's Word exists independently of current trends and prejudices, independent of any audience for that Word. While often ignored and rendered invisible, lesbians themselves do not go away. Finally, a glimpse of two women in love is a gratuitous gift from God, a miracle of courage, daring, and integrity. Such a sight is a delight offered by God to those able to see.

Lesbian spirituality resembles Christian spirituality when it is visionary, sacramental, relational, and transformational.[2] One woman's love for another is possible only if she is willing and able to perceive reality/God in a new way at odds with the predominant culture around her. It is possible only if she is willing and able to create a life which concretizes that new vision of woman-centered relationship. As creations of God, lesbians are imbued with the spirit of God and are mediators of the divine. Our love for each other relates us to God and brings us to God; it can bring others to God, whether they are gay or non-gay. Love between women heals, renews, brings, joy, sustains hope, and allows us to touch God through our touch of one another. Being lesbian invites a woman to live out the knowledge that there is more to life than meets the eye. In so doing, we enflesh the divine. Women who love women are indeed fortunate to have been set apart for such delight.

NOTES

1. D. Austin, "On becoming a theologian: In praise of the ordinary life," *Harvard Divinity Bulletin,* Oct.-Nov. 1982, *13* (1), 14-16.

2. R. McBrien, *Catholicism* vol 2. (New York: Winston Press, 1980), 1057-1058.

It is important to remember that heterosexuality and the Western institution of marriage are by no means universals. As a well-known maxim states, "Other cultures, other customs." Anthropologists have indeed documented an astonishing variety of behavioral forms within the human family. The concluding piece in this anthology, entitled "Wife Lending: Sexual Pathways to Transcendence in Eskimo Culture," talks about an ethnic custom that most of us will find quite outlandish but that should make us thoughtful rather than judgmental. The much-misunderstood Eskimo custom of sharing one's wife with an outsider, as reported by anthropologist Chris Moyers Gove, is not a sexually motivated practice at all but springs from the desire to create eternal kinship bonds. We tend to feel enormously possessive about our sexual partners, and the idea of wife lending (rather than wife swapping) stirs up feelings of jealousy in most of us. Possessiveness, however, is correlated to the notion of our sexual partner as property over which we have certain rights. It is also connected with our egoic tendency to put our own "individual" interests above those of the group to which we belong. The Eskimos think and feel differently. The traditional view presented in Moyers Gove's essay affords a poignant contrast to our egocentric world-view with its shattered feelings for kinship and the sacred. Any attempt at creating an erotic spirituality for ourselves must necessarily involve a thorough reevaluation of our ideas and beliefs about community and what this means in sexual terms.

WIFE LENDING: SEXUAL PATHWAYS TO TRANSCENDENCE IN ESKIMO CULTURE

By Chris Moyers Gove, Ph.D.

Visitors to Eskimo villages in Alaska frequently return with stories of exceptionally promiscuous and aggressive local women who invite sexual contact without expecting "anything" in return, not even payment, much less an ongoing relationship such as marriage. Meanwhile, the Eskimo men are reported as submissive and insecure, who even allow strangers to "use" their wives sexually. Few visitors ask the Eskimos their view of what is going on, and so they usually miss the fact that they are taking part in a religious rite that could spiritually obligate them forever.

The European settlers in Northwestern Alaska called the natives "Eskimos," without knowing what the name meant. It was an Indian word learned from Athapascan tribes contacted by the settlers on their way northward, and it means "flesh eaters," referring to the major component of the Eskimo diet, for little vegetation grew where they lived. These are the lands that Europeans and Americans later called the "barren north." But neither name gives a clue to the Eskimos' character, behavior, or spirituality. The Eskimos, in their own language, are called "Inupiat," which means "the People." Only kinship ties could make anyone a person endowed with a spirit, or higher consciousness, and able to speak the language of human beings, as well as worthy of participating in religious and sexual rites.

Before attempting to understand the Eskimos' sexual behavior, it is essential to look at several Eskimo beliefs that are very different from the European or Euroamerican world-view. First, Eskimo tradition does not make a radical distinction between the spiritual nature of humans and that of animals. Animals used for game were traditionally thought to have a collective soul or spirit. A portion of this spirit was contained in the individual animal, and it returned to the collective at the time of death. Another portion entered each new game animal at the time of birth. If the animal was killed for food, certain parts of the animal had to be ceremonially returned to the environment to make sure the soul could properly reincarnate. Decline in game populations were attributed to improper handling on the part of hunters.

Dogs and humans, on the other hand, were thought to

have individual spirits, which remained individual and moved to a different plane upon death. These could become re-embodied as another individual at birth, often a descendant, and always a member of the kinship group. The spirit was usually recognized by the parents and other relatives shortly after birth. The infant was then named for that ancestor; this was done without regard to sex, and so an infant girl could be called by her grandfather's name and was given the honor and status within the family that the grandfather had earned during his lifetime. Since Eskimo names did not connote gender, and since men and women had equal status, this custom did not seem unusual or cross-sexed, as it would in modern American culture, where, for example, the title of Johnny Cash's popular song "A Boy Named Sue" strikes us as odd.

Second, the spirits of humans were thought to be not always confined to the corporeal body, but capable of leaving the physical frame to explore other realms under certain conditions. This was routinely accomplished by shamans during the performance of healing rites and by hunters while investigating the migration patterns of game. Anyone could explore the spirit world before making a life transition, such as progress into adulthood or in preparation for death. Such journeys into the spirit realms could also happen during sexual intercourse, especially where they were an integral part of a religious or social rite; Eskimos considered such rites as much of a religious transition as a European of that time might consider baptism, marriage, bar mitzvah, or mass.

Third, a person's spirituality was thought to affect not only the individual, but all of the kinship group. Faith and belief were not spiritual elements that could be embraced by an individual alone, but needed to be held in common by an entire kinship group in order to be effective. For example, prayers from one person could not be heard, but two or more praying together could influence supernatural intervention. This, in turn, could affect transcendental aspects of life for the whole kinship group, such as survival after death, as well as mundane aspects such as attracting needed game animals. In this capacity, sexual acts could serve as a ritual which bound kinship ties and lead to spiritual ties, which were necessary in order for transcendental group experiences to occur.

One's spiritual experiences were thought to affect the person's intuitive sense of right or wrong behavior, and the behavior of an individual could affect the survival of the entire kinship group or village. This is easy to see in such practical contexts as hunting and fishing, where cooperation is essential, but is less readily apparent in spiritual terms.

The Eskimos believed that when a person's behavior was harmful to others or forbidden by supernatural powers, such as beating a child or violating the incest taboo, natural consequences would follow. For instance, a hunter might be avoided by game animals or a woman might be rendered childless or a shaman might lose the way to the "hidden" world of the animals, resulting in beginning a migration at the wrong time. Any of these could lead to the destruction of the individual, the village, or the entire kinship group.

There is no near equivalent to this concept in present American life, although it has been mistakenly described as having a son pay for the sins of his father, expanded to include the extended family group. It has also been mistaken for the Hindu notion of karma, wherein a person's actions determine the experiences of the next incarnation or later suffers in proportion to whatever pain has been caused by deliberate actions. The Eskimos had no such concept, however. There was no sin or evil, as such, and wrong behavior was not punished by a supreme being. Natural consequences followed behavior in much the way a dropped object follows the "law" of gravity, and the Eskimos did not think prayer would change this.

The "self" was viewed (and experienced) as including not only the individual but all his relatives and those with whom he had developed kinship ties, such as present and past wives. (This also applied to women, and in the Eskimo language, there is a nonspecific personal pronoun meaning "a person of either sex." English has no equivalent at the present time.)

A person without kin was unthinkable in aboriginal times, not because such a person was considered "polluted" in body or spirit, but simply because he or she did not exist. A man and a woman, together, could exist in the Eskimos' environment, but either alone could not survive. Everything that was necessary— hunting, building shelters, straining the animal oil into fuel, cooking, chewing the hides and sewing them into clothing and insulation, fishing and smoking the fish, training dogs and breeding them with wolves, and other duties were so diverse and complex that no one person could do it alone. An example from more recent times is the expedition to "discover" the North Pole. Robert Peary and Matthew Henson were accompanied by a group of Eskimos that included a woman, because the trek was thought by the Eskimo guides to be impossible without her help. After the Eskimo people were exposed to European diseases, for which they had little resistance, individuals without kin became common. Such a person was thought of in terms similar to the modern concept of insanity—likely to be unpredictable and without normal restraint, not necessarily to be blamed or condemned for bad behavior, but simply to be avoided. Such "unfortunate" people were ostracized, not formally by a ritual or legal ceremony, but simply because no one wanted to associate with them.

On the other hand, even very small kinship groups had total access to spiritual powers. Eskimo legends abound with accounts of supernatural intervention that saved families in danger or that gave dispensation for activities that were normally forbidden, such as cannibalism or incest. But the common European excuses for bad behavior, insanity and drunkenness, were not excuses for the Eskimos. Alcohol and psychoactive plants were unknown, and "insanity" would have been dismissed as a person who had surrendered control of emotions or actions without the sanction of a powerful "transcendental" experience, such as the vision of a shaman.

A person was eternally responsible for any action performed at any time during that person's lifetime. For example, the Eskimos' practice, described as "wife-swapping" by early explorers, was actually a sacred ritual that involved both sexuality and kinship extension, and was looked upon as a sacrament as much as marriage was in the European context. This custom was connected with another, potentially more lethal custom: When a stranger arrived in the village, it was mandatory that he should be killed, for he was, by definition, not a real person; he had no spirit, because he had no kinship ties. The only way that he could be saved was if a member of the group claimed kinship to him. (The pronoun is used advisedly, because records include only incidents in which men were the strangers.) If he was not recognizable as a relative, he could be invited into the kinship structure only by marriage. For the Eskimos, this did not include elaborate preparations, or an exchange of property, or a certification of virginity or widowhood, as in European society at that time. It required only a simple act of sexual intercourse.

This kinship extension was called "wife-lending" when reported in European accounts, because it was thought that the Eskimo husband commanded his wife to have intercourse with the strangers. This was not the case, however. Such behavior could not have been ordered or even requested by the Eskimo husband; to do so would have meant a loss of status, for it would have meant that he was attempting to force his wife to do something against her will, not for her own benefit, but for his. This was disgraceful behavior for the Eskimos, and would have brought on the wrath of his wife and all her kin. "Wife-lending" therefore was usually at the request of the wife; it was strictly forbidden that it be done against her will. Women and men had equal control of their own lives, and neither was considered the property of the other. Each could initiate courtship, request marriage, and pass on property to designated children. By engaging in intercourse, the spirits of, say, a European man and an Eskimo woman, were forever entangled, and the social liaison was a kinship that had obligations throughout the present life, and even extending into any future life.

It was a liaison so permanent that no European could—or would—understand. Once made, it could not be broken, even by divorce or death. The husband of the hour, no matter how brief, was the husband for all time. If his wife left, and his children were motherless, the transitory wife must care for them, even if her own children had less to eat, or even if her husband of many years must work harder to provide for them. The spiritual tie was permanent, a bond that could be frivolous in times of plenty or life threatening in times of starvation, but lasting forever. The Europeans, who recorded stories of wife-lending, and often told their stories as if they had participated in the rites reluctantly, never recorded that they understood their obligations in this kinship tie.

Another aspect of Eskimo life that has remained obscure to Europeans and Euroamericans is the function of sexual relationships in spiritual life. Part of the problem is that it is hard for us to see sexuality from a point of view that is not our own, and often we do not realize that it is a question of point of view rather than a question of right and wrong or good and evil. Perhaps this point is easier to appreciate if we reverse the perspective. The idea is to try to see ourselves from the point of view of someone outside our own culture; this process often tells as much about the other culture as about our own. Much has been written by imagining how Eskimos would see us, but this is often less than satisfactory. A better way was suggested by Charles Case, an anthropologist specializing in Native American culture, who said, "when all reasonable anthropological methods fail, you might try asking an Eskimo."

Taking this idea literally, an investigator asked Collins Avesiq, an Eskimo living in Nome, Alaska in 1981, to comment on his view of Euroamerican sexuality. He was old enough to remember when the first "whites" came to his village. He said:

> "To you, it is not fun. It is not a good thing except if you do not do it, like a priest. Or to make babies. You do not laugh, and you feel guilty afterwards. Better you should not do it."

Regarding spirituality, he continued:

> "The preacher talks and the people listen. We have learned to listen, too. Like you. Long ago, we all talked. Each man, he had his special song. No one else could sing his song. He taught it to a child, perhaps his grandson. No one else could sing it. It was his. Only his. If he did not teach it, no one else would ever sing it. There were other times, when we all sang and played and danced together. Sex? Yes, we made loving and laughed together. That was part of the songs and the games. Then we went to other places in our minds. Places we could not go except together singing the songs, where those dead already still can talk, and where the spirit-woman makes the winds blow. You say it is not good to do these things in your church. You only do that in the bars when you drink booze. Also, then, you dance and then that sex thing is okay for you. In church you say don't do these things. But then you do them, after, in the bars, but you do not laugh, and you feel bad after. In the church, you sing, but you do not dance, and not laugh then either. I never quite understand how the heaven thing works."

It was also hard for the Eskimos to understand the importance of Easter, which seemed to them to be a celebration of death. At the same time, the Euroamericans tried to stop the Eskimo dance festivals ("Inviting-In" is an example), which shared everything the village could offer, including material wealth and sexuality, and which would often lead to transcendental experiences. These included "out-of-body" experiences in which the spirit traveled to another realm inhabited by the spirits of dead relatives and the spirits of game animals. Persons having these experiences would later give accounts of meeting the spirits of dead relatives and receiving information about impending hunting trips. These experiences were not limited to shamans, or even elders, but could be undergone by any "real person," including women and children.

A typical festival might begin like this: Members of a nearby village were sighted several days before arrival, and the host villagers prepared gifts, food for the feast, prizes for the games, and extra camping-sites for the sleds and dogs. A special group of shamans, dressed in decorative feminine costumes, went out to greet the visitors. These shamans were men who had been raised to develop mystical powers, which required them to wear female dress from birth and to learn all the skills of a woman and to perform sexually as a woman. This was not an unusual custom among Native Americans, although the reason for this practice is not clearly understood.

These cross-dressed shamans left the village and met the travelers far out on the road, escorting them into the village. The other villagers remained hidden until the shamans had led the newcomers into the village, and then they appeared, giving gifts, and offering food. Then the festivities began: races, games, joke-telling (the first to laugh loses), blanket-toss (the person to toss highest wins), gift-giving (the person giving the most valuable gift wins). Feasting following the games included food from both the hosts and the guests. The last night consisted of drum-music and dancing, usually in a large enclosed structure; it began with men and women in separate dances, and culminated, many hours later, with a dance in which men and women danced together. This was one of the few dances in which men and women performed together, and was the only time that the villagers were likely to come in close contact with visitors of the opposite sex.

This last dance began with a long musical (mostly drumming) performance, accompanied by chanting in which everyone present participated. As the hours passed, a trance-like state was attained by most of the participants. It was during this time that the transcendental experiences occurred. The final dance was performed in this state. This was not a formal or practiced dance as the preceding dances had been, but was completely spontaneous, beginning and ending as each individual felt inspired.

During and following this final dance, while still in the trance, couples often performed sexual intercourse; this was done openly, with no need for privacy, because the Eskimos did not consider sex a secret or shameful act. Usually the partners were a host and a guest. Anthropologists have often interpreted this behavior as a survival mechanism. This idea is based on the fact that villages usually consisted of a very small number of people, and marriages were likely to occur within this group, and therefore intercourse with those from other villages served to introduce new genes and make the next generation more viable.

There is, however, a point that is missed by both anthropologists, who have interpreted this sexual behavior as a mechanism of "genetic variability," and missionaries, who have interpreted it as a "condemnable primitive rite." That is the point of view of the Eskimos themselves: the transcendence of one's everyday ego in sexual ecstasy, the transcendence of possessiveness or jealousy into an extension of kinship, the transformation of separate villages into partnership and kinship. This included the extension of the spiritual self, and the recognition of a spiritual kinship within all the Inupiat—all the People. It is hard for those from a European cultural background to understand how sexuality can be part of the pathway to spiritual experience and meaning, as it was for the Eskimos. It is easier to see how transcendental experiences might be produced by control of the mind, such as meditation in some Christian sects, or the control of the body, such as the postures of Yoga. For the Eskimos, however, spirituality extended beyond the individual to include others in the kinship group. Spiritual transcendence was not attained alone, but always in a group ceremony. Therefore, it is not surprising, in this context, that sexuality was one of the ceremonial devices in which spiritual experiences could occur.

Contributors

MANTAK CHIA was born in Thailand where he learned Thai Boxing, Aikido, and Thai Chi Chuan. Later in Hong Kong he studied with Master Pan Yu who has created a synthesis out of Buddhism and Taoism. Chia is the spiritual head of the Healing Tao centers in the United States, Europe, Australia, and the Far East. He has authored *Taoist Secrets of Love: Cultivating Male Sexual Energy* (written with Michael Winn), *Healing Love Through the Tao: Cultivating Female Sexual Energy* (written with his wife Maneewan Chia), and several other books. Mantak Chia can be contacted through The Healing Tao Center, 2 Creskill Place, Huntington, New York 11743-1194.

ARTHUR COLMAN, M.D. is a psychiatrist in private practice and an associate clinical professor at the University of California Medical Center in San Francisco. His wife LIBBY LEE COLMAN, PH.D. is a part-time teacher. They co-authored two books, *Pregnancy: The Psychological Experience* and *Love and Ecstasy*.

DA FREE JOHN is an American-born spiritual teacher whose writings have affected tens of thousands of people in the United States and abroad. Among his numerous books are *The Knee of Listening* (his spiritual autobiography), *Love of the Two-Armed Form, The Enlightenment of the Whole Body*, and *The Dawn Horse Testament*. He is the spiritual head of the Free Daist Communion, which can be contacted at P.O. Box 3680, Clearlake, CA 95422.

DODY H. DONNELLY has a Ph.D. in classics and a Ph.D. in theology. She is adjunct professor of theology at San Francisco Theological Seminary and also teaches at the Institute in Creation Spirituality. Her books include *Radical Love, Team*, and *Thomas Moore*.

GEORG FEUERSTEIN, M.LITT., is well known for his numerous publications on Hinduism, especially the philosophy and history of Yoga. He did postgraduate research in Indian philosophy at the old University of Durham, England, is a founder-member of the Indian Academy of Yoga (Benares Hindu University), and a former co-director of the Center for Yoga Research, Durham. Among his many publications are *Introduction to the Bhagavad-*

Gita, The Philosophy of Classical Yoga, Structures of Conscious-ness, and *Yoga: The Technology of Ecstasy*. He is also editor of *Spectrum Review*, a quarterly newsletter, and editor of the *Paragon Living Traditions* series of encyclopedic dictionaries. He lives and works with his wife Trisha in the mountains of Northern California.

JULIE HENDERSON, PH.D. is a bioenergetic analyst, hypnotherapist, sexologist, and actress. She lectures around the world and offers training emphasizing direct pleasure in being. She is a consultant to the Human Interaction Laboratory, Langley Porter Neuropsychiatric Institute, University of California at San Francisco. She authored the book *The Lover Within*.

LORA HOCHSTEIN, a former religious studies educator, is a licensed psychologist. She has a doctorate in pastoral psychology and works in private practice as a pastoral psychotherapist. Her special area of interest is the effect of organized religion on lesbians and, more important, the effect of lesbian spirituality on organized religion and on practitioners of organized religion.

SAM KEEN, PH.D., a former professor of philosophy, is a freelance writer living in Sonoma, California, who has lectured and con-ducted groups at more than 200 colleges, universities, and corporations in the United States, Europe, and Russia. He is a contributing editor of *Psychology Today* and a regular contribu-tor to numerous popular magazines and academic journals. Among his many books are *Apology for Wonder, To A Dancing God, Life-Maps, The Passionate Life*, and *Faces of the Enemy*. The PBS documentary "Faces of the Enemy" was nominated for the Emmy Award in 1988.

JEAN LANIER is a therapist in private practice in San Francisco and a former counsellor at Matthew Fox's Institute in Culture and Creation Spirituality in Oakland, California. She has authored *Diagnoses and Other Poems* and *The Wisdom of Being Human* and is a contributing editor of *Creation* magazine. She is married to Sidney Lanier with whom she co-founded a residen-tial center for human potential in Spain.

GEORGE LEONARD was senior editor at *Look* magazine for seven-teen years and is a former president of the Association for Humanistic Psychology. He is the recipient of many US national awards for his educational writings and author of the bestsellers *Education and Ecstasy, The Transformation,* and *The Ultimate Athlete,* among other books.

EDWIN M. MCMAHON, PH.D. and PETER A. CAMPBELL, PH.D. are Catholic priests and psychologists of religion. They have been studying religion for thirty years in order to understand how religious practices contribute to health or pathology. They are co-directors of the Institute for Research in Spirituality and conduct workshops and retreats. Their books include *Becoming a Person in the Whole Christ, The In-Between: Evolution in Christian Faith, Please Touch,* and *Bio-Spirituality: Focusing as a Way to Grow.* They have also authored a series of pamphlets, which include topics such as "Addictive Religion," and "Teaching Children to Focus." These are available from The Institute for Research in Spirituality, 6305 Greeley Hill Road, Coulterville, CA 95311.

DEENA METZGER, PH.D. is a poet, novelist, playwright, and psychotherapist. Her books include *The Woman Who Slept With Men to Take the War Out of Them* (a drama novel) and *Tree* (a diary novel), both published by Wingbow Press; *Looking For the Faces of God* (poetry) by Parallax Press; *What Dinah Thought* by Viking/Penguin. She is currently working on *Writing For Your Life: Creativity, Imagination and Healing,* to be published by J. P. Tarcher. She is married, has two sons, and lives at the end of a dirt road with her wolf, Timber.

CHRIS MOYERS GOVE, PH.D. is director of the Institute of Preventive Psychology and is investigating techniques of detecting and preventing family situations leading to abuse and various dysfunctions. Most of her anthropological research was done during the six years she lived in Alaska, teaching college classes in remote locations. She is married to Jim Gove, a San Francisco poet.

DAVID ALAN RAMSDALE conducts workshops on Tantra and works as a psychic and astrological consultant. He is the author of the widely read book *Sexual Energy Ecstasy* (with Ellen Jo Dorfman). In addition to the Tantric seminars, books, and tapes, his company is preparing a Tantric educational video. His address is: Peak Skill Publishing, P.O. Box 5489, Playa Del Rey, CA 90296.

DOMINIC S. RAPHAEL is a widely published and pastorally active Roman Catholic author writing here under a pseudonym. Both Church and society need healing ideas in the area of sexual ethics. A pseudonym may help toward healing, by avoiding personal controversy and promoting objective discussion. At any rate, D. S. R. is in good company: Benjamin Franklin used no fewer than 57 different pseudonyms in the course of his life.

DAVID A. SCHULZ, PH.D. is a part-time professor, Episcopal priest, and wood sculptor residing in California. He is the author of *Human Sexuality, The Changing Family,* and other books on human relationships. He has taught seminars on sexuality and sexual harassment. His manuscript "Sacred Shrines and Thirsty Fishes: Celebrating Ordinary Lives" is nearing completion.

DELL SOKOL, PH.D. is a clinical psychologist in private practice in San Francisco. Her special clinical interest is in counseling women in mid-life crisis and transition. She is a founding member of West Portal Counseling Associates, San Francisco, and a staff psychologist of the California Counseling Institute, under the auspices of the Episcopal Church. She has been a student of the way of radical self-transcendence taught by Da Free John for sixteen years. She has been married for twenty-five years and is the mother of four children. She has traveled extensively in Europe, South America, and Asia, visiting sources of spiritual power and healing.

STUART SOVATSKY, PH.D. is a psychotherapist in private practice and director of the Kundalini Clinic in San Francisco. He is on the faculty of JFK University, the California Institute of Integral Studies, and the Rosebridge Institute in the Bay area. In addition to academic and popular articles, he is the author of *Tantric Celibacy.*

ROBERT E. SVOBODA, PH.D. is the first Westerner to obtain a degree in Ayurveda, graduating from the Tilak Ayurveda Mahavidyalaya in Poona, India, where he studied with Vasant Lad. He is the author of several books, including *Prakruti: Your Ayurvedic Constitution,* published by Geocom, and *Aghora: At the Left Hand of God,* published by Brotherhood of Life, which introduces to the West the little-known Tantric tradition espoused by his late teacher Vimalananda. He has lectured and conducted workshops throughout the United States and Canada, has traveled to over fifty countries in the world. He and his family spend much time in India.

LEWIS THOMPSON (1909-1949) was born in London and lived in India as a wandering poet for sixteen years. Edith Sitwell called him a "poet of genius." His remarkable book *Mirror to the Light* was published posthumously in 1984.

FRANCES E. VAUGHAN, PH.D. is a psychologist in private practice in Mill Valley, California. She is on the clinical faculty of the University of California and was formerly president of the Association for Transpersonal Psychology and the Association for Humanistic Psychology. She is author of *The Inward Arc: Healing and Wholeness in Psychotherapy* and *Spirituality and Awakening Intuition*, as well as co-editor of *Beyond Ego: Transpersonal Dimensions in Psychology, Accept This Gift*, and *A Gift of Peace*.

MICHAEL WINN, who was born in San Francisco and lives in New York, is a journalist, photographer, and widely traveled expedition guide. He is also general editor of the *Taoist Esoteric Yoga Encyclopedia*. A student of Mantak Chia, he has practiced various kinds of meditation and Tai Chi for the past twenty years.

Select Bibliography

The literature on sexuality is vast. Most books deal with the medical, psychological, or sociological dimensions of sexuality. Works delving into the religious and spiritual aspects are a trickle by comparison. The following titles represent a brief selection for readers with a spiritual interest wishing to inform themselves further. Some of the books are referred to in the essays of this volume.

Baker, Robert and Frederick Elliston, eds. *Philosophy and Sex.* Buffalo, NY: Prometheus Books, 1984.

> An anthology of thoughtful essays on monogamy, adultery, feminism, homosexuality, abortion, etc.

Evola, Julius. *The Metaphysics of Sex.* New York: Inner Traditions International, 1983.

> A masterful philosophical treatment of eros, agape, and sex.

Gold, E.J. and Cybele Gold. *Tantric Sex.* Playa del Rey, CA: Peak Skill Publishing, 1988.

> A practical introduction to neo-Tantrism.

Hurcombe, Linda, ed. *Sex and God: Some Varieties of Women's Religious Experience.* New York and London: Routledge & Kegan Paul, 1987.

> A delightful anthology of stories, poems, and essays by women concerned with understanding the connection between sexuality and the Divine.

Keen, Sam. *The Passionate Life: Stage of Loving.* San Francisco: Harper & Row, 1983.

> A wonderfully readable examination of the unfolding of love in a person's life.

Lilar, Suzanne. *Aspects of Love in Western Society.* London: Panther Books, 1967.

> A brilliant historical review of Western notions about love and sex, including sacral love.

Lyon, Harold. *Tenderness is Strength: From Machismo to Manhood.* San Francisco: Harper & Row, 1977.

A plea for the cultivation of sensitivity in men.

May, Rollo. *Love and Will.* London: Collins, 1972.

One of the first books to insist on the reintegration of eros and sex as well as spiritual and emotional values.

Moore, John. *Sexuality & Spirituality: The Interplay of Masculine and Feminine in Human Development.* San Francisco: Harper & Row, 1980.

A helpful attempt at integrating our thinking about sexuality and spirituality.

Morgan, Robin. *The Anatomy of Freedom: Feminism, Physics, and Global Politics.* Garden City, NY: Anchor Books, 1984.

A powerful book on feminist philosophy that is important not only for women but also men.

Nelson, James B. *The Intimate Connection: Male Sexuality, Masculine Spirituality.* Philadelphia, PA: Westminster Press, 1988.

A well-written examination of the shift toward a spiritually oriented sexuality in our culture.

Szasz, Thomas. *Sex by Prescription.* Harmondsworth, England: Penguin Books, 1980.

An iconoclastic critique of contemporary sex therapy.

Packard, Vance. *The Sexual Wilderness: The Contemporary Upheaval in Male-Female Relationships.* New York: David McKay, 1968.

A classic work that is still worth reading.

Qualls-Corbett, Nancy. *The Sacred Prostitute: Eternal Aspect of the Feminine.* Toronto: Inner City Books, 1988.

A Jungian exploration of the feminine.

Welwood, John, ed. *Challenge of the Heart: Love, Sex, and Intimacy in Changing Times.* Boston: Shambhala, 1985.

An excellent anthology.

Index